THE BEST OF FELLAS

The Story of Bob Wooler
Liverpool's First D.J.

by Spencer Leigh

DRIVEGREEN
PUBLICATIONSLtd

In association with Jim Turner

ABOUT THE AUTHOR

Spencer Leigh was born in Liverpool in 1945. His *On The Beat* programme has been broadcast on BBC Radio Merseyside for nearly 20 years and he has written for several magazines including *Country Music People, Goldmine, Mojo, Now Dig This, Record Buyer, Record Collector* and *Radio Times*. He also writes obituaries of musicians and songwriters for *The Independent* newspaper. He also puts original material on his website www.spencerleigh.demon.co.uk.

Spencer Leigh's books are *Paul Simon - Now And Then* (1973), *Presley Nation* (1976), *Stars In My Eyes* (1980), *Let's Go Down The Cavern* (with Pete Frame) (1984), *Speaking Words Of Wisdom: Reflections On The Beatles* (1991), *Aspects Of Elvis* (edited with Alan Clayson) (1994), *Memories Of Buddy Holly* (with Jim Dawson) (US 1996), *Halfway To Paradise, Britpop 1955 - 1962* (with John Firminger) (1996), *Behind The Song* (with Michael Heatley) (1998), *Drummed Out - The Sacking Of Pete Best* (1998), *Brother, Can You Spare A Rhyme? - 100 Years Of Hit Songwriting* (2000), *Baby, That Is Rock And Roll, American Pop 1954 - 1963* (with John Firminger) (2001) and *Sweeping The Blues Away - A Celebration Of The Merseysippi Jazz Band* (2002).

Published by Drivegreen Publications Limited
in association with Jim Turner
KNB House, 7 Rodney Street, Liverpool L1 9HZ.

Design & Typesetting by
Emso Creative Media
36 Seel Street, Liverpool Telephone (0151) 707 2448

Front cover design
Anthony Brown

Printed by Ashley Printers Limited
25 Dickson Street, Liverpool L3 7EB   Telephone (0151) 236 4415

ISBN 0-9543839-0-7

CONTENTS

FOREWORD
by Jim Turner

Bob Wooler's contribution to the Mersey Beat scene is immense and quite possibly, the scene with all its many stars would not have happened without his efforts at the Cavern. Certainly, it would have emerged in a very different way and *The Best Of Fellas* shows, perhaps for the first time, the extent of the debt that the musicians owed to him. His enthusiasm, creativity and energy at the Cavern and other Merseyside venues helped to establish the Beatles, Gerry and the Pacemakers, the Searchers, Billy J. Kramer, Cilla Black, the Merseybeats and many other performers.

I wasn't one of those musicians, but I did play in the Texan Skiffle Group with Rory Storm and Johnny Guitar. I was on washboard and double-bass and we banged anything that could be banged. Then I became the booking manager for Rory Storm and the Hurricanes and this developed into the Arcade Variety Agency where I managed many of the local acts including the Cyclones (Mark Peters' original backing group), Faron's Flamingos, Ian and the Zodiacs, Lee Castle and the Barons, the Kansas City Five and the Kubas. I was also the booking agent for Denny Seyton and the Sabres and for several acts outside the area. Carl Perkins, Sonny Boy Williamson, John Lee Hooker, Tom Jones and Gene Vincent have worked for me on occasion.

I met Bob Wooler at the Cavern early in 1961 and thought he was a very impressive DJ as his voice was excellent. He had a sharp and sardonic wit and he would call me Texan Turner. The Cavern was switching from jazz to rock'n'roll and Bob and I would negotiate over booking fees. I would start high and he would be low and we would meet in the middle. Bob might want two one-hour Saturday night spots for £10 and we might agree on one spot for £15. It was difficult for Bob once Mersey Beat had become established as Liverpool bands could command fees of £25 to £75 in other cities simply because they came from Liverpool.

In 1963 we had the Beatles at the Odd Spot when they were No.1 with 'Please Please Me'. There were 1,000 people queuing in Bold Street and we couldn't cope with the demand. Brian Epstein was only getting £15 but he honored the booking. Bob's comments on Brian Epstein indicate that he always acted in an honorable way. I also totally agree with Bob about Freddie Starr - Bob was always worried that Ray McFall would choose the wrong moment to emerge from the manager's office, and I felt the same way. You never knew what Freddie would do and the five directors of the Odd Spot were even more staid than Ray McFall. I also have the impression that Bob was very fond of Gerry and the Pacemakers. I would agree - if the Beatles had not arrived, Gerry and the Pacemakers would have had all the glory. They were always very reliable and very professional.

Although Bob mentions Epstein's gambling at the Odd Spot, he was told little about it because Brian knew he didn't approve. Gambling was very male oriented then and a lot of lonely men gambled late at night, though I don't know if Brian went there to find people similar to himself. He wasn't a big gambler - I have seen fortunes won and lost - and I doubt if he ever lost more than £500 in a night. That sounds a lot but Brian came from a wealthy background. If he had been really reckless or foolish, I am sure that my Jewish directors would have informed Brian's parents.

I knew Bob Wooler for forty years, but many of the interests in Spencer's book were new to me. I love dance band records and the work of great songwriters like Cole Porter and Irving Berlin and I wish I had known about his passion for this music while he was alive. I moved into property and I was amazed to find that I had purchased the very house in Calthorpe Street in which he was raised and renovated it. Perhaps I could have sold it back to him, had he known!

It was very interesting to learn that Bob had had the opportunities to be on national radio and to work in London, but that he preferred to remain on Merseyside. Whilst much wealth was created through his efforts, he was working as a bingo-caller. This seemed very unfair at the time, but I can see now that it was partly his own doing. He was a man who was afraid of success.

I was amused by the story of Bob's birth certificate and to learn that his Christian names, Frederick James, are the same as mine. I must agree with him though that Bob Wooler sounds much better.

ACKNOWLEDGEMENTS

The first person to thank is Bob Wooler who gave me so much of his time, but as you will see, the meetings were a double-edged sword. I really, really regret that this book couldn't be published in his lifetime. I think he would have enjoyed its publication, but he was so pernickety that it would never have had final approval.

My thanks to *Record Collector* for permission to use parts of my interview with Bob Wooler, published in July 1998 and to reprint my feature on Liverpool cover versions from February 1999. Thanks also to Bill Harry for permission to reproduce some of Bob's work for the *Mersey Beat* newspaper. Then there is Bob's friend, John Seddon, who loaned me his "BW File". Bob would send him letters for the file and I was mortified to find that there were some about me. One says, "Please keep this strictly between ourselves - Spen must not know." As it was his comments on some of the draft pages for the book, you can see what I was up against. From reading the letters, I am sorry that he found it so stressful, but I think that, by that time, Bob found anything stressful.

I am very grateful to Tony Brown for his artwork, design and photography. Tony witnessed at first hand the frictions between Bob Wooler, Allan Williams, Joe Flannery and Rex Makin when his portrait of Brian Epstein was unveiled at the Neptune Theatre. As we came out reeling from some back-stabbing speeches, BBC Radio Merseyside's Arts Correspondent, Angela Heslop, said to me, "That's appalling. I feel so sorry for Tony Brown." "So do I," I said, "but wasn't it fun?"

Naturally, I am very pleased that Jim Turner of Drivegreen Publications has had such faith in the project. It is very flattering that someone should venture into publishing simply because he likes a book so much. I was delighted that the excellent Liverpool artist and designer, Tony Brown, was available to design the book as he made such a good job of *Brother, Can You Spare A Rhyme? - 100 Years Of Hit Songwriting* in 2000. Many of the photographs and items of memorabilia in this book come from the colletions of Bob Wooler, Jim Turner and myself. In most instances, the original copyright owners have been lost with time, but their names can be added to any future editions of the book. Our thanks to the *Liverpool Daily Post and Echo* for permission to reproduce news cuttings.

My thanks to everyone who has spoken to me about Bob and to Mark Lewisohn, with whom I shared many telephone conversations discussing the various issues. Thanks to Tim Adams, Steve Bailey, Steve Barnes, Tony Barrow, Lew Baxter, Mike Brocken, Jean Catharell, Geoffrey Davis, Ron Ellis, Peter Grant, Bill Harry, Bill Heckle, David Horn, Dave Jones, Mick O'Toole, Harry Prytherch. Viv Robinson, John Seddon, Howard and Melissa Storey, Norman and Cheryl Williams and my wife, Anne. Anne had long conversations with Bob on days that I wasn't there: Bob was delighted to find someone who disliked Bob Dylan even more than he did. Finally, my thanks to Allan Williams and Beryl Adams. Throughout this book, Bob's relationship with them is fairly spiky, but they are going to miss him more than anyone.

Spencer Leigh, October 2002

ROBERT WOOLER
21 Waverley Road
Liverpool L17 8TZ

(0151) 728 9064 (ExD)

1 TELLING TALES
Keith s Wine Bar

"It is so easy to make things up and we must avoid all this."
(Bob Wooler to Spencer Leigh, January 1998)

Bob Wooler was the disc-jockey at the Cavern during the 1960s and the compère and promoter at many other Merseyside venues. He was there at the start of Mersey Beat, saw it develop and watched the Beatles' rise to fame. He is a reliable witness, keen to point out that his stories are "from the horse's mouth and not from the other end." From time to time, authors have asked Bob for his reminiscences and, in particular, he has assisted Philip Norman (*Shout! - The True Story Of The Beatles*) and Ray Coleman (*John Winston Lennon, Brian Epstein - The Man Who Made The Beatles*). He said no to Albert Goldman (*The Lives Of John Lennon*), but he did find it highly comical that Goldman referred to him as "the scoutmaster". He would sometimes call me and say, "This is the scoutmaster here."

Several personalties connected with the Mersey Beat scene have written their autobiographies - Cilla Black, Brian Epstein, Len Garry (of the Quarry Men), the promoter Sam Leach, Gerry Marsden, Paul McCartney, Pete Shotton, Freddie Starr and Allan Williams. Alistair Taylor has written two books and Pete Best, with his newly published history of the Casbah Club, three. The memoirs of the local impresario Joe Flannery and of Faron (of Faron's Flamingos) should be published shortly and a second volume of Allan Williams' reminiscences is also in hand. In addition, many others have written extensively about their personal involvement with the Beatles, notably Tony Barrow and Bill Harry. George Harrison wrote a book, *I Me Mine*, which only mentioned John Lennon 11 times and Paul McCartney nine, which reveals a lot about their relationship.

Both fans and journalists had been pestering Bob Wooler for his reminiscences. For many years, he had given the impression that he was working on a book and that it would be published posthumously. "It's in the book" was one of his catchphrases. When he died in February 2002, the *Liverpool Echo* stated that he had lodged the text with the solicitor Rex Makin fifteen years earlier. Untrue. Bob was a world-class prevaricator and he had not even started the book, much less deposited it with a solicitor.

The basic material was there as Bob has kept memorabilia and made notes over the years, and at least three authors (Tony Barrow, Mike Evans and Bill Harry) had encouraged Bob to tell his story to them. Invariably, Bob got sidetracked or went coy whenever a cassette recorder was switched on. I never even tried myself: I interviewed Bob for a BBC Radio Merseyside series, *Let's Go Down The Cavern*, in 1983 and found him so cagey and hostile that I never wanted to interview him again. I remember him jeering, "And you'll probably add that Wooler made these remarks with a bottle in his hand." I didn't, of course, but it was an indication that Bob was both aware of his heavy drinking and ashamed of it.

Bob insisted that the interview was for broadcast purposes only and so, much to my regret, his comments were missing from my book of the same name. Mark Lewisohn, the author of *The Complete Beatles Chronicle*, had a similar experience. "When you ask Bob a question," he told me, "he first assesses whether he should answer it." It is understandable - Bob made little money from the Mersey Beat explosion - and he was wary of young (or even middle-aged) Turks exploiting his memories for personal gain.

By 1997 I had the rights of my *Let's Go Down The Cavern* book back and I was considering a much fuller, much longer version - indeed, I still have that as a long-term objective. First, I have to find a publisher willing to risk a 200,000 word book on Mersey Beat and then I have to clear the decks of most of my other commitments for a year. Whilst I was considering the way forward, I realised that Bob Wooler's story had still not been published and, in view of his advancing years and deteriorating health, it was about time something was done about it. Instead of seeking permission to quote him in a general book about Mersey Beat, I thought his own story should be told. This is sounding pretentious but I believe history should be preserved wherever possible. Bob was very astute and I felt that his perceptive opinions should be on public record. And they were opinions - it was hard to debate anything with Bob, he would prod me in the chest to emphasise some of his thoughts.

So many Mersey Beat musicians owed so much to Bob Wooler that I did consider a book which would combine his thoughts with their comments. However, that would be boring as they would say virtually the same thing, namely, Bob's a great bloke and he gave us bookings and encouragement. His support was most important and as Bob said, "Instead of being bitchy, I have always tried to encourage people." That is not wholly true as there is an affable bitchiness to many of his observations. This is one of the reasons why he didn't want a book published in his lifetime. He didn't want to hurt those that he might meet, and yet his comments, no matter how critical, were always affectionate. He could say with John Lennon, "In my life I've loved them all", although whether that included Lennon himself is a moot point.

Outside of the Mersey Beat contingent who owe him so much, not everyone shares this affection for Bob Wooler. Over the last twenty years and largely because of his association with the Beatles' first manager, Allan Williams, he had become a joke figure. At Beatle Conventions and elsewhere, Allan Williams gave the impression of making it up as he went along, and, indeed, there are enough inaccuracies and fabricated stories in his book, *The Man Who Gave The Beatles Away*, to merit it being filed under 'Fiction' in a library. As a Mersey Beat historian, I prefer the true stories without the embellishments, but Allan's anecdotes are colourful and highly entertaining. I like him a lot, more so in recent years because he has mellowed and has had Bob's welfare as a priority, although he couldn't resist goading him. The Williams and Wooler cabarets at Beatle Conventions did absolutely nothing for their credibility, but they featured compulsive, knockabout banter. In order to give you a flavour of their double act, I've included a transcript of two of their public appearances in the text.

After the 1997 Merseybeatle Convention, I asked *Record Collector* if they would commission a long, detailed interview with Bob Wooler. They agreed and, because Bob was not thought to be in a strong financial position, a fee was agreed, which is unusual for interviews. So far so good, but Bob kept delaying our meeting and by December 1997 I had given up hopes for the interview, let alone a book. I told him that his favourite record must be Peggy Lee's 'Mañana', not a bad guess as it happens.

Then, just before Christmas 1997, I had John McNally of the Searchers on my BBC Radio Merseyside programme, *On The Beat*. When I got home, I found four telephone messages from their former drummer, Chris Curtis, with the programme on in the background: "I'll talk," he said, "You can interview me at last." After many years of being silent, Chris Curtis told his story for both *Record Collector* and my radio programme. The success of the piece prompted *Record Collector* to ask for more Mersey Beat material and they wanted the Bob Wooler interview quickly. I told Bob it was now or never. For once, he agreed, and the resulting feature showed that we could work together - his words were not distorted and it came out how he wished. We could start on the book.

But Bob's health was poor - a stroke, a heart attack, diabetes, oedema, gout, arthritis and insomnia had left him with a huge regime of pills. I saw him leave a chemist with what seemed like a good proportion of their stock. He joked, "Where is Lord Woodbine now that I need him? I need some joints for my joints, anything to alleviate the pain." Bob no longer had the strength or will-power to write a book, but he did want to tell his story, to ensure that true accounts of many events were preserved for posterity and to add many anecdotes which were known only to him. I admired him for that but I was never sure - and I still don't know - whether working on the book kept him going or added to his troubles.

Probably fearing, quite correctly, that I would go rummaging through his memorabilia, Bob would not let me into his flat. We drank tea on Saturday mornings at Keith's Wine Bar near Sefton Park, which is about four miles from the city centre, and we had 25 two-hour sessions. As I walked down Lark Lane, I was unsure what I was going to find. Bob was exhilarating, exasperating, amusing, gloomy, razor sharp, blunted, mischievous, paranoid, superkeen and supercold about the book - and that's just one meeting. The worst meetings were when he changed his mind about telling me something or refused to let me use something from the previous week. It took a month to get the story about Brian Epstein and the little-known Liverpool singer Clay Ellis because Bob only told it to me in parts.

Whatever the outcome of a particular meeting, I was glad to be there as our rendezvouses could be cancelled at short notice, usually because of his health - or at least that's what he told me. I taped all our interviews and although Bob rambled and could be repetitious, it didn't matter because of the cut-and-paste facilities of today's computers. "I wish I had a red light which would come on to indicate that I have already told you something," he surmised, renaming the place on one of his more mournful days, Keith's Whine Bar. Even on gloomy Saturdays, the wit was usually present: "If I get married again," he surmised, "I would have to spend my honeymoon at Viagra Falls."

Bob Wooler was a Liverpool Oscar Wilde as he is known, even revered, for aphorisms. All the favourites are within these pages, but because of his constant pain, he felt that he had lost the capacity to mint witty phrases. He was wrong and as the weeks went by, more and more new Woolerisms were unveiled. One morning he sat down at the table and said in his very clear and distinct voice, "John Lennon went from rage to riches. Will that do for today?" Many of his Woolerisms, as you will discover, are devastatingly funny. He described the book as 'bile with a smile'. His suggested title, *Those Zany Grainy Mersey Beatle Days*, was a play on Nat 'King' Cole's 'Those Lazy Hazy Crazy Days Of Summer', but I didn't like it at all. The next week he offered me an alternative, *Those Witty Gritty Walter Mitty Mersey Beatle Days*. Not quite, Bob, but much better. Next time it was *A Hard Night's Daze*.

I have greatly enjoyed getting to know Bob Wooler, but he was suspicious and secretive and resented so many of my questions. "You're at it again," he would snap, "You're putting me through the Jerry Springer wringer." I would be irritated that he was pulling down the shutters. Sometimes he would refuse to take my calls, fearing I would upset him further. The prime difficulty was getting Bob to discuss, or even acknowledge, the fight between himself and John Lennon at Paul McCartney's 21st birthday party. "The readers will understand that I don't want to talk about it," he would say. "Not if they're paying good money for a book," I retorted. Quite simply, secretive people shouldn't write autobiographical books.

Bob was steeped in, and surrounded by, nostalgia, although he kept up to date on world affairs and often drew parallels between the 60s and the 90s. As he said, "The reason I remember so many things about the Mersey Beat days is because I haven't let them go. If you let them go, they vanish from your mind. I find that if you don't let go, no matter how way back it is, you keep it fresh in your mind. Once this book is written, I can undergo a kind of catharsis and let my mind go free and unfettered."

This book, however, is not Bob Wooler's autobiography. It could have been, it should have been, it almost was, but it isn't. Bob Wooler died in February 2002 before the book could be completed, but even that isn't the reason. Bob had a good cop, bad cop personality: the good cop wanted to write his memoirs, the bad cop fought against it. The good cop wanted me to ghost his book but so often he would say he was sorry for wasting my time, that this book would never be published. "If people read this," he would say, "they will accuse me of having foot in mouth disease."

Ironically, it is Bob's death that has made this book possible. If he were still alive, he would still be prevaricating, wanting to rewrite certain sections - every section - and then going back to the beginning. "This is speech, Spencer," he would say, "I wouldn't write it like this." "But you're never going to do that, Bob," I would argue, "and besides it is your speech, and what people love is the way you speak." "No," he would say, "I can't let this through. I didn't expect to be smelling of roses, but when I read it, I see I am smelling of neuroses." He would add, "Don't let it bother you. You are still in my Family and Friends for discounted telephone calls."

Despite the many inconclusive meetings, we had, I think, completed about 80% of the book. I told him that if he rang me one morning and said, "Come to Keith's Wine Bar and I will answer anything you ask", we could have finished the book. I knew that would never happen, and after a year of waiting, I decided that I had had enough and amongst other things, I wrote a history of the Merseysippi Jazz Band, *Sweeping The Blues Away*, where, in complete contrast, all the participants were very helpful. I told Bob that if and when he wanted to complete the book, we could meet up but otherwise we were going round in circles. Bob sent me a letter, "I cannot and will not assume further feelings of guilt and have it said of me that I was responsible for delaying it or even not having it come out at all. That would be all I need to complete my grief." Still, nothing happened.

I wouldn't claim to be a personal friend of Bob Wooler's but we spoke from time to time about other matters. Bob had an excellent knowledge of old-time songwriters and if I was writing an obituary for *The Independent*, we might discuss that person's work - and he sometimes mentioned the book. "We must get it out," he would say, "Look at what so-and-so is saying in the papers. I can tell the true story." The bad cop, however, would refuse to complete the project. I met Allan Williams who said, "I know what you're doing, Spencer. You're keeping all this until Bob dies and then you can publish it and keep all the royalties for yourself." That had never crossed my mind, but Allan's words rankled me for so long that I determined never to publish the book.

Bob's funeral changed all that. Bob's former wife, Beryl Adams, asked me to say a few words about him and I decided that they should be Bob's words. I hadn't looked at the draft chapters for some months and I found myself laughing at the sharpness of his wit: this is terrific stuff, I thought, it should be published. I chose a few paragraphs near the end of the book where Bob is talking about *Desert Island Discs, Room 101* and becoming *The Ghost Of Mersey Beat Past*. The paragraphs were packed tight with Woolerisms, many of which would have been new to the mourners and his pointed observations were aimed at some of them. Bill Heckle, a director of Cavern City Tours, said, "I could imagine Bob in his coffin rocking with laughter as you read that."

After the service, it seemed like the entire congregation was saying to me, "You must publish this book." Jim Turner, a Liverpool club manager and agent from the 1960s and hence, a contemporary of Bob's, offered to publish it, and here it is. I didn't look for a London publisher as I thought it was fitting that Bob's book should be published in his home town. In keeping with his shambolic life, Bob died intestate but not impoverished - he wore the same herring-bone jacket and he called Oxfam his tailors, but he had £25,000 in his bank account. Bob wanted the Institute of Popular Music (IPM) at Liverpool University to have his papers and I hope that comes to pass. From time to time, he would arrive at Keith's with a few of his numerous files as he had kept notes, photographs and press cuttings on almost anything or anyone connected with Liverpool. He also had an impressive collection of Merseyside newspapers and magazines. How he lived in the midst of so much clutter is beyond me. I considered delaying the book until the outcome of the files was known as, with access to them, I could flesh out the chapters. However, that is another project - perhaps for me, perhaps for someone at the IPM.

The Best Of Fellas is the story of ghosting Bob Wooler's autobiography and I can imagine Bob saying, "Revenge, Spencer, you're getting your revenge." I wouldn't deny it, but the background to the book tells you a lot about Bob Wooler. You will find Bob's autobiography within the text in direct quotes. You can imagine him saying every word. As indeed he did.

SIDETRACKED

Lyrics by Bob Wooler, as arranged and recorded by Phil Brady and the Ranchers.

Just when I started doing instead of thinking,
Even started saving up my pay,
She pulled the cork and had me drinking,
I guess I got sidetracked on the way.

I guess I got sidetracked on the way,
There ain't nothing more that I can say,
It was ever thus, I'm like the wayward bus,
Forever getting sidetracked on the way.

And then there was a time that I decided,
That from the straight and narrow I'd never stray,
But she tempted me and all the things that I did,
I guess I got sidetracked on the way.

I guess I got sidetracked on the way.
There ain't nothing more that I can say,
You'll always find I've got a tangled mind,
Forever getting sidetracked on the way.

I've always been so full of good intentions,
That I hope the Lord on judgement day,
Will pardon me if I should mention
That I got sidetracked on the way.

I guess I got sidetracked on the way.
There ain't nothing more that I can say,
Like I said before, I know the drifters' law,
Forever getting sidetracked on the way.

Story of the CAVERN

THE CAVERN... A Tomorrow Kind of Club! *by Bob Wooler*

Number 10 Mathew Street, Liverpool - the most famous Beat music address in the world - a disused warehouse basement and one-time bomb shelter which was opened as The Cavern Club in January 1957 as a Jazz cellar. During the course of the next nine years it changed hands and its music policy.

It was to become the most publicised, visited, talked of, written about, photographed, filmed, televised Pop music shrine in the world.

Like a magnet it drew people from all walks of life. When in Liverpool the international 'in' thing was to visit Mathew Street. Rolls Royces rubbed bumpers with battered groups' vans. A case of if-you've-never-seen-The-Cavern-you've-never-lived!

Recorded in The Cavern's V.I.P's visitors book are the signatures of such celebrities as Arthur Fiedler, Nancy Spain, Dave Clark, Lord Derby, George Martin, Rex Harrison, Chet Atkins, Stanley Baxter, Lionel Bart, Anna Neagle, Marlene Dietrich, and many others.

The Cavern has a proud history of being the U.K's leading launching pad for Pop artistes. The show biz luminaries who have achieved world-wide acclaim with the help of The Cavern are legion. It will always be regarded as the Top Cellar that produced so many Top Sellers!

An A to Z of hit parade artistes who during its long history have kept The Cavern in the forefront of popular entertainment venues by appearing at the club would read like a Who's Who of the international Pop scene.

The high standards of top quality entertainment established in the past will be maintained in the future. The aim will be to enhance even more the reputation of the club; to make the name The Cavern synonimous with all that is important and exciting in teen appeal happenings.

In the very near future the ultimate in popology will be achieved. The combined premises of Nos. 8, 10 and 12 Mathew Street will resemble a kind of subterranean Disneyland Poporium! A Cavernanza, with dancing, star entertainment, coffee lounge, beauty salons, souvenir shops, boutiques, bowling alley, mini-cinema, amusement arcade, closed circuit television, fashion shows, charm school.

A sort of Beatique, specialising in Superpop! That's The Cavern - a tomorrow kind of club!

BOB WOOLER - Mr Mersey Beat himself; Radio Luxembourg compere; disc jockey, agent, manager, Beat music columnist, promoter, songwriter, broadcaster, Pop music consultant; has appeared in many TV programmes including 'Thank Your Lucky Stars', 'A Whole Scene Going,' and 'Scene at 6.30,' also several video films for U.S. release. During his five years association with the old Cavern, he presented The Beatles there 292 times! His role with the new Cavern will be chiefly as Entertainments Co-ordinator, in charge of bookings and general publicity,

From the programme for the reopening of the Cavern in 1966.

15

The Best Of Fellas - The Story Of Bob Wooler.

Bob Wooler

Bob Wooler and Kingsize Taylor

Keith's Wine Bar, Lark Lane, Liverpool

'Live At The Cavern' Album cover

16

2 I REMEMBER IT WELL?

DOB - Childhood - Schooldays - Second World War - Army service

*"I was not born like Lee Marvin under a wandering star. I was born
under a wondering star and my whole life is full of questions."*
(Bob Wooler)

After several drafts, we had, I think, a terrific start.

Bob Wooler: "I don't know how the song came to be written but I like to think that Carl
Sigman looked at Francis Lai's melody, scratched his head and thought, 'Where do I
begin to tell my story?' He realised that his words fitted the melody perfectly and a hit
song was born.

"So, where do *I* begin to tell my story? I am not sure how much you want to know about
me. It's a fair supposition that you have bought this book for my memories of the
Beatles and the other Mersey groups. I will give you this, plenty of this, and I can vouch
for its accuracy. Many autobiographies embellish the truth and, in lots of cases, simply
lie in order to give the impression that they are authorities on the subject when, in truth,
they had very little involvement at all. There is none of that here. I am going to tell
you the truth. I don't want to win the Booker Prize, which is awarded each year for
books of fiction. And couldn't there be a wonderful new award - the prize for the
autobiography containing the most lies?

"The first casualty of war is said to be the truth - the first casualty of a phenomenon, I
submit, is also the truth as so many people are jockeying to stress their own importance
and connections and to come over as Mr. Clever. You know the sort of thing - 'When I
first saw the Beatles in 1960, I knew they would make it.' Imagine people possessing
an inbuilt trait whereby their noses would become like Pinocchio's when they started to
lie. Their noses would become bigger and bigger, and there would be a lot of people
around Liverpool who could audition for the role of Cyrano de Bergerac. I take so
much of what I read with a cellarful of salt, and I shall separate Mathew Street from
Mythew Street as the book develops.

"Of course, I should have written this book many years ago, but I am a terrible plodder,
I prevaricate and I seldom get on with things. I'm not attempting to excuse myself by

saying this is a common fault because I know it can be most frustrating for myself as well as for the people I deal with. Now I can say it is my health holding me back, but what excuses do I have for the years before I had my stroke? In 1997 Spencer Leigh wanted to ensure that my reminiscences didn't die with me and I gloomily told him that he'd better be quick as I didn't think that I would make the Millennium. We have had many meetings, usually in Keith's Wine Bar near Sefton Park, and he has asked me many pertinent, and some impertinent, questions in his quest to capture my story. It is not an easy task: some stories I will gladly tell a dozen times, others I don't want to discuss at all.

"As far as I'm concerned and I cannot stress this enough, this book is not written in any way to boost my ego. My sole reason for writing the book is to tell the truth. I want to have something available for researchers that they can consider as fact and not fiction. Many of the other Beatle books are little more than fiction. I will separate the facts from my opinions as I am fully aware that someone might see the same things as me and form a completely different opinion."

All this was very commendable, a good declaration of intent, but Bob Wooler did not arrive, fully formed, into the beat clubs of 1960. I needed Bob's background. We must begin at the beginning.

"I suppose you mean my DOB," grumbled Bob, "I was born on January 19. I am a Capricorn, born on the cusp. Everything is rather grim with Capricorns and, by and large, they take things too seriously. I conform to that pattern: Capricorns can be irritatingly orderly and like things just so. I was organised at one time but rock'n'roll took its toll and I developed a tangled mind."

"And the year?"

"Haven't you read Bill Harry's *Encyclopedia of Beatles People*: 'Bob Wooler was born on 19 January 1932'?"

"That's what the book says, but I don't believe it. You're very careful not to give many details about your past, but your tastes betray your age. I think you were born earlier than that."

"Does it matter?"

"Yes, it does. Jimmy Savile didn't give his age in his autobiography and it looks ridiculous. You have to come clean. I always like to know someone's age. It is much easier for readers to relate to you once they know how old you are."

"1932," said Bob.

"Well, think about it and tell me next Saturday."

"There's nothing to think about. It's 1932."

"And your full name?"

"Ah, I will reveal something here. In the past, I have told people that my full name is Robert James Wooler, but that is only half-true. It is Robert Frederick Wooler, which sounds so old-fashioned."

"Wooler is a very unusual name."

"I don't know where my name 'Wooler' comes from - Wilfred Wooller, the cricketer, has two L's. My name is often misspelt with two L's but there is enough 'ell in my life as it is. One day at the Cavern a lad came to the bandroom and said that he had the same name as me, but he wasn't from these parts. He only had one L, and apparently the spelling of my surname is a rarity. If you look in the Liverpool telephone book, you won't find another 'Wooler'. I did have some relations in Leeds but I drifted apart from them years ago. There is seemingly no-one else extant in Liverpool. There is a town called Wooler not far from Holy Island and I thought several times of going there out of curiosity, but never did."

During the next week, I spoke to Ritchie Galvin, the drummer with Earl Preston and the TT's. Bob was the best man at Ritchie's wedding and he was sure that Bob was born earlier. Bob remained adamant about 1932. The writer, Mark Lewisohn, was going to St. Catherine's House for research connected to his biography of Benny Hill, and I asked him to obtain a copy of Bob's birth certificate. He searched for Robert or Bob Wooler and got nowhere. With a little more information, he returned and obtained the details. I had some ammunition for my next visit to Keith's Wine Bar.

"Bob, when were you born?"

"We're not going into all that again. 1932, as Bill Harry says."

"Bob, I have a copy of your birth certificate."

"Oh." (Long, long pause) "19 January 1926. Allan Williams knows my actual age, and he was born in 1930. He said, 'According to Bill Harry's book, I'm older than you and it should be the other way around.' I said, 'Let it be, Allan. It suits me fine.' I was born in Liverpool, I don't know precisely where, on 19 January 1926. It was a memorable

19

year because of the General Strike, the only such strike that we've had here. Her Majesty the Queen, Bill Haley, Chuck Berry, George Melly, Brian Matthew, Alan Freeman, Marilyn Monroe, Rod Steiger, Burt Bacharach, Roger Moore and Ken Dodd are my contemporaries. George Martin was born a fortnight before me."

"So why is it such a secret?"

"It is very difficult to imagine that a decrepit person like me was the disc-jockey at the Cavern nearly 40 years ago, and I have always been reluctant to give my DOB. This is because I have always regarded rock'n'roll as essentially teenage music, music for young people to perform and get involved in. I didn't think it was music for a person over thirty to dabble with, no matter how young thinking he may appear to be. At least, this was my view in the embryo days of the 50s. Things are very different now as rock'n'roll has become an established form of music just as jazz did eventually. Daddy-O can be Granddaddy-O." (Indeed. Owen Clayton at the age of 66 is playing with Juke Box Eddie's - Liverpool's first rocking pensioner.)

"And Bob, you're not even Bob Wooler. You were born Frederick James Wooler. We can't have this deception. If the book is published with wrong information, a critic who knows the real picture can tear it to shreds."

"No one knows," said Bob, "And you wouldn't if you hadn't gone prying. I can't stand this. The book is off." (Silence)

"Okay, I'll go now and call you during the week."

"Let me see that certificate." I placed it in front of him.

"My father was Thomas Henry Wooler (I don't even know if he was called Tom) and my mother's name was Florence. My birth certificate describes him as a jobbing gardener, which sounds rather ordinary, but I know he had a farm in Aigburth Hall Road near the cricket ground. It would be a dairy farm, but again I am vague about the details. There were a lot of dairy farms then and George Smith also had one. He was John Lennon's uncle and married to Aunt Mimi, and John lived in their house in Menlove Avenue for half of his life."

"What about your mother?"

"She was from Scarborough and I don't know how she met my father, who was from Aigburth. He died of cancer when I was four and my mother died when I was 15, so no-one can answer these questions. I don't think I ever asked her about my background: when you're 14 or 15, you're not very enquiring. There was nothing big about my father's farm and my mother didn't inherit anything. After my father's death, my mother was granted a weekly allowance by the PAC - which is the Public Assistance Committee - but it was means-tested and meagre."

"How did your father die?"

"My father died on 2 June 1930 at the age of 54. My mother told me that my father used to drink a lot with his friends at the Aigburth Hotel and I wonder if it is a case of like father, like son. I have always been conscious that heavy drinking runs in the family, but it's not a wagging finger hanging over me. When it's Operation Elbow, you don't give a damn. I have seen people being destroyed by drink all the time. Most of the beat groups had one member with a self-destruct button. The Big Three had all three, but fortunately they are still active today, although one of them owes his survival to AA. I love that story about Del Shannon. He was feeling bad on a UK tour and he asked a young, inexperienced roadie to take him to the AA. The roadie took him to a garage to get signed up. Some people would have us believe that addiction to the bottle is an illness, but that sounds like an excuse. It is surely more like a weakness and calling it an illness is simply camouflage for one's own inability to give it up."

Week after week I would return to Bob's childhood and I would get no more than a handful of words each time. Like the Del Shannon story, he would find some way of going off at a tangent. Bob told me of his brother, Jack, who was two years older than himself, but he immediately regretted giving me that information as he knew it would lead to more questioning.

Piecing together Bob's various snippets about the pre-war years, I have come up with the following.

Bob Wooler: "We were living in Calthorpe Street, Liverpool 19, which was a two-up two-down terraced house without a bathroom in Garston. A Coronation Street world. I lived at the top of St. Mary's Road, which was the main street in the village, and the gasworks, the bobbin works and Bryant and May's matches were close at hand. My old house is still there and a few years ago, I took a sentimental journey to see it which was a ridiculous thing to do - places are never the same as they were and you can't recapture the past. 20 Forthlin Road in Allerton where Paul McCartney lived was a cut above our house. We had gaslight and it was all very frugal, but I am not trying to enlist your sympathy.

"To quote from *A Tale Of Two Cities*, they were the best of times, they were the worst of times. We didn't complain as we were not aware of the mod cons, the niceties that were available to those with money. These days there is a car at every door in the street, but a car was a rare thing in Garston. Our houses didn't have garages, and the coalman delivered hundredweight sacks of coal on a horse-driven cart. It was as though we were living in the Victorian age. I remember reading *The People Of The Abyss*, a novella by Jack London about the terrible conditions in the East End of London, and that was even more appalling than where we lived.

"Like millions of others, we had nothing - no hot water, no fridges, no toasters and no vacuum cleaners. We had cold water and everything had to be boiled on the gas oven. We only had gaslight. When the war came, they stopped all the conversions from gaslight to electricity because the authorities didn't see that as important. They had their priorities and this was not one of them. We were not converted until after the war and we had to put up with gaslight and, of course, a wind-up gramophone. However, I would stress that I am not trying to appear hard done by - as I keep saying, there were millions living like us or in even worse conditions."

Most people I know have a repertoire of well-proven anecdotes about their schooldays. Bob Wooler had none. He would rather be at the dentist than talk about his childhood. "I have no school stories," he would say, "but if I was AW, I could make something up." Occasionally, there was a shaft of light.

Once I asked him if he had ever been caned. He replied, "School punishments were more severe and humiliating than they are today. At the school assembly, the Headmaster would say some prayers and then proceed with the Riot Act. He would call out some boy's name and the poor lad would go on to the platform. He would tell us what the boy had done wrong and say he was going to be punished. The cane would be wielded and he would have two strokes on each hand, which was quite fearful in a way. We all willed the lad not to break down and cry. Most of them would leave wringing their hands with pain and tears in their eyes, but they didn't break down. I was lucky. This humiliation never happened to me, thank God."

One day, to my immense surprise, he came to Keith's Wine Bar with a school report from Gilmour Heath Road. Bob had good marks for geography and science, but maths was 'a most disappointing result'. "The constant criticism wore me down," said Bob, "The art teacher praised Jack, who was a good artist, and he would say, 'You're not as good as your brother.'"

I pointed out that being good at maths is a prime requirement for a promoter: "Well, I am no good at mental arithmetic, I can add and subtract but I am lost with percentages and fractions. I was punished by the class teacher for doing my maths poorly. If you got less than 50% in the tests, you had to go to the front and receive a thwack. The teacher never put much effort into it, but there was a certain indignity attached to it."

There were ways around this. "You would give your answers to the person sitting alongside you. He would mark your paper and you would mark his as the correct answers were being written on the blackboard. One day there was a smart lad alongside me and I asked him if I could copy his answers and he said yes. As the low scoring boys went to the front to receive their thwack, the teacher said, 'Is that all? Isn't there anybody else, what about you, Wooler? You're usually out here.' The lad said, 'No, sir, he's got them right.' The teacher thought something was up and he arranged a complete switcharound, so I got a thickhead next to me. He didn't let on that he didn't know the answers so I was copying the wrong answers. He joined me in the front of the class for his thwack. That was supposed to be inculcating us, but it did nothing of the sort for me. I'm still lousy at mental arithmetic."

Mostly, however, the mention of school brought out his Woolerisms:

• I had an inquiring mind, but having a lot of whys does not necessarily make one wise.

• School taught me the traditional three R's - reading, writing and arithmetic - which also tells me that teachers can't spell. My mother taught me the other three R's - respect, and the difference between right and wrong.

Bob's school effectively ended when war was declared in September 1939: "The Government decreed that all places where people assembled such as cinemas, theatres and sporting events were to close down. The ban was soon lifted for reasons of morale. Schools initially were also affected. Token lessons were given to small groups of pupils using front rooms of houses for the purpose, courtesy of the tenants. One hour lessons might be held in a house several times a week. Afterwards, the teacher would go to another house and instruct the pupils who were there, so it was all rather makeshift. I was 14 in January 1940, but I left earlier, at Christmas. I was not sorry to leave. They were not the happiest days of my life, and I couldn't wait to get away. My schooldays never filled me with joy. I found them fraught and anxious and I was glad to leave when I did."

Bob reflected, "I don't want to use my flimsy schooling as an excuse for not doing more with my life. I have no time for people who say their whole life has been ruined by their childhood. I try not to subscribe to self-pity, and I accept the precept that we all make our own way in life, although now I am sounding like Mrs. Thatcher or the *Daily Mail*. Eric Morley and Leslie Thomas go on about being Barnardo boys and ask us to look at what they have made of their lives, but I don't want to blame anyone but myself.

"The war years were terribly difficult for everyone. London was the hardest hit of course, more so than all the other UK cities put together, but Liverpool, Birmingham and Glasgow suffered very badly. Both sides of the Mersey were mercilessly hammered for one unforgettable week in May 1941 by Hitler's Heinkels. My brother wouldn't give a damn and continued sleeping in his bed even when the shrapnel was falling like hailstones on the slates on the roof. It was more an act of defiance than being macho. If your name is on the bomb, he thought, what can you do about it? I would hear a cacophony of sounds, and would hurriedly get up and go under the stairs, supposedly the safest place. I did feel the pressure to be like my brother and remain in bed, but didn't manage to do so.

"Without piling on the agony, it was unnerving as you never knew what was in store for you. It wasn't so much the bombs as the shrapnel from the anti-aircraft guns. The shells would be aimed at the 'planes, the casing would explode and a shower of shrapnel would hurtle downwards and hit the roofs. In the morning, you could see the shells lying in the streets. I was lucky as I escaped the bombing and there were no casualties in our street. There was a landmine in the garden of a house in nearby Whitehedge Road, and a bomb landed in the gasworks, which was about a mile away, but didn't explode. God knows what would have happened if it did.

"We didn't have an Anderson shelter in the back yard - you had to have a garden for that. The Government did build some big shelters above ground on either side of the street, but not everyone went there. You could get about 50 people in, and the walls were very thick with equally thick concrete flat roofs. There is still a pillbox in Clark Gardens near the cemetery in Allerton: this was a gun position. They would site them all over the place, usually behind hoardings or at bridges, so that they weren't visible. The guns would be put in the ports and they would put holes in the hoardings.

"The shelters were not lit or heated and we went there with candles. There would be the odd armchair and we would sit on benches shivering and making desultory talk against the crunching sound of the ack-ack shells. The louder sounds would signify a bomb had been dropped somewhere nearby. The bombers were usually Heinkel HE 111's or Junkers 88's, and they would bomb Liverpool and thereabouts for an hour or so and return to Germany via the Irish Sea.

"My mother died of a heart attack two days before my sixteenth birthday on 17 January 1942; she was 53 years old. She was worried about us going into the army and that may have been a contributory factor, although she had suffered from angina for some years."

When Bob told me of a conversation in the bandroom at the Cavern where John and Paul had been discussing losing their mothers at a young age, I asked him if he had told them of his similar loss. "No, no, I wouldn't reveal that to them, but I knew how they felt about their losses."

When Bob's mother died, he was working on the railways as a junior clerk, and his brother was a gardener: "I worked for a railway company, the LMS, but it was on the goods side, not the passenger trains. Garston Docks were R.O.D. - railway owned docks - and the railway lines went into Garston Docks for coal to be exported, usually to Ireland. We also collected the pit props from the ships and dealt with many other wartime commodities. The Elders and Fyffes banana boats no longer plied their trade, although that did resume once the war was over."

His friend, Doug Evans, who worked with him, recalls, "I was born in 1926 so we were both 17 but I went in as a clerk, which was very posh in those days, and he was a messenger boy who moved into the clerical ranks. We became friends and we were both in the wages department. We would make up the wages bills for the dockers. He also worked in the estate office and he liked that as it had to do with maps. One of his jobs was showing school parties around the dock estate. Even then he was a loner, but he wasn't bothered about being on his own at all. As I discovered, when he wasn't on his own, he did like to be the star of the show. And he always spoke in that wonderful way, no trace of a Liverpool accent at all."

Bob Wooler: "My mother had died, Jack was called up and I was by myself then. It was difficult, but the neighbours were very good. My brother wasn't the sort of person who could adapt to army life. He was not at all outgoing, and it must have been murder for him as he was a total misfit, but then how many were really suited to this life? He was in the Royal Artillery and he was stationed in this country. I was spared for a time because they were deferring people who worked on the railway. Eventually I joined the army and went as far as Singapore. Much later in the 1960s, the Fourmost pop group told me, 'We've got a nice booking on a cruise on the Dunera', which was the troopship on which I went to the Far East.

"I got through the army okay by simply conforming and not making waves. I am a maverick at heart, but I realised that toeing the line was the wisest move. I did what I was told to do, which was terribly routine and dismal. You see films like *From Here To Eternity* where they kick over the traces and do outrageous and outlandish things, but I did none of that and I never met anyone who did. I didn't even drink in those days. I was in the Coordination and Procedures Office in 23BOD (Base Ordinance Depot) in Singapore. I was in charge of a section, rather than being in charge of men. The second lieutenant in charge told me I was to go on a CADRE course and I said, 'Do I have to?' He said, 'Why not? It will be promotion for you, and you are interested in promotion, aren't you? If you're not, then you're no good to us.' So I had to go. Incidents like this give a flavour of my truculent tolerance of the army."

In trying to get stories of Bob's army life, I got an amusing aside. "I'm not Tom McKenzie serving on an ack-ack site during the war and 'darning his socks in the night when there's nobody there.' He compèred six shows by the Beatles in Northwich in 1962/3, and he claimed to be the Father McKenzie in 'Eleanor Rigby' which is tenuous, to say the least."

In a revealing moment, Bob removed his stripe when he returned home so that his brother would not know of it. I've no doubt that Bob's dysfunctional upbringing affected his later life. He would have made an ideal subject for Radio 4's *In The Psychiatrist's Chair*. He disliked so much about himself that he resembled a character in a Samuel Beckett play.

What happened to brother Jack? "I don't know. He wasn't interested in popular music to the extent I am. I do remember him saying how marvellous Liszt's *Hungarian Rhapsody No. 2* was, and I would, in turn, point out that 'Love Walked In' was a very good composition, but he wasn't terribly impressed. Jack and I drifted apart because I became associated with rock'n'roll. He wanted to be a painter and sculptor, and it wasn't until the 1970s that I met him again and he had returned from Australia. I asked Arthur Dooley if he could be considered for any sculpturing jobs but nothing came of it. Then I lost touch with him again."

In the search for relatives following Bob's death, it came to light that his brother had died but he had known nothing of it. "That super-optimistic song, Blue Skies, was written the year I was born. It's not me, is it?"

THANKS FOR THE MEMORY (PARODY)

This is a lyric that Bob wrote in the services. 50 years on, he was not proud of it but he appreciated that it gave a good feeling for the times. It also made his point that budding lyricists should write new lyrics for existing songs as practice. I know that Bob would want me to say that the original, Oscar-winning song had words by Leo Robin and music by Ralph Rainger and was performed by Bob Hope and Shirley Ross in 'The Big Broadcast Of 1938'.

Thanks for the memory
Of Smith and Waterworth
Of yearning for some earth
Of flesh and sweat
And people I've met
And moodiness and mirth
How futile it was.

Thanks for the memory
Of bromide in the tea
Of wild, delirious sea
Of heat and haze
And salty sprays
And a longing to be free
How futile it was.

Many were the times of frustration
And many the times of elation
Ever present the engine vibration
Life was grim, and hearts grew dim, so

Thanks for the memory
Of fantastical hide and seek
Of quickly drying teak
Of sweaty socks
And talks on pox
And an hour is a week
How futile it was.

Thanks for the memory
Of hammocks on the hooks
Of greasy native cooks
Of sour salads

27

And Oakley ballads
And pornographic books
How futile it was.

Thanks for the memory
Of decks that won't keep still
Of seas that make one ill
Of latrine troughs
And nightly coughs
And a surreptitious thrill
How futile it was.

Many were the moments of madness
And many the moments of sadness
And sometimes we knew of gladness
But that was rare, so why should we care, so

Thanks for the memory
Of kippers and of grease
K.D's without a crease
Of pulpy bread
And a wary tread
And a constant search for peace
How futile it all was.

*Bob Wooler commented: "I wrote this at the time as a diary entry and I am somewhat
reluctant to use it as it is not well-written. Some lines have just been included for the
rhyme and the scansion could be better. Comments are needed to explain some
references:*

*"Smith and Waterworth were two trifling Signals captains in charge of the troop-deck;
they fussed the voyage away giving stupid orders. Later on, there's a reference to
Oakley, who was a corporal and a terrible, boozy-voiced baritone. He sang 'Friend Of
Mine'. He wasn't.*

*"Bromide was put in the tea as a sex sedative. It made the tea taste rotten. We also had
weekly lectures on the ravages of syphilis and gonorrhoea. There was, however, plenty
of salacious literature on board.*

*"The 'hide and seek' wasn't intentional. It was amazing how long it took to find people.
Somehow they contrived to move to the port side when you had crossed to the starboard,
and vice versa.*

"Each morning the Indian crew would clean the decks with sea water. The sun would come up and steam the decks bone dry in a few minutes.

"K.D. is khaki drill. We had to wash our clothes as best we could. Usually, we went on parade looking pretty baggy."

Calthorpe Street, Garston, 2002.

Bob Wooler and Doug Evans, 1943.

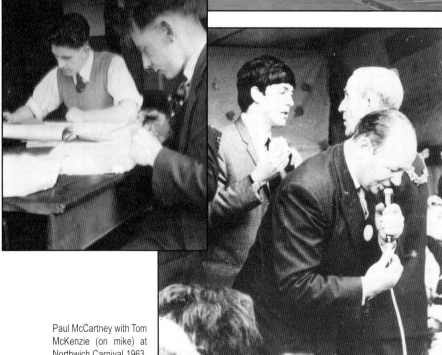

Paul McCartney with Tom McKenzie (on mike) at Northwich Carnival 1963.

29

The Best Of Fellas - The Story Of Bob Wooler.

CERTIFIED COPY OF AN ENTRY OF BIRTH

GIVEN AT THE GENERAL REGISTER OFFICE

Application Number ....G002708......

REGISTRATION DISTRICT   West Derby

1926. BIRTH in the Sub-district of ...Kirkdale........................ in the ......County of Liverpool C.B......

No.	When and where born	Name, if any	Sex	Name and surname of father	Name, surname and maiden surname of mother	Occupation of father	Signature, description and residence of informant	When registered	Signature of registrar	Name entered after registration
Columns:-	1	2	3	4	5	6	7	8	9	10*
229	Nineteenth January 1926, Stanley James Hospital W	Frederick James	Boy	Thomas Wooler formerly Brown Liverpool	Florence Wooler formerly Brown	Getting 1/13 arguildHall 13 Blond Arguild Hall Liverpool Road	T. H. Wooler father arguildHall March Road 1926	Fourth	ArthWall Registrar	

BXBY 624947

CERTIFIED to be a true copy of an entry in the certified copy of a Register of Births in the District above mentioned

Given at the GENERAL REGISTER OFFICE, under the Seal of the said Office, the ....19th.......... day of .... May .... 19 ..99..

*See note overleaf

CAUTION:- It is an offence to falsify a certificate or to make or knowingly use a false certificate or a copy of a false certificate intending it to be accepted as genuine to the prejudice of any person or to possess a certificate knowing it to be false without lawful authority.
WARNING: THIS CERTIFICATE IS NOT EVIDENCE OF THE IDENTITY OF THE PERSON PRESENTING IT.

Dd 0096 197M 7/98 Mcr(203574)

30

3 THE TRADICAL
Religion - Politics - Liverpool life - Scouse accent - Liverpool films
- Scouse pride

*"I have evolved a Woolerism with regards to my politics
- I am a radical with traditional views, so I am not a radical,
I am not a redical, I am a tradical."*
(Bob Wooler, 1998)

The majority of this book is about music, but Bob Wooler had strongly held views on a wide variety of subjects. "I am an old codger who is given to cogitating," he told me, "so call me an old codgitator."

Bob rang me on 7 February 2000. He told me that he had a question in the *Daily Mail* that he asked under a pseudonym. He wanted to know if there was a perfect way to collect ransom money. You could never tell what was going to interest him next - and what did he want to know it for?

Bob Wooler and Religion

"I was born Church of England but long ago I renounced all religions not because it is easier that way, but because I am firmly convinced that most wars are caused through religious intolerance. However, when it comes to beliefs, I would still say that I am a Christian. When I was working on the railway, I befriended a devout Catholic and people said, 'Wooler's on the road to Rome.' When someone found a *Daily Worker* in my desk, they said, 'Wooler's on his way to the Kremlin.' I said, 'I can't be going both places, can I? How can I be going to Rome and to Moscow?'

"I would love to know what happens when we die. Scientists are pioneering new frontiers all the time, especially with regards to the creation of life, but no one ever mentions the other side. What will happen to us at closing time? And what would happen if we knew? I don't think anyone wholeheartedly believes in God; everybody has a percentage of doubt. If we could be sure that we would go to Paradise, then everybody would commit suicide tomorrow. Why would we bother to stay around? We can't be certain and this is the reason we keep on living.

"Forgive one of my aphorisms, but isms can cause schisms. I am thinking of Catholicism, Protestantism and, of course, racism. The one that comes most natural to us all, whether tall or small, is narcissism. As far as history of Mersey Beat is concerned, the most dangerous is revisionism."

Bob Wooler and Politics

It can be hard to put the thoughts of Chairman Wooler into a logical order - and sometimes I don't want to. This is a good example of his rambling speech. He starts with the monarchy and brings in politics, the Americanisation of England and shows produced by Brian Epstein. When Bob was on a roll, his speech could be a roller-coaster ride: you weren't sure what was coming next.

"I have no time for the royal family and I would support Willie Hamilton, Eric Heffer, Tony Benn and the various other critics over the years. I have been against the royal family since boyhood as I have never understood why we have one. I don't understand why people should be privileged by dint of birth. And how the hell did it all start? They got those privileges by force and it has been passed down the line. Nowadays, of course, our royal family is benign, but I would still abolish them. I wouldn't say, 'Put them in the tumbrels and off with their heads' but I'd quote Cole Porter, 'Get Out Of Town', which says tough things in a romantic way: it suggests someone might 'retire to a farm, and be contented to charm the birds off the trees.' I'm surprised the royal family are still around. When I was on the railway in the 50s, I gave them until the end of the century.

"I like the idea of a president, and Tony Blair would be an excellent first choice. It is not just the party he leads, as John Major was impressive too. But why not have a President? We would soon accept it as we are so Americanised now. It's all baseball hats, trainers and McDonald's, and most people sing in an American accent. Geographically, we are not much further away from America than Hawaii, so if they can become a state, why can't we? Instead of all this business about going into Europe, we should debate whether we should become the 51st or the 52nd state - the exact number depending on Puerto Rico.

"We've also acquired from America the concept that politics should be totally media driven. In the 1960s the politicians realised the importance of television and of looking televisual and it's developed from there. You see old pictures of them at the hustings, and there is Aneurin Bevin on the back of a lorry with no security around.

"I admired William Hague for his keen sense of humour, which is unusual in a politician. Harold Wilson called Harold Macmillan 'Mack the Knife' when he sacked half of his cabinet and he said Edward Heath was a shiver looking for a spine to run up - very, very witty but I wonder if he wrote it. Mrs. Thatcher's famous line about 'The lady's not for turning' was written by Ronald Millar, who wrote the musical *Robert And Elizabeth*. He and the Maigret composer, Ron Grainer, wrote the stage flop, *On The Level*, which Brian Epstein produced in 1966.

"Garston, where I grew up, was a Labour stronghold and we didn't see how the other half lived. The 1945 election was a lot like the 1997 election where the public had had enough of the Tories. Here they had had enough of the Churchill brigade, and it was time for a change. The new Prime Minister, Clement Attlee, struck me as insignificant but clearly he was not. I gather that he was very dogmatic and quite punchy in a way, but the fact that he won the election is remarkable. Can you imagine how the Conservatives must have felt? Churchill must have thought, 'How dare they do this to me? I have led the country through the War.' History does repeat itself, so Tony Blair will be at pains to avoid what happened to the Labour party in the late 1940s.

"I must have been aware of the Cold War, but it didn't make a strong impact on me. As far as I know, none of the musicians in the beat groups were involved with the Ban The Bomb movement. I was with the Beatles constantly for three years and I knew John Lennon's views on lots of things, but at no time did he fly the pacifist flag or take part in any protests. Some books say he showed his feelings by not being photographed with the other Beatles at the Arnhem War Memorial, but when I asked Allan Williams about that, he said, 'John Lennon stayed in the van. He couldn't be bothered to get out.' Did he realise that 'Their name liveth for evermore' was going to apply to Allan Williams and Lord Woodbine? The memorial happened to be there, that's all: just like the photograph of Harold Wilson outside 10 Downing Street as a child. What a wonderful line 'Their name liveth for evermore' is: Ecclesiastes must have been the first showbiz writer.

"In 1961 a couple of Cavernites said that they were going on the Aldermaston march and invited me along. It wouldn't have been easy as I worked at the Cavern and relied upon freelance DJ work around jive halls in the evenings, especially at weekends. Anyway, I never felt committed to the CND movement. Because the Japanese are so fanatical, the loss of life would have been so much greater had those bombs not been dropped in 1945. Half a million people were killed, but invading Japan would have been a slaughterhouse not only for them but also for the American troops. I don't know how deeply these adolescents thought about banning the bomb. Those two wanted to rough it, as people do now: it's like people saying, 'How was the mud in Glastonbury?' 'Oh, it was great.' How can a festival be great when you are knee-deep in mud?

"The 60s was when the dependency culture really got under way. Ever since there has been a dependency culture with people living on the dole, and not just in this city. The 1960s made it automatic but if I criticise it, I know I sound like Thatcher and Tebbit. I don't call the decade the Swinging Sixties but the Whinging, Unhinging, Syringing, Swingeing Sixties. We have been stigmatised as a nation of Giro tyros and the question is, 'Who put the dole in adolescence?'

"I was disheartened by what was happening in Liverpool in the 1980s. To me, it was summed up by the state of our phone boxes. I would go to make a call and they would invariably be vandalised. I had a secret admiration for Maggie Thatcher, as undoubtedly Neil Kinnock and Tony Blair have. She would put her foot down and say, 'I'm going to have these phone-boxes repaired.' It seems trivial but it was part of her rebuilding of the country. Very quickly, she got the phone-boxes working. In the end, she went too far and instead of 'The lady's not for turning', I came up with 'The lady's not for returning'.

"Derek Hatton was a Cavernite, who told me his favourite Mersey Beat group, apart from the Beatles, was the Searchers. I have never been a very staunch left-winger and I didn't like what he did to Liverpool. I know many people who were all for him, but I think he was posturing and I doubt if he believed all he was saying. What was most amazing was that he wasn't even the leader of the Council. That was John Hamilton, and Derek Hatton was his deputy. It's like Gordon Brown saying he is more important than Tony Blair. The real leader was older and not as eloquent, and he gave Hatton his head. In his way, Derek Hatton was just as dictatorial as Maggie, and he was determined to mess it all up for her."

Bob Wooler and Liverpool life

"Unlike, say, Sheffield, Liverpool is full of contradictions, and that is the most intriguing aspect about it. It is not just the people with their opposing views, but it has a flavour of perverseness.

"Liverpool people are very proud of their heritage. When the pop singer Sonia said something bad about Liverpool, she immediately fell out of favour, and many people put the Beatles down because they stopped living here. Pete McGovern's 'In My Liverpool Home' is a very perceptive song as it summarises how people feel about the city.

"I don't know what a Scouser is, or a Wacker for that matter. As far as I'm concerned, this is one large conurbation which happens to be divided by a river. Some people feel that the two communities - Birkenhead and Liverpool - are separate and different, but I don't see it that way.

"The city has had a number of white elephants over the years, and the Garden Festival of 1984 springs to mind. It was a flower power that was purely cosmetic with no lasting benefits. The biggest white elephant has to be St. John's Beacon. It was so stained when it was erected that it was as though the city had run out of money. You look at beacons in other cities - I think of Berlin - and they are so impressive. This is shabby and pathetic and when I see it, I think, 'Call Fred Dibner'. Somebody proposed something like the Hollywood sign on top of the Beacon, which was a pathetic idea. Next, it will be letters 50 foot high outside the city proclaiming L I V E R P O O L. Why not a Liverpool Mount Rushmore with four king-sized heads?

"One of my dreams is to have a bridge across the Mersey. A suitable point would be from the Pier Head to Birkenhead where the river narrows to about three-quarters of a mile, so it would be feasible and even viable. Like the Brooklyn Bridge or San Francisco's Golden Gate, you could allow people to walk over it with traffic in the central lanes of the bridge. There could be restaurants, a multiplex, shops, a dance hall - 'the ballroom on the bridge' - and a huge conference and concert centre. The possibilities seem very attractive. During the early 60s, I got the management of Mecca's Locarno dance hall in Liverpool enthusiastic about the concept and they said they would put it to their HQ in London. Like most of my ideas, nothing came of it.

"I've never been interested in football. To many people, Liverpool is synonymous with the Beatles or a Liverpool football club, but that is not necessarily so, and this is why I've never thrust the Beatles upon people. I try to find out what they are interested in, and if it is possible to talk about that subject, I will. I have only taken an interest in sport as a talking point. The Cavern audiences did not initially respond to the Manchester groups, and when I asked why they were lukewarm to them, it came down to Manchester boasting a rival football team of note. I suppose tribal instincts are bindingly strong in us all."

Bob Wooler and the Scouse accent

A subject that recurred in nearly all my conversations with Bob Wooler was the Liverpool accent. Although Bob was born and raised in the heart of the city, he had no trace of an accent and he wished other Scousers were the same.

"Until the Beatles came along and Liverpool became fashionable and emancipated, people weren't generally aware of what a Liverpool accent sounded like. Ken Dodd doesn't speak with a Scouse accent and there is no accent when he sings. The same goes for Tommy Handley, Arthur Askey and many other broadcasters, comedians and actors. I wonder how Billy Fury with his Liverpool accent really got on with the London boys like Marty Wilde, Tommy Steele and Joe Brown.

"I did evolve an expression - Liverpool's an ace apocapatin' place. I have reached the conclusion that you are not considered to be a genuine Scouser unless you apocapate words, especially ones ending '-ing', because they all, sheeplike, do it now. Just look at the Channel 4 soap opera *Brookside*, it is not just the h's at the beginning of words that suffer but the g's at the end. Call me a snob if you like, but surely the slavish apocapating of words is a kind of reverse snobbery. The constant Scouse accent in *Brookside* grates on me. Vince Earl plays Ron Dixon but he never spoke with such an exaggerated accent when he was in the Teenage Rebels and other groups in the 50s and 60s. Neither did the Beatles, they put it on a bit. What about Cilla Black? Can you imagine her speaking like that at home?

"The result of the three B's - *Brookside, Bread* and *Boys From The Blackstuff* - has been that people want a Scouse accent. I have never been able to detect different accents in Liverpool - I don't even think Professor Higgins from *My Fair Lady* could distinguish between someone from Garston and someone from Waterloo, and now it has become totally impossible. I've heard people in nearby towns such as St. Helens, Runcorn and Widnes talking Scouse, and even Chester is beginning to sound like Scouseville. There are also those who affect the deadpan vocal delivery of John Lennon and the Liverpool-born DJ, John Peel.

"There is a deliberate attempt, a very successful attempt, to apocapate words, which is mainly derived from the Irish influence here. The attitude of Scousers seems to be, If you don't do that, then you're not one of us. Willy Russell doesn't do it, but Alan Bleasdale goes out of his way to do so. Of course, it is not confined to Liverpool, but it predominates here. Somehow the idea of dropping your g's can make you sound a hard man. Frank Sinatra and Dean Martin, for instance, dropped their g's, but they knew when they did it that it was slovenly and colloquial. If they were singing slow, serious ballads, they would not apocapate their words.

"Jim Laker's cricket commentaries really irritated me. He would say, 'The bowlin' leaves a lot to be desired and the catchin' is poor and so is the wicketkeepin'. It's easy to be battin' out there but I don't like the runnin' between the wickets.' William in Just William talks like that too. I have read an interview with the New York songwriter, Stephen Sondheim, in which he states that he was self conscious at school about being the smartest boy in his class. He says, 'I would purposely drop my g's because I spoke English too well.'"

Bob Wooler and Liverpool films

"I have always been interested in films and plays about Liverpool. *Violent Playground* was made by Michael Relph and Basil Dearden, who were responsible for a number of socially aware British movies of the 50s and 60s. *Violent Playground* was released in 1958 and it starred Stanley Baker, David McCallum and a young Freddie Starr. I rate the film very highly, but apart from its real life Liverpool locations, its attitudes and accents were far from authentic.

"People talk about Hollywood on the Mersey, but we have no studios here - just a few locations and some buildings which are of interest to filmmakers. This filmmaking is far from unique to Merseyside as many other places in the UK are used: Birmingham, Bristol, Glasgow, Newcastle, Sheffield, Belfast and Manchester, not forgetting London, of course.

"Cameramen may have difficulty in masking TV aerials and yellow lines in the road in a period drama set in Liverpool. In one film they covered the yellow lines with leaves, but they were shooting in a street with no trees, so where did the leaves come from? So that the TV aerials wouldn't be shown, they didn't shoot too high - it would have been too costly to take them down."

Bob Wooler and Scouse pride

"Some Scousers like to make out that they were responsible for the trends of the twentieth century. They have the Kilroy syndrome - Kilroy was always here first and he was a Scouser. Someone even told me that Scousers had invented Cockney rhyming slang and another claimed that a Scouser had discovered America some 300 years before Columbus. If Scousers invented anything, it was spindoctoring.

"Of course, Scousers can't compete with the braggadocio of some Americans, who claim credit for everything. To their great delight, John Lennon settled in New York and became Americanised. I once described the Beatles to a visiting American as an episode in my life. Aghast, the American said, 'My god, you call them an episode, surely they were the most important thing in your life.' My PR training prevailed and I didn't challenge his OTT declaration.

"Please do not get the impression that I am in any way anti-Liverpool or anti-Scousers. I am not, and the words of my song 'Oh, Liverpool' express how I feel. However, I am constantly against claims which cannot be substantiated. I even have reservations about the famous Liverpool humour. A lot of British humour like *Monty Python's Flying Circus, Fawlty Towers* and *The Goon Show* has nothing to do with Liverpool. However, Stan Boardman would have you believe that Liverpool is the heart of the nation's humour. Ken Dodd says you have to be a comedian to live here, but he should come to Lark Lane - there are plenty of miserable people around. Ken Dodd himself is very funny and the Beatles' natural humour was a significant part of their charm. It is true that you'll find a comedian in every pub, but that is true of other cities as well. Liverpool was a seaport renowned for its ocean-going liners, and now it's renowned for its one-liners. Merseyside has become Mirthyside."

Liverpool's waterfront

OH, LIVERPOOL
Lyric by Bob Wooler

Bob Wooler: "'Oh, Liverpool' is just one of several different lyrics which have been set to the musical notation of the original tune of 'The Londonderry Air'. Some others this century have been : 'Acushla, Mine', words by Terry Sullivan; 'Far Away', words by Dr. George Sigerson; 'O Mary Mine', words by Count John McCormack; and the most famous version of all, 'Danny Boy', with words written just before the Great War by Fred E. Weatherly. The use of an Irish air for a song about Liverpool is particularly apt as the Celtic influence has been very strong in Liverpool for over a hundred years.

"'Oh, Liverpool' is a tribute to a town of triumphs and tribulations ... a seesaw kind of a city with more downs and ups than a Lewis's lift! This unashamed homage, with its bitter-sweet overtones and internal rhymes, is a poetic panegyric to the tradition of songs like 'New York, New York', 'Manhattan', 'Chicago', 'I Left My Heart In San Francisco', 'Wonderful Copenhagen', 'The London I Love', and other soft-focus treatments of places around the world.

"Allan Williams did record the song at the Take 1 Studios in the Albert Dock some years ago. Allan is a good singer of the traditional kind. His silver tones suggest a counter-tenor to me, which is not a bad way of putting it, considering he is often given to regaling one at counters - bar counters!"

Oh, Liverpool, am I a fool to love you so;
To hold you dear wherever I may go?
For right or wrong I sing the song that praises you;
For me there'll be no other that's so true.

Your sights and sounds abound within my eyes and ears;
They're all around me everywhere I turn.
You are to me my smiles and frowns, my sighs and tears.
Oh, Liverpool, for you my heart will always yearn.

Oh, Liverpool, you'll always rule where I'm concerned.
Such a pool of talent I have learned.
I can't ignore you, I'm all for you, my top town.
You sport so jauntily your shining crown.

Your sights and sounds abound within my ears and eyes;
They're all around me everywhere I turn.
You are to me my smiles and frowns, my tears and sighs.
Oh, Liverpool, for you my heart will always yearn.

Tommy Steele with his statue of Eleanor Rigby, Stanley Street, Liverpool

The opposition was a team of girls

★   ★

MERSEY BEAT XI

(Red Shirts/White Shorts)

The Team, subject to availability, will be chosen from amongst the following Groups :—

Rory Storm — Captain

The Hurricanes   The Escorts   The Kinsleys   The Hideaways

Chick Graham   The Nocturnes

Earl Preston's Realms

Billy Butler   Eddie Parry (if fit)

REFEREE — TONY KAY (EVERTON F.C. & ENGLAND)

★

★   ★

★

N. Reade — Captain

G. Lynn   H. Leister   I. Walsh   C. Wilson   A. Warehow

S. Malloy   F. Daniels   B. Parker   I. Walker

L. Shepherd   Reserves — D. Upton   L. Doyle

KICK OFF by Mrs. Bessie Braddock, M.P., at 3-0 p.m.

Commentary given live by Bob Wooler ... ...: Cavern Club D.J.

We wish to express our sincere thanks to the LIVERPOOL & DISTRICT SUNDAY FOOTBALL LEAGUE and also McBAIN SOUND SERVICES for their kind co-operation in the arrangement of this fixture.

4 USE YOUR MENTALITY
Songwriting

"No one can change what is destiny,
Can't rearrange what was meant to be."
(Johnnie Ray, "No One Can Change Destiny", 1953)

Although Bob Wooler was an excellent conversationalist, it was very much on his own terms. There were certain topics that he would never discuss and others that he would argue about all day. His enthusiasm for pre-war Tin Pan Alley and Broadway songwriters never faltered. This chapter is the only part of Bob's autobiography that could be called complete.

Bob Wooler: "Many of the songs and hymns that they sang at school assemblies seemed silly to me, so I used to just mouth the words in a silent protest. I knew that other voices would make up for my miming act. I was, however, impressed with the Gilbert and Sullivan songs we had to sing, and this was the beginning of my appreciation for cleverly written songs with a strong melody. Quite apart from the obvious reasons for welcoming the end of term, I used to look forward to seeing the music teacher in the assembly hall letting his hair down as it were and playing at the piano contemporary dance band tunes like 'Pennies From Heaven' and 'Cheek To Cheek'.

"I was born in 1926 so it wasn't until the 1930s that I was old enough to be aware of popular music. I don't want to convey that I was a whiz-kid, but when I was about 10, I heard 'I've Got You Under My Skin' on the wireless. I thought, fancy calling a song 'I've Got You Under My Skin'. To my tender years, I found it disturbing and daring and, although I didn't know the word then, risqué. Undoubtedly, the song has had a profound and lasting effect on me. At that age and at that stage of my awareness, I was not into who wrote a song, so the name Cole Porter meant nothing to me, apart from sounding somewhat amusing. But, from that moment on, I began to sit up and take notice and I started to compare one song with another. I suppose my awareness of the impact a song lyric can have on the listener is a couplet in that song, 'Use your mentality, Wake up to reality'. Other songs didn't use words like that, and little did I know that, purely by chance and without anyone pointing it out, I had stumbled upon the greatest words and music songwriter of the twentieth century, namely, Cole Porter.

"I started listening, really listening to lyrics and gradually I came upon songs that deserved more than casual listening. Songs like 'Mean To Me', 'Brother, Can You Spare A Dime', 'Thanks For The Memory', 'Anything Goes' or 'I Wish I Were In Love Again' with its hilarious reference to 'the faint aroma of performing seals'. I'm still the same and I much prefer to listen to songs through headphones because it helps to concentrate the mind and enables me to hear the lyrics clearly. Sadly, that doesn't apply to the vast majority of today's pop songs. You can't dumb down these so-called lyrics as they are already at rock bottom.

"A common obsession when you're young is to play your records as loud as possible which is as much to annoy your elders as anything else. We had a wind-up gramophone and I used to favour the thick steel needles so I could play my records as loud as possible, but they did sound better that way. The gramophone needles were sold in little tin boxes and the manufacturers would say 'use once only', which I'm sure was a con. They just wanted to sell more needles. I would always use a needle for both sides of a 78rpm and possibly even more if I was running out of needles. This all sounds so primitive now.

"Every week I would buy a 78rpm record, maybe two. I bought 'Warsaw Concerto' from the wartime film, *Dangerous Moonlight*. It was a 12-inch record that was continued on the other side. I had some jazz records - Fletcher Henderson's 'Stealin' Apples', which was written by Fats Waller, was one of my favourites - and there was Jimmy Dorsey, Glenn Miller, Tommy Dorsey and Woody Herman. My favourite vocalist was Frank Sinatra. He chose such good songs, and it was always a case of the song, not the singer, with me, although in the case of Sinatra, he was as important as the song. I went for the songs. I also liked Peggy Lee, Ella Fitzgerald and later Doris Day.

"I'm absolutely sold on Ella Fitzgerald's Songbooks, which were produced by Norman Granz. Each album features a great songwriter or songwriting team and they chose the songs together. Just to take two examples, how can you top 'Ev'rytime We Say Goodbye' or the Gershwin songs? They are beautifully done and, in my reckoning, she is the female equivalent of Frank Sinatra. However, I don't like everything Ella did as I don't care for scat singing. I once penned a piece of doggerel with Ella in mind:

> *Drat that scat singer, she's no humdinger,*
> *Ignoring the words is strictly for the birds.*

Scat, to me, is an irritation and my dislike is all to do with my adulation of words. Van Morrison is an excellent singer and could make a wonderful album of standards, but whenever he sings them, he includes some bit of business that I don't like.

42

"The Richard Rodgers and Lorenz Hart song, 'Manhattan', was written in 1925. In that song, Lorenz Hart comes out with, 'And tell me what street / Compares with Mott Street / In July?' It made me wonder what was so special about Mott Street and, indeed, I did look it up on a street map of New York. It was there in the Jewish quarter, but what was so special about it? The original lyric says that they will take their children to *Abie's Irish Rose*, 'I hope they'll live to see it close.' Apparently, this operetta ran and ran and ran. I wonder how Hart would have updated it? I tried to write a similarly bright eulogy about Liverpool, but I found it difficult because of my misgivings about the place. That is why I say, 'For right or wrong, I sing the song that praises you.'

"I liked the fact that good songwriters could encapsulate a story in so short a time, and I was inspired to write songs myself with this in mind. I didn't know the restriction of 32 bars then, but I did later on because I had a friend, Tony Anderson, who could both read and write music. He was a fellow railway clerk who happened to have a piano at his home in Garston. I realise that he indulged me because he wasn't very keen at writing songs. He would say to his wife, 'We'll go into the front room', which is where the piano was, and we would analyse songs for a couple of hours - their technical construction and the like, none of which matters today. I often visualise staff writers in publishing houses shaking their heads in disbelief when they are trying to make sense on sheet music of what they hear on cassettes. Setting out a song in manuscript form would be beyond most of today's songwriters.

"The Three I's dominated show business in New York City - the Italians, the Irish and the Israelites. They were given to music, and most of the great songwriters are Jewish. The Jews had emigrated from Europe to America at the turn of the century. The English language was not their natural language, yet they certainly showed us how to use it. So, in my endeavours to get songs published, I assumed a Jewish name. I was writing with Tony Anderson, whose son was called David. I thought I would take something from the name of one of my favourite lyricists, Mack Gordon, and I became David Mack. It didn't do the trick though - my work was still rejected. I would console myself by remembering that thousands of songs, books, plays and scripts had been turned down over the years, so the message was like Robert Bruce and the spider: try, try, try again. To this day, at the end of my three score years and ten, I'm still trying. It's amazing how we delude ourselves.

"I love coming across unexpected words in popular songs. There's an example which intrigues me in the 1944 film, *Meet Me In St. Louis*. The song is 'Have Yourself A Merry Little Christmas', which was sung by Judy Garland and written by Ralph Blane and Hugh Martin. Part of the lyric is: 'Until then we'll have to muddle through somehow, So have yourself a merry little Christmas now.' The notation of the music had called for a two syllable word with the accent on the first syllable, and the writers had chosen 'muddle'. The word conveys a rather confused and fumbling state, which is true of the teenage mind and perfect for the film's story. The song also captures the feeling of the actual time (1944 in wartime), and I wonder how many other words Blane and Martin considered before they settled for 'muddle'? This is an example of songwriting at its thoughtful best.

"Incidentally, I see nothing infra dig about using a rhyming dictionary. Most of the great songwriters used them and indeed, Sammy Cahn compiled one. I am obsessed with rhymes, yet one of my favourite songs, the 1946 composition, 'Moonlight In Vermont', does not include a single rhyme. The melody is marvellous but the whole song is very unusual with only 26 bars instead of the established 32. It was Tony Anderson who showed me how to count up the bars and it is intriguing to discover how the great songwriters varied it.

"I will give all aspiring songwriters a good exercise. Cole Porter's 'You're The Top' is a perfect song, full of fantastic witticisms and really clever rhyming. It is very enjoyable to try and parody or update the lyric while observing the perfect scansion and absolutely pure rhymes of the original. It requires a lot of effort and perseverance, I can tell you. One TV commercial which parodied 'You're The Top' was a total disgrace, being loaded with half-rhymes and quirky scansion. Chappell, the publishers, should never have granted permission without ensuring the parody preserved the spirit and skill of the original. This is a parody that I wrote in 1956 for a *Daily Express* competition. It took me several weeks to complete, which was far too late for the competition, but then I always have trouble with deadlines. I'm pleased with it though, because it did at least achieve the interior rhymes laid down by the great Mr. P.

You're the top
You're the captain's table
You're the top
You're the legs of Grable,
You're the C-scope movie
About Vesuvius
You're a western duel
You're smokeless fuel
You're a Greyhound bus.

You're supreme
You're the US White House
You're the beam
From the Lizard lighthouse.
I'm a worried frown
A broken-down jalop
But if I'm the fertiliser
You're the crop.

"The first payment I ever received from a publication was from a letter I wrote to *Everybody's Weekly* about Cole Porter - two guineas, no less.

"Most of the great songwriters were American but I gladly acclaim the Irish songwriter based in London, Jimmy Kennedy, who wrote, among many other hit songs, 'South Of The Border', 'Harbour Lights' and 'My Prayer'. He recounts short stories in his songs and 'The Isle Of Capri' is an excellent example - it starts off, it develops, things go wrong and it's goodbye to the Isle of Capri, all in 32 bars, which is only a couple of minutes. I tried to do the same and encapsulate short stories in 32 bars. At times I said, 'I need another eight bars to complete this', but then I would say, 'No, it has got to be done within 32 bars.' Of course, Cole Porter was so revered that he could throw convention to the wind when he wanted to - I don't know how many bars there are in 'Begin The Beguine' but it goes on and on, building up like Ravel's *Bolero* to a stunning climax. I would put 'Hey Jude' in the same category as it has an orgasmic ending.

"Most of the key songwriters of the day worked in partnerships - a lyricist and a musician - and that continued into the rock'n'roll era. Irving Berlin wrote on his own, but most writers formed a partnership. Cole Porter said, no doubt jokingly, in the presence of Rodgers and Hart, 'Fancy needing two people to write a song.' Richard Rodgers put up with Lorenz Hart's waywardness because he knew he was fantastic. The reason Lorenz Hart was able to write so quickly and so brilliantly was because he didn't want to waste good drinking time - he went from one set of bars to another! Many of the writers including Lorenz Hart, Cole Porter and Noël Coward were homosexual, so they were all singing from the same 'him' sheet. They didn't always disguise their feelings - look at Noël Coward's 'Mad About The Boy'.

"In 1952 I wrote to the BBC and requested that they played a vocal version of Cole Porter's 1930 censored song, 'Love For Sale'. I was intrigued to know what the lyrics were and why they should have been banned. I failed to get my request played so I wrote to Chappell and bought the sheet music for 3/6d (17p). When it arrived, I realised why they didn't play it on the air. It was about prostitution and very cleverly written. The word 'Love' is held on for a couple of bars, rather like a street vendor crying out, 'Mangoes, chillies, love for sale'. It is a brilliant song and includes such daring lines as 'If you want to buy my wares, follow me and climb the stairs, Love for sale.' After you've been exposed to a mature song like this, it makes the vast majority of the others seem trite and trivial.

"'The macabre 'Strange Fruit', with its lyric by the poet Lewis Allan, was also controversial, but I suspect that lots of people didn't realise what the song was about as its subject-matter was disguised. I didn't realise it myself at the time. I thought it was about unusual berries hanging from the trees, but it was really about corpses. These people had been hung - it was a fantastic image and a brilliant song performed by Billie Holiday, although I first heard it by Josh White.

"The Searchers made a record that was similarly oblique, 'What Have They Done To The Rain?', an excellent folk song by Malvina Reynolds. It was about life after a nuclear disaster, but you wouldn't pick that up on first hearing. It dates from 1964, and not even the Beatles were recording any provocative material at that time.

"The language of popular song is also very interesting. It was even controversial to put the word 'damn' into a song before the War. Noël Coward used the word 'bloody' in one of his wartime broadcasts - calculatingly of course, it wasn't a slip of the tongue. Coward felt that we were fighting for our lives and the thought of the troops being prim and proper was ridiculous. He thought they would appreciate 'bloody', which they did, but it was quite startling at the time. In the original version of *My Fair Lady, Pygmalion* from 1912, George Bernard Shaw has Eliza Doolittle saying, 'Not bloody likely', which was highly shocking. By the time of *My Fair Lady* in 1956, 'bloody' was such a meek word that Alan Jay Lerner knew it would have no impact to repeat it.

"My favourite lyricist is Sammy Cahn, who wrote for Sinatra. He is so very New York: he betrays nothing romantic when he speaks and yet you have to be romantic to write words like that. He wrote beautiful ballads like 'The Second Time Around' and 'All The Way' and top-class novelties like 'High Hopes', which I view as a companion to Bing Crosby's 'Swinging On A Star'. Sammy Cahn is the lyricist who took the mantle of Lorenz Hart on his shoulders.

"As well as Sinatra, Sammy Cahn and Jimmy Van Heusen wrote some songs for a Liverpool performer, Frankie Vaughan. In 1960, this Frankie went to Hollywood to make a film with Marilyn Monroe and Yves Montand, *Let's Make Love*. He acquitted himself quite ably and the songs are excellent.

"Sammy Cahn wrote a marvellous song with Jule Styne called 'Brooklyn Bridge', which was just a throwaway song for Sinatra to sing in *It Happened In Brooklyn*, a 1947 film with Jimmy Durante. Sinatra is fresh from the army and he is going round the places that mean so much to him. He goes onto the Brooklyn Bridge on the East River because it epitomises New York, and the words are simply marvellous. In the same film, there is a really beautifully-crafted song, 'Time After Time', which has deservedly become a standard. I commend it to anyone who wants to know what skilful songwriting is all about.

4 USE YOUR MENTALITY

"When they were working together, Jule Styne played a new melody for Sammy Cahn. He went, 'It seems to me I've heard that song before.' Style said, 'What are you? A tune detective?'

"Oscar Hammerstein had a hard time with Jerome Kern. Kern would give him the music and say, 'Those are the dots, don't alter them', and he didn't want to go through that again when he teamed up with Richard Rodgers for *Oklahoma!* He stated a preference for doing the words first and Rodgers went along with this. Rodgers was such a professional, capable of composing a tune to an existing lyric as well as the other way round (which was the case when Hart was his collaborator). I wonder how many tunesmiths are prepared to accommodate their lyricists this way? Very few, I'll bet. Composers often think they are being somehow inferior if they compose a tune to a lyric.

"There is at least one exception to the way that Oscar Hammerstein worked with Jerome Kern. He loved Paris and he gave Kern a poem, 'The Last Time I Saw Paris', which Kern set to music. It was included in the film, *Lady Be Good,* and won an Oscar. Kern then said it was wrong that a song that had not been expressly written for a film should be nominated for an Oscar, and the Academy changed the rules. However, he only said that after he had won the Oscar for 'The Last Time I Saw Paris'.

"I saw the Fred Astaire / Ginger Rogers films, *David Copperfield,* the various Broadway Melody musicals and lots of others including the Saturday afternoon serials. So you see, I was not brought up on Gene Vincent but Gene Tierney and Gene Autry - I guess you could say that the movies are in my Genes. Those singing cowboy films were quite impossible: the whole concept was risible - they never shot anyone badly or if they did, it was in the shoulder or the arm. They weren't shot in the guts, and it was all so phony, just conveyor-belt stuff that never caused you to think or question anything. They all led to the typical Hollywood ending of 'Everything's gonna be alright'.

"I did like some western songs (*'Tumbling Tumbleweeds', 'The Last Round-Up'*) and I did like country and western music - Jimmie Rodgers, who was pre-war, and Hank Williams, who was post. They were both very down-to-earth - look at Hank Williams' 'Half As Much' which is a perceptive song about keeping up appearances, but I was more inclined to the urbane, sophisticated songs of Cole Porter and his contemporaries."

Although he was often searching, Bob could never find a collaborator for his own songwriting. Doug Evans: "He did ask me to write some music for him from time to time, but I was stupid and always said no. I didn't have the confidence, but I was a good pianist and I do feel now that we could have done something worthwhile. We both enjoyed the same type of music and he could write good lyrics."

Frankie Connor from the Hideaways: "Bob was grumpy and grouchy a lot of the time and that could be down to his frustrations. More than anything else, he wanted to be Cole Porter. He could put words together wonderfully well - just look at his Woolerisms - and I liked to send him my own lyrics. He was like a schoolmaster and he would be encouraging: 'That's quite good,' he would say, 'but what does this bit mean? I can see there are many Connor-tations here.'"

Doug Evans: "I never went to the cinema or the theatre with him, but he would analyse everything and something had to be good before he would praise it."

Billy Butler: "In the 1960s, I had assumed that Bob was all for beat music. It was only when I started to go for meals with him after the Cavern had finished that I appreciated his other interests. He told me that his favourite singer was Ruth Etting, whom I only knew from a Doris Day and James Cagney film about her life, *Love Me Or Leave Me.* He once told me that his favourite record was 'Creole Jazz', which was an Acker Bilk B-side."

Bob Wooler: "I was influenced by the great lyricists of the pre-rock period - Cole Porter, Irving Berlin, Johnny Mercer and the like - but I could never find a collaborator, someone whose heart was in it as mine was - and still is, for that matter. I admired Lionel Bart who started in rock'n'roll and became a legitimate songwriter, if I may put it that way. He lived in London, which helped a great deal. It all happened in London as I was to learn, as the Beatles were to learn, as everybody was to learn. I did tout some lyrics around Denmark Street but no-one wanted to know. I would be advised to submit a complete song, words and music, but there was still no guarantee that the work would even be played, let alone considered. Years later, when rock'n'roll dictated my life, I was to learn in disbelief that the vast majority of cassettes submitted to record producers and music people by wide-eyed wannabes were binned. Most A&R men never bothered to listen to them. Maybe this cavalier attitude came about in order for them to preserve their sanity against so many puerile and unoriginal songs, with boring, repetitive, lobotomised lyrics. This may result in quality offerings falling through the net, but not too many.

"Having said that, I am intrigued that Jack Brooks, the lyricist of 'That's Amore' and 'Old Buttermilk Sky', came from Liverpool. He worked in Hollywood for Universal and Paramount Pictures, writing songs with Harry Warren and Hoagy Carmichael and having his songs recorded by Dean Martin and Jerry Lewis. However, I have never heard him praised as a musician who came from Liverpool.

"There was a photograph in the *Daily Mail* of Lena Zavaroni who revived 'Ma, He's Making Eyes At Me' with its lyricist, Sidney Clare. The article said he was a pensioner in the Liverpool suburb of Huyton, but I don't know whether he was from Liverpool originally. This, naturally, intrigues me, but I am also interested in the fact that, around 1920, when he was a young man, he sold his lyric for £10 outright. He was not to know that his lyric, set to a tune by Con Conrad (who later co-wrote the first Oscar-winning song, 'The Continental') would become a huge hit for Eddie Cantor, netting best-selling royalties, none of which came his way. But was he treated badly? £10 was a considerable sum in 1920 as it was two weeks' pay for a skilled worker and he may have been urgently in need of cash. Incidentally, he is not the same Sidney Clare, who wrote 'On The Good Ship Lollipop' and 'Please Don't Talk About Me When I'm Gone', but some books assume they are the same person.

"I've never been sure about the television playwright, Dennis Potter. I did appreciate his love of old songs and the idea of featuring so many of them in *Pennies From Heaven* and *The Singing Detective* was tremendous. 'Pennies From Heaven' is a marvellous song title. Johnny Burke's lyrics are full of high hopes and so many of them have philosophic themes, for example, 'Aren't You Glad You're You', 'Going My Way', 'I Haven't Got Time To Be A Millionaire' and 'Swinging On A Star'. I like songs with this quality. A song of a similar ilk is 'It's Only A Paper Moon', in which the world has no substance until the singer meets the girl. Then there's Cole Porter's 'After You, Who?', that is so cleverly done. In other words, why bother to talk about anyone else for, as Porter says, 'After you, who?'

"I also love 'Are You Lonesome Tonight', which was also written in 1926, the year I was born. I love the reference to the 'chairs in your parlour'. It takes me back to the front parlour, which you rarely went into. It was for special days. Alan Bleasdale called his play about Elvis Presley, *Are You Lonesome Tonight,* and a more apt and perceptive title would be hard to find. In his later years, Presley was essentially baubles, bangles and beads of sweat with an uncontrollable vibrato. Cabaret songs like 'My Way' are embarrassing parodies of his former dynamism and weren't his forte.

"The reader may find it tedious that I seem to be obsessed with old songs, largely those that preceded rock'n'roll. This is not so, for I could list many songs from recent decades that I, and others of the 'old school', consider to be worthy of acclaiming. The main reason why I constantly cite pre-rock songs as being commendable and rewarding is because so many of them are so well-crafted and thought out with meaningful and often witty lyrics. This should apply to all popular songs, but, alas, the vast majority of today's songs are so slapdash that they are not worth one's indulgence to try and make sense of them.

"Leo Robin's lyric for 'Diamonds Are A Girl's Best Friend' is witty, very clever and quite brilliant. The Beatles never wrote a song that could equal it for wit and cleverness and being so brilliantly rhymed and crafted. This is why I question the 'greatness' of so much of Lennon and McCartney's output. I shall return to this subject in I Blame The Beatles!"

ARE YOU GOING TO STRAWBERRY FIELD?

Lyric by Bob Wooler

Bob Wooler: *"I was thinking about the structure of Simon and Garfunkel's 'Scarborough Fair' and it struck me that the scanning would fit, 'Are you going to Strawberry Field.' There is a reference to St. Peter's and Quarry Bank, 'Just as it did in yesterday years; oh, how nostalgia adds its veneers.' That is what nostalgia does, it makes everything much prettier than it was in reality. My days of the 30s were not glowing and flowing - those were the days, my friend - they were like hell.*

"The first verse is as though it is a film being unreeled. 'Those sepia days' imply olden times, but 'blue summer skies' seems like a contradiction: they always seem to be blue summer skies, but they weren't. I imagined that John Lennon used to swing on the gates, but I don't know how true that was. Lennon was a working-class boy really although he lived with his Aunt Mimi. He was middle-class in that sense, but he liked to portray himself as working-class. He does mention the tree in 'Strawberry Fields Forever'. I can't understand why he sang 'Strawberry Fields Forever' as he must have known it was Strawberry Field."

Are you going to Strawberry Field?
There to have some past times unreeled,
To close your eyes and visualize,
Those sepia days with blue summer skies.

Are you going to Strawberry Field?
That's St. Peter's church bell that pealed!
Just as it did in yesterday years;
Oh, how nostalgia adds its veneers.

Are you going to Strawberry Field?
What impressions might it all yield?
The gates are still there as they once were;
Oh, to swing on them and have not a care.

Are you going to Strawberry Field?
Where working class lad lived, 'midst the well-heeled,
Lived out his dreams, had schemes to explore,
And quarried songs that were to endure.

Are you going to Strawberry Field?
Where once trees with apples appealed,
And tempted lips to sample the joys,
Of forbidden fruit - but boys will be boys!

Are you going to Strawberry Field?
Imagine one whose lips are now sealed.
Perhaps you'll see the very same tree
He used to climb when time seemed so free.

Are you going to Strawberry Field?
Its secrets will remain unrevealed.
For now they're all just dead memories,
Like leaves that fall from tall silent trees.

Spencer Leigh and Judi Spiers at the Strawberry Fields gates

51

A Bob Wooler Show
(Of Course)

CAMBRIDGE HALL
LORD STREET, SOUTHPORT

THE JOE BROWN SHOW

starring

Joe Brown and his Bruvvers
THE BEATLES
The North's No. 1 Recording Group
THE DAKOTAS with PETE MACLAINE
B.B.C. and TV Star Group
GERRY and the PACEMAKERS
BILLY KRAMER with the COASTERS
THE FOUR JAYS
Late Licensed Bars

THURSDAY, JULY 26th. 7-30 to 11-30
Buy your Tickets now at 6/- (in advance), from Aldridges, Morrison's
Travel Agency, H.P. Radio, Nems (Liverpool), Cambridge Hall and usual
Agencies (7/- at door)

It's a Bob Wooler Show — Of Course

Cole Porter

52

5 THE PREFAB, PRE-FAB DAYS
Early 50s concerts - Rock n roll - The first Liverpool groups
- Carroll Levis - The first DJ.

"Mister, Mister DJ, keep those records playing,
'Cause I'm having such a good time dancing with my baby."
("Having A Party", Sam Cooke, 1962)

After the war, Bob Wooler returned to his administrative job on the dock railways. Reluctantly. You were only allowed a certain amount of time in which to reclaim your job, and Bob reclaimed his at the last possible moment as he had no idea of what he wanted to do. His passion was to go to the Liverpool Empire and watch such American stars as Nat 'King' Cole, Vic Damone and Al Martino. If the Americans weren't performing, he would enjoy the talents of Dickie Valentine and Lita Roza, the first singer from Liverpool to have a No. 1 record, albeit with the novelty "How Much Is That Doggie In The Window?" in 1953.

Bob Wooler: "I saw Frank Sinatra in 1953 and I paid 3/6d (17p) for my ticket - and threepence (1p) for the programme. He was playing the Moss Empires and he was in Liverpool for a week. Relatively speaking, he was on the skids. All the bobbysoxers had been screaming for him at the Paramount in New York and now nothing was happening. I saw him on Tuesday at the Empire in a half-empty house, and in the interval, I moved to a seat in the front stalls. I'm glad I did because Sinatra did the whole of the second half with Bill Miller at the piano and the orchestra on stage. I remember him going into the wings and coming out with a cup of tea and saying, 'It's tea, I can assure you.' He was given the tea by Ralph Webster's wife, Dorothy, who worked at the Empire, and you'll be meeting Ralph later on. Sinatra gave a very good concert, and then *From Here To Eternity* came along and re-established him as a major star. Pavarotti said that Sinatra was the Mozart of singers, which is a good way of expressing a truism.

"Some years later I saw Dick Haymes when he was down on his luck and he had a much worse time than Sinatra. I went with Beryl and Dougie Evans, a railway clerk, who, through me, became the pianist upstairs at the Blue Angel, to see him at the Empress Club in Widnes. It was so terrible to see him doing 'It's A Grand Night For Singing' to a noisy audience. It was pathetic that they treated him that way.

"Frankie Laine at the Empire was a different story. He was so loud that the message was, 'You'd better be quiet while I'm singing.' His hardened voice and unresonated singing has definitely influenced generations of vocalists. By way of contrast, the songwriter Hoagy Carmichael had a nice easy manner and I liked him very much. I had mixed feelings about Guy Mitchell. I didn't care for his novelties like 'She Wears Red Feathers' but I liked the ballads. Johnnie Ray's singing sounded fine to me but he wasn't able to sustain his success. His hearing-aid was ostentatious, to curry sympathy as it were. I thought it was crocodile tears when he sang 'Cry' and he wasn't my cup of tea. He did write one very good song, 'I'll Never Fall In Love Again' and I loved 'No One Can Change Destiny', which is closely related to his private life. When I met him backstage, he seemed quiet and withdrawn."

That famous decade, the Swinging 60s, did not start, except in a temporal sense, in 1960. The phenomenon of the Beatles in 1963 is the real starting point, although Bob felt the change had been coming since the mid-50s. "That was when youths were earning better money and were spending it, and we can't ignore the Teddy Boys with their defiant dress and behaviour. I liked them as they brightened, if not enlightened, the scene. These were grim days - the days of prefab houses, the pre-Fab days, the prefab, pre-Fab days. Some would say how deplorable rock'n'roll was, that was when the rot set in, but those years were a prime influence on this country. They prepared the ground for the 1960s. The music changed and the attitude of youth changed as they became more defiant.

"It was during 1956 that I became aware of rock'n'roll. There was no such thing as a discothèque then but there was a fairground in Garston Park that would blare out 78s - the Crew-Cuts' 'Sh-Boom (Life Could Be A Dream)', Kay Starr's 'Rock And Roll Waltz' and the Platters' 'Only You'. Commentators overlook the importance of fairgrounds to the development of rock'n'roll in the UK. Rock'n'roll records always sounded good at fairgrounds and teenagers would stand around listening.

"There had been trouble in other cities for Bill Haley's film, *Rock Around The Clock*, but the press blew it out of proportion. It was a copycat business and little more than jiving in the aisles, but the newspapers had them wrecking the cinemas, so that managers would remove fire extinguishers, curtains and moveable furniture before they screened the film. The film was banned by some authorities but it was shown in Liverpool at the Gaumont in Camden Street. Despite what some claim to remember, I can assure you that any riots in Liverpool for *Rock Around The Clock* are a myth. No damage was done and no arrests were made."

Bob used to listen to my radio programmes and he would ring me if anyone stepped out of line. One day I was talking to the rock'n'roll singer, Karl Terry, who said, "I was the first person to sing rock'n'roll on Merseyside. I was doing it in 1954." Bob exploded, "This is nonsense. No-one could have been singing rock'n'roll on Merseyside before 1956 and I doubt if anyone was doing it even then. Why didn't you challenge him?" I said, "Very few listeners are concerned about dates, all of us get the years wrong, and Karl Terry was making a simple mistake." Bob would have none of it and criticised me for allowing such rubbish to be broadcast uncorrected. As it happens, Bob was in at the start of rock'n'roll on Merseyside.

Bob Wooler: "By the mid-50s, I knew that I wanted to be a professional songwriter. I had bought a portable Philips reel-to-reel tape recorder so that I could record the songs I was writing. Not many people had tape recorders then, but I never recorded the beat groups later on. I missed out there, but this is hindsight talking. Anyway, I took this tape-recorder to the office Christmas party in 1956, just to lark around. Two of the lads from another department were there. They had formed a skiffle group and they asked if they could hear what they sounded like. I took my tape recorder to where they practised and they asked if I could get them any bookings. I didn't know any dance hall promoters but I knew one or two clubs and that was the thin end of the wedge. They called themselves the Kingstrums and the first booking I got for them was for ten shillings each. I remember them playing the All Britain Skiffle Competition at the Pavilion Theatre - the Pivvy - but they didn't last long. They were a skiffle group doing some rock'n'roll and I could see that Lonnie Donegan had served his purpose. The teenagers had learnt from Lonnie the simplicity of playing music. Skiffle and rock'n'roll were do-it-yourself forms of music as they didn't require you to learn an instrument properly as you might a trumpet or violin - and slinging a guitar round your shoulder looked rather cool as well. What other instrument allows the performer to stand up, sing and look cool at the same time? The cost was a problem, but the hire purchase houses did well out of it. They still do.

"The Kingstrums went to see *The Girl Can't Help It* for a second time just to write down the words for Eddie Cochran's 'Twenty Flight Rock'. They told me about the American rock'n'roller, Charlie Gracie, and I was so intrigued that I got a 78rpm of him singing 'Fabulous'. I said, 'It's a great number, why don't you do it?' but they never did. They could do Elvis numbers but not 'Heartbreak Hotel' as it involved echo. They also sang 'Bye Bye Love' which got me very interested in the Everly Brothers and their harmonies. The Beatles did a lot of harmonies but, strangely enough, I never heard them discussing the Everly Brothers. I love 'Wake Up Little Susie', which is the epitome of innocence - teenagers would never react that way today. The Kingstrums' final booking was on New Year's Eve, December 1957 at Bryant and May's club in

Garston. It's a common complaint - they wouldn't dedicate themselves to the music. Groups need to spend more time rehearsing and shaping their act and less time arguing. You can say that they were young, but that is excusing them. They were old enough to go into the army, to carry a rifle and kill someone."

By 1957 Liverpool rock'n'roll groups were starting to proliferate and indeed, I contend that the first example of Liverpool rock'n'roll on record is a private recording by Paul Murphy and Johnny Guitar of "Butterfly" and "She's Got It". Bob Wooler: "Duke Duval had one of the first rock'n'roll groups on Merseyside, Duke Duval's Rockers. He was a disciplinarian and he kept his group under tight control. He would tell them where they were playing next, what time he wanted them and when they were rehearsing. He was older than the others, and a couple of years can make all the difference. Most groups wouldn't have put up with him but he impressed me because he was a go-getter. I thought he would have had some success later, but he didn't. There were seven in his group at one stage and I remember recommending them to the promoter Wally Hill, who said, 'Seven, I'm not feeding seven.'

"I went to see Russ Hamilton at the New Brighton Tower where he was topping the bill - it is amazing to think of all the entertainers who have come from Liverpool. I find it fascinating that he made the Top Three here with 'We Will Make Love' and did equally well in America with the other side, 'Rainbow'. That should have made him an international star, but it never happened. It was the usual story: the managers and the agents made the money, and not Russ. On the bill with Russ, was our local Elvis impersonator, Tommy Jordan, who was backed by Bob Evans and the Five Shillings.

"I missed Buddy Holly at the Philharmonic Hall in 1958, but I did go and see Cliff Richard as I was very impressed by his first record, 'Move It'. The girls were screaming their heads off, 'Oh Cliff! Oh Cliff! Oh Cliff!', and an attendant lifted up one of the girls and put her back in her seat with the words, 'Oh Cliff! Oh Shite!' In 1960 I went to the Empire to see Bobby Darin, who was a favourite of mine. He reminded me of Sinatra with his phrasing and ebullience, but he could also write songs and I appreciated that. George Harrison had gone to see Duane Eddy, who was on the same show. George loved listening to guitarists and sometime later I took one of my records, an LP by Les Paul and Mary Ford, and played 'How High The Moon' one Cavern lunchtime. George loved the multi-tracking so I gave him the record: he gave me a Gene Vincent LP in exchange, which I reluctantly accepted.

"I went to the Essoldo, Birkenhead in November 1958 to see a Larry Parnes extravaganza starring Marty Wilde. I didn't know Brian Epstein then, but he came to admire the impresario Larry Parnes very much. He wanted to emulate his stable of stars and he was a parallel to BE - very theatrical, of the faith and of the persuasion. That night, Larry Parnes thrust a local boy, Ronnie Wycherley, onto the stage, and he became Billy Fury. There is talk of sticking a Billy Fury statue in Mathew Street, but that has no relevance whatsoever. Billy Fury never played the Cavern, which is my mistake as I did turn down a booking. The most appropriate site would be the Essoldo, Birkenhead, which is where he strummed those songs and it all began for him. He wrote good, but not fantastic, songs, and they had beginnings, middles and endings like 'Maybe Tomorrow' and 'Margo'. There was a little story in each of them, which is what good songs should have.

"The importance of Larry Parnes and the TV producer Jack Good are paramount to the development of rock'n'roll in the UK. Parnes had several of the best artists on his books and he brought over American names like Eddie Cochran and Gene Vincent. Jack Good put rock'n'roll onto the TV screen with *6.5 Special* and, when that wasn't exciting enough, he moved to ITV for *Oh Boy!* I used to talk endlessly about that programme - I was an old boy of the *Oh Boy!* network. Later on I attempted an *Oh Boy!* presentation at the Queen's Hall, Widnes with the Merseybeats and the Big Three but the blackout effects weren't very good and it didn't have the speed that I wanted. Nowadays it would be a doddle to do something like that.

"Allan Williams, who owned the Jacaranda coffee bar, told Gareth Pawlowski for his book (*How They Became The Beatles*, Macdonald) that the Liverpool beat music scene started in the city centre, but it didn't. The action was out in the suburbs and it was only later that they came into Liverpool. Ian Edwards of the Crosby group Ian and the Zodiacs said on Radio Merseyside last year that the biggest decision he ever took was to accept a booking in the city centre. These groups had no transport to speak of and so travelling six or seven miles to a booking involved considerable planning.

"I saw the Bobby Bell Rockers at Holyoake Hall in Wavertree, who were one of the first rock'n'roll groups in Liverpool, but I didn't see them regularly and they made little impact on me. If I only saw a group every couple of months, they would have no particular impact, because, believe me, if they were good, I would have been seeing them regularly. A lot of the groups, it has to be said, were very ordinary, and that remained true throughout the 1960s. I would rather spend an evening listening to the Merseysippi Jazz Band, who often had Clinton Ford as their guest vocalist. Their name appealed to me, it was a wonderful pun, and their performances were always very lively. They did 'Creole Belles' and 'Muskrat Ramble' and even today they put a lot of meaning and feeling into whatever they play.

"In 1958 at the Winter Gardens, Garston, Vince Earl was in a group called the Teenage Rebels. They were 16 year olds from Birkenhead and he was the Elvis of the group. I am convinced that if any group could have challenged the Beatles, it would have been the Teenage Rebels, but it never happened. He went into Vince Earl and the Attractions and I put them on a Jerry Lee Lewis show in 1962. Vince became a comic and he has been Ron Dixon in Brookside for several years. Freddie Starr, Bobby Kaye, Johnny Sandon, Lee King and Tom Pepper also became comics, clearly with varying success."

One of the canniest promoters was Carroll Levis. Rather than have stars on his theatre shows, he would pack the bill with local talent. Tony Fisher, who now leads the Bert Kaempfert orchestra recalls, "Carroll Levis was the star of the show - he was a Canadian who brought an American-style talent show to the UK. He didn't sing or dance himself - well, he was 20 stone - but he was a very good presenter and a very good showman. Before he came to the Manchester Hippodrome in 1949, there was an ad saying he was holding auditions. I was a small 13 year old boy playing the trumpet and he must have liked the gimmick of that as I got special permission to leave school and join him on the road. He had a company of eight or nine performers who would appear on his stage shows and his radio programmes, and he would fill up the stage shows with local talent. In some towns, hardly anyone would come to the auditions - in others, there would be 200 acts to choose from. You never could tell. A lot of people got their start in his show including Barry Took and Jim Dale and he often used Morecambe and Wise. The Carroll Levis Discoveries Show did a lot of business: we worked most weeks of the year and even if we were playing the London Palladium, it would be full. Hughie Green saw what Carroll Levis was doing and did virtually the same thing on television with *Opportunity Knocks.*"

Bob Wooler: "They would hold heats for the Carroll Levis show at the Empire, staging the heats during the week and hoping the audience would return on Saturday night to see who'd win. With a bit of luck, you'd get a core of people who would attend, and pay, every night of the week. Carroll Levis had a good thing going as he got all the local acts performing for free, but it gave me a bad feeling about talent nights. If I got involved in them, I felt I was cheating the performers unless I was paying them. I had to give them at least 30 bob (£1.50) to cover the cost of transport."

The first known appearance by John Lennon's Quarry Men was at a Carroll Levis show at the Empire in June 1957. They were beaten by the Sunnyside Skiffle Group from Speke with the comedian and singer, the four foot Nicky Cuff on lead vocals and tea chest bass. In later years, John Lennon would recall "being beaten by a midget". Harry Prytherch, the Remo Four's first drummer, was there two years later: "We passed an audition and took part in the heat on Tuesday night. We did the Jerry Keller song, 'Here Comes Summer', and we only had one amp. As soon as we started singing, the amp blew up and Carroll Levis came on from the wings and apologised and gave us another

58

chance. We were beaten by a snake dancer, and Derry and the Seniors with Howie Casey also got through to the finals."

Bob Wooler: "There was a girl singer whom I first met at the Peel Hall in Peel Street, Dingle with Bob Evans and the Five Shillings in 1958. She was an attractive person and she had some feelings towards me. She called herself Carol Crane for stage performances - her real name was Yvonne - and through her, I learnt an important lesson. I was backstage with her at one of the heats for the Carroll Levis Show at the Empire and she was in two minds as to whether to sing 'The Day The Rains Came' or 'Stupid Cupid'. Her voice wasn't absolutely spot-on so I persuaded her to do the Connie Francis number, 'Stupid Cupid', and she didn't win the heat. She said, 'If I'd stood to my guns and done the Jane Morgan number, I could have won.' I shrivelled up as I was being blamed for this. From that moment on, I realised that I should never advise someone to do a song because if it doesn't work out, I'd be blamed." Quite by chance, I met Carol Crane a few weeks ago and she was surprised that Bob had maintained his guilt for 40 years.

It never happened, but Carol Crane might have been a suitable soulmate for Bob: he certainly thought so. "I was so obsessed with writing songs that I could think of nothing else but songs, and Carol indulged me because we could talk about them. She wasn't as committed as I, but I took her to see the film musical, *Gigi*, and I loved 'I Remember It Well'. I loved the way Maurice Chevalier was constantly being corrected by Hermione Gingold. When he confesses and says, 'Am I getting old?', she still feels impelled to correct him and say, 'Oh no, not you'.

"Carol phoned me from Runcorn a few years later, and we arranged to meet at the Kardomah café in North John Street. She asked me to mention her to Brian Epstein. I thought that was impossible. The voice may be good but the torso was more so with Brian. If she had been a delightful boy, Brian would have been interested, but he would have simply said, 'Why are you recommending her, Bob?', and I couldn't come out, in all honesty, with superlatives about her. Brian already had Lennon leaning on him and saying, 'Give Cilla a break, you fucker.' It would have been useless recommending her and anyway, she was married with children."

One of the first rock'n'roll promoters on Merseyside, if not the first, was Wally Hill. Wally remembers, "I was working at the Rialto Ballroom and jive was not allowed, it was strictly ballroom dancing, and we had to keep breaking them up because they would be doing a bit of jive in the corners. I spoke to the wife and I said, 'There is a market here', because jive wasn't allowed in any dance halls in Liverpool at that time. The manager of the Rialto thought he would run ballroom dances in Garston and so off we went to Garston. He didn't anticipate the trouble there, he didn't like the bloodshed and so he packed it in, but my wife and I said, 'We'll have a go at rock'n'roll. We opened for business and it was great. Bob Wooler came along and asked if he could do the records."

Quite by accident Bob Wooler found himself the first, and for a long time the only, rock'n'roll disc jockey on Merseyside. At that time, it was unusual for someone to announce the records and take requests. Bob would also play obscure but appropriate records while the bands were changing over. Not too many though - Bob started by playing records that were in the Top 20 or thereabouts. One day he showed me a list of records he had played at the Winter Gardens, Garston in 1958: 'I Got Stung' (Elvis Presley), 'Say Mama' (Gene Vincent), 'Love Makes The World Go Round' (Perry Como), 'The Day The Rains Came' (Jane Morgan), 'Hoots Mon' and 'Wee Tom' (Lord Rockingham's XI), 'Mason Dixie Line' (Duane Eddy), 'Stood Up' (Ricky Nelson), 'To Know Him Is To Love Him' (Teddy Bears), 'Real Love' (Ruby Murray), 'Problems' (Everly Brothers), 'The Diary' (Neil Sedaka), 'Break Up' (Jerry Lee Lewis), 'Livin' Lovin' Doll' (Cliff Richard), 'Chantilly Lace' (Big Bopper), 'Beep Beep' (Playmates), 'Babyface' (Little Richard), 'Gotta Travel On' (Billy Grammer) and 'Tom Dooley' (Lonnie Donegan). "That was the start of things," says Bob, "I was known as the Daddy-O of DJs on Merseyside because I was the first person to do an Alan Freed and specialise in playing rock'n'roll records."

Wally Hill: "I'm surprised 'Rave On' isn't on that list. Sometimes Bob would play 'Rave On', then another tune, and then 'Rave On' again. I said, 'Bob, what are doing?' He said, 'Casey likes 'Rave On', I've got to play it.' Casey was a local hardcase. Another one was Crowee. Bob once held a talent contest and picked him as the winner even though he was the least talented of the contestants. Bob said, 'I daren't let him lose.' The Garstonites didn't like anybody foreign in the dance hall, and by that I mean anyone from the Dingle or anywhere else. Nobody but Garstonites was allowed into a Garston dance hall. If a stranger wandered in, he was found in the toilets, or what was left of him. When we had the ballroom dances for the manager of the Rialto, he thought it would be civilised to have commissionaires on and they would last about 15 or 20 minutes and we would have to escort them to the bus stop, so it was rough."

The Winter Gardens was opposite the police station but that didn't stop regular bouts of fighting. The police soon tired of it and the venue was closed in December 1958. Despite the fiasco at the Winter Gardens, the promoter Wally Hill saw the potential for dances in the area and for using Bob Wooler. In February 1959, he started rock'n'roll evenings at Holyoake Hall in Smithdown Road, just round the corner from Penny Lane.

Wally Hill: "It was different at Holyoake because we had an army of bouncers. We advertised in the *Liverpool Echo* and we got replies, loads and loads of them, for baby-sitters. Nobody knew the word 'bouncers' then and they thought we wanted 'baby-sitters'. The national press wanted to know what a 'bouncer' was and did a story about it. We had between 11 and 16 a night, paying them the princely sum of £1 which went up to 25 shillings (£1.25) and then 30 (£1.50), which wasn't bad money then. Howie Casey said to me once, 'When you book us here, do you want me to be a bouncer as well so I can get a bit extra?' There was a row of terraced houses opposite Holyoake Hall and the neighbours would arrange their chairs in the front windows to watch the goings-on for the evening. I thought at the time that they were a bit sad, but it must have been quite interesting."

Wally's wife, Mickey, adds, "I used to take the studded belts off them as they went up the stairs. We weighed one once and it was seven pounds. It was like the western films where you would see a row of gun-belts in the saloon. Some of them were very heavy. If they had kept them, they would have been swinging them round their heads to stop anyone getting near them."

Wally Hill: "We dealt with the front of house, Bob controlled the stage, and the bouncers the dance floor. The stage was high up at Holyoake and Bob felt safe. He knew how to fade away at the first sign of trouble, but the rest of the time he was dynamite."

I KNOW

Lyrics by Bob Wooler, music by George Martin.
Recorded by Billy J. Kramer with the Dakotas as the B-side of their single,
"I'll Keep You Satisfied".

I'm the one who always felt so lonely,
Now you've said you'd be my one and only.

I know how the angels feel,
I know heaven must be real,
I know, I know
What makes the world go round,
This love we found
Surely makes the world go round.

You smile and my dreams come true,
Just smile, my heart enjoys the view,
For I was unaware
Of the love we two could share,
And now I know, I know, yes, I know.

For I was unaware
Of the love we two could share,
And now I know, I know, yes, I know.

George Martin

I KNOW
By GEORGE MARTIN & BOB WOOLER

RECORDED

BY

BILLY
J. KRAMER

WITH
THE DAKOTAS

ON

PARLOPHONE

2/6

JAEP MUSIC LTD.

6 THE STUFF THAT SCREAMS ARE MADE OF

Liverpool, 1960 - Gerry and the Pacemakers - Hamburg - Litherland Town
Hall - Tony Sheridan - Fairweather friends

"Don't interrupt us. We're fucking stars. Where do you think we
are? In the Jacaranda?"
(John Lennon to an engineer at the "Get Back" sessions, 1969)

Relatively few rock'n'roll stars came to the UK during the 1950s and those who did
would not stay long. The three month tour by Eddie Cochran and Gene Vincent early
in 1960 was therefore a special event and a unique one as it offered the chance to see
two US rock'n'roll stars performing live. For a variety of reasons, Gene Vincent's
career was on the rocks in the States: he had burned every bridge, been blacklisted by
his union and even his group, the Blue Caps, had stopped working with him. Cochran
was the new kid on the block, as good-looking as Vincent was haggard and as self-
assured as Vincent was lacking in confidence, but both liked rock'n'roll - and drinking
hard.

Georgie Fame, who played piano on the tour, told me, "Eddie was a wonderful guitarist
and a terrific performer. He was a really nice guy and more than anyone else, he was
responsible for introducing Ray Charles' music to the masses in England. Very few
people had heard of Ray Charles until Eddie Cochran came over. He played 'What'd I
Say' on stage and he recorded 'Hallelujah I Love Her So'."

Also on the tour was the guitarist Big Jim Sullivan: "Eddie and Gene used to drink a
bottle of bourbon before they went on stage. They were the first men I'd ever seen who
really drank. They drank shorts so they weren't like beer drinkers. Eddie was so drunk
at the Liverpool Empire that we weren't sure that he'd make it to the stage. It had one
of those microphones that comes up from the floor. We positioned Eddie so that it
would come up between his body and his guitar and he could balance on it. He sobered
up after two songs and untangled himself. He still gave a good show, so he never had
anything to apologise for."

The tour was promoted by Larry Parnes, who added his own artists including Billy Fury
and Joe Brown to the bill. They played the Liverpool Empire for the week of 14 March
1960 and would finish with a week at Bristol Hippodrome starting on 11 April. The
stars would take a break but the tour was so successful that Parnes had arranged further

bookings for May. While the package was playing at the Liverpool Empire during March, Allan Williams, the owner of the Jacaranda coffee bar, told Parnes of his plans for a huge rock'n'roll extravaganza at the Liverpool Stadium on 3 May. Nothing like this had ever taken place in the UK before and Parnes was impressed. Together they would promote the concert and Eddie and Gene would star.

Tragedy struck on the last night of the tour. The car carrying Eddie and Gene crashed on its way to London. Eddie was killed and Gene, who was crippled anyway, suffered further injuries. Vincent returned to America with Eddie's body on 20 April, and, allowing little time for recuperation, he was back in the UK a fortnight later for the new tour. The posters for the Liverpool Stadium deleted Cochran's name and had Vincent as the sole top of the bill. Most intriguingly, the concert was to feature local bands, who would have rarely played to more than a handful of people.

Bob Wooler: "Allan Williams was providing the local groups, and he didn't include the Beatles because they had difficulty in finding a drummer and I don't think Allan rated them too highly. I recommended Gerry and the Pacemakers as I had seen a lot of them and knew they were a very well organised and well-liked group. They were originally called the Gerry Marsden Trio, and I was at Holyoake when their first pianist, Arthur McMahon, came up with the name of the Pacemakers. He was watching sport on television and the commentator said, 'He's a pacemaker.' Arthur announced, 'That's it. We're no longer the Gerry Marsden Trio but Gerry and the Pacemakers.' That was a great improvement as the name, the Gerry Marsden Trio was too square and reminded me of the Modern Jazz Quartet."

Freddie Marsden, drummer with the Pacemakers: "Bob Wooler was the main man and we owe what happened to us to Bob Wooler. In 1959 when we were trying to get going, he got us into Holyoake and then into Blair Hall. He was always promoting us and we felt really good when he introduced us on stage. We'd think he was talking about another group because he made us sound so good."

Bob Wooler: "Philip Norman says in his book, *Shout! The True History Of The Beatles*, that Gerry was the hit of the stadium show. I told Philip Norman that Gerry was singing the Jack Scott song, 'What In The World's Come Over You?' but he changed it to 'You'll Never Walk Alone', presumably to make it a better story. Gerry didn't even know the song at that stage. Tony Sheridan used to do 'You'll Never Walk Alone' in Hamburg, and he, in turn, had heard it from Gene Vincent. That's how Gerry learnt it, over in Hamburg in 1961. I used to encourage Gerry to do it at Cavern lunchtime sessions. It was ironic that the Kop should adopt the tune as its anthem in December '63 as Gerry was an Evertonian in his youth."

It was Johnny Gustafson, a member of Cass and the Cassanovas, who caught Larry Parnes' attention. Gus recalls, "I was a young lad of 17 and Larry Parnes spied me and thought, 'Star quality' and invited me to London. We did a recording test in Denmark Street of me singing 'Money Honey' with an electric guitar which wasn't plugged in. He treated me very well, buying me clothes and things, but I had had a lecture from my dad before I went and I was very wary about him. We didn't have a bath at home, we used to go to the public baths, and the fact that he had one in his flat was a huge luxury. There was a huge mirror in the bathroom, and I found out later that the mirror was double-sided. He had a little room round the corner and he would be sitting there watching me. Later on, when he wanted to get into bed with me, I decided that I had had enough and I left in the middle of the night and came back to Liverpool."

For whatever reason, Larry Parnes was impressed with the local talent and told Allan Williams he was looking for a regular backing group for Billy Fury. Williams arranged an audition for Liverpool bands on 10 May at the Wyvern Social Club in Seel Street. Alan Schroeder from Cliff Roberts and the Rockers remembers, "Bob Wooler asked us to go along and I remember Howie Casey and the Seniors and Cass and the Cassanovas being there. All I can remember about Billy Fury was his long fingernails - it was obvious he wasn't a manual worker. We did our bit and when the Beatles went on, I walked out. I thought they were terrible. Still, they got the job, or at least a job, of backing Johnny Gentle in Scotland."

None of the groups got the prize of backing Fury, but the Beatles, then the Silver Beatles, were asked to accompany Parnes' protégé, Liverpool singer Johnny Gentle, on a short tour of Scotland. Bob Wooler: "I've heard Johnny talk about this - indeed, he has written his autobiography - but I feel he talks with hindsight, which is so easy. He paints a glowing picture of the Beatles; they are gentle on his mind as it were, which I'm sure doesn't represent his views at the time.

"I am convinced that Johnny Gentle went to Scotland with this group of unknown, fellow Scousers, who had a different style of music from his own. They were his backing group, although they also performed in their own right, and I have a feeling that it was not a successful tour. Otherwise, Larry Parnes would have been on to Allan Williams and saying 'I must have another tour with Johnny Gentle and the Silver Beatles, they were fantastic.' But what happened? He dropped them. He never offered the Beatles anything after that, so the Scottish tour must have been a bit of a disaster."

The Beatles did not have a drummer when they appeared at the Wyvern Social Club, although Johnny Hutchinson had helped out. They took that most unknown of all Beatles, Tommy Moore, with him. Bob Wooler: "I knew him from my days on Garston docks as he had worked there. He was a messenger boy who was crazy about drums. He took drum lessons and held the sticks correctly - that is, the conventional dance band way, which has gone out of fashion now. His wife was very contemptuous about beat groups and she never thought that working with the Beatles would lead to success. She ordered him to stick to his job driving a fork-lift truck at Garston Bottle Works."

But there was another reason. "Tommy Moore came in for the Lennon treatment. Moore was a very working class lad and he was not able to cope with the Lennon attitude and, taking his lead from Lennon, McCartney could be similar. At times, they reminded me of those well-to-do Chicago lads, Leopold and Laeb, who killed someone because they felt superior to him. It was known as the crime of the century and the Alfred Hitchcock film *Rope* was based upon it as well as an Orson Welles film, *Compulsion*. Lennon and McCartney were superior human beings and poor Tommy had to mind his p's and q's with them. He was so forlorn because their IQs were miles ahead of his."

Although Bob knew the Beatles, he did not see them perform until they returned from Scotland. "I first saw the Beatles perform at the Grosvenor Ballroom in Liscard, Wallasey on Saturday 2 July 1960, and I'd gone to see Gerry and the Pacemakers who were on the same bill. Johnny Gentle, who had come back to Liverpool for the weekend, was there as well. He may have done a few numbers with them but I don't know about that as Gerry wouldn't let me see them. As soon as the Beatles got on stage, Gerry said, 'Aren't we going to Burtonwood Ales?', and I only saw one number. It was the Pacemakers I was rooting for then and I regret going for that pint now."

At that time, the Beatles featured John, Paul, George and, on bass, Stuart Sutcliffe. Bob Wooler: "I don't think that the Beatles ever carried passengers and, if he was as lousy as some books suggest, he would have got the order of the boot. I could imagine Lennon saying, 'As a guitarist, you're a fantastic painter', but he never did - at least, not in my presence. Stu's true ambition was to be a painter but ever since Lonnie Donegan and Elvis Presley, rock has obsessed the majority of youngsters. It's the done thing. Even Tony Blair was in a group, so it was natural that Stu should be in one too."

In the late 50s, early 60s, London had its fashionable basement coffee-bars, notably the Two I's in Old Compton Street. Naturally, several people in Liverpool wanted to follow the trend; Allan Williams had the Jacaranda and Neil English the Sink. Mona Best opened the Casbah in the basement of her house with the help and encouragement of her sons, Rory and Pete. Rory Storm tried to establish the Morgue, and there was another called the Masque in the centre of Liverpool. Many commentators remark on the Cavern having no liquor licence but that was hardly significant as it applied to most places. It wasn't an essential requirement back then, although it would be now.

Bob Wooler: "It was in 1960 that I decided to go pro. I would say to my fellow clerks on the railway, 'This is not my station in life', and so on, and they would say, 'Wooler's gone off the rails.' All very funny, but they couldn't believe I would pack in my job for the precarious business of disc-jockeying. I was given a job at the Top Ten club in the roughest area in Liverpool. Allan Williams, who launched the club in Soho Street, took the name from a similar establishment in Hamburg. It lasted five days and then someone got careless with the Bryant and May's. At one Beatles Convention, I said it was a torching job and I glared at Allan. He said, 'What are you looking at me for?' I was to learn about incinerations as that was not the only place in Liverpool to go up in smoke." Indeed not, I was in a pub with a Mersey Beat group a few years back and one of them said to me, "That's Tommy the Torch. He's done more damage to Liverpool than Adolf Hitler." However, in this instance, although the insurance company was suspicious and took Allan Williams to court, the allegation was not proved.

Allan Williams: "The first group to play at the Top Ten was Howie Casey and the Seniors and they blew the place apart. The only snag was that it was in a tough area known as the Four Squares and the locals said it was their club as though it was their local youth club. I don't know how it would have developed, but the premises were fantastic. It was like a barn with thick wooden beams and we had to write notices, 'Please duck your head'. I had absolutely no reason to burn down the club and it loused up my plans. I had even selected Bob Wooler as the right person to run it. I had persuaded him to give up his day job, and five days later the poor feller was out of work."

Strangely perhaps, I find myself agreeing with Allan Williams. He had no reason to burn down the place. He says now, admittedly with hindsight, "History would have been altered if the Top Ten had not caught fire. That would have been my Cavern club. The Cavern was only doing jazz at the time and there wasn't a venue in the centre doing rock'n'roll. Still, I opened the Blue Angel and that was a luxurious night club."

Bob Wooler: "When the Top Ten went up, a promoter in the north end of Liverpool, Brian Kelly, came to my rescue and I worked on his circuit of dances. The Remo Four told me about the Cavern and I went there one lunchtime in December 1960. At the end of his set, Johnny Hutch of the Big Three thrust a Reslo mike at me and said, 'Make an announcement'. I'd had a little wine and I said, 'Remember all you cave-dwellers, the Cavern is the best of cellars.' The owner of the Cavern, Ray McFall, heard me - and that's how I got the job of introducing the Cavern's lunchtime sessions."

So Bob's most famous Woolerism had come into being that first day at the Cavern. "I didn't top 'the best of cellars' but I used to run newspaper ads for the Cavern which said, 'The venue with the menu with the mostest' or, even worse, 'Meet the beat that's reet for the feet.' I did try and put some humour into my ads. I remember, 'What is geological music?' and the answer was 'Rock, rock, rock.' One of the ads for Hambleton Hall announced 'Bob Wooler's married' and added 'to the best rock sessions in Liverpool', but that was inserted by Vic Anton and not by me. I thought it ridiculous to give me prominence in this way and besides, it wasn't even a good joke.

"The Cavern was a dreadful place really, a forbidding place, a Black Hole of Calcutta, noisy and initially menacing. In its favour, it couldn't be torched as only the chairs were flammable. There was no back exit or entrance. The ventilation left much to be desired and I was sure I was going to get tuberculosis."

When Bob discussed the Beatles with Allan Williams, either publicly or privately, the conversation would return to one key point: "1960 was your Beatles year, Allan, you never saw them after that." Although that is true, Bob did acknowledge Allan's contribution. "He was the first person to spot the Beatles' charisma, and he did do something about it. He got them the bookings in Scotland and he arranged for them to go to Hamburg, but it was also the year that he got rid of them. They had come from Germany in December 1960 somewhat crestfallen as they had been extradited for starting a fire and, in George's case, for being under age. If the music hadn't happened, maybe they could have got jobs torching clubs in Liverpool - or perhaps not, as they were caught in Germany!"

Stu Sutcliffe remained in Germany and John, Paul, George and Pete Best were looking for work. Bob Wooler: "Allan was preoccupied with the demise of the Top Ten and the opening of his new club, the Blue Angel, which wasn't for beat music. The Beatles would have played the Top Ten on their return but, in the event, they had come back early with no work on offer. Anyway, Allan said to me, 'You get them work. Try Brian Kelly. He has a string of dance halls and you have some connections with him.' They asked me about bookings and they didn't want to go back to playing Allan's coffee-bar, the Jacaranda. I agreed with them - it was a former coal cellar and had no stage, no lights and no microphones. It was totally unsuitable for showcasing a group. It was also very small, and I doubt if you could get 50 people in there. On the other hand, Litherland Town Hall, Lathom Hall, Aintree Institute and Hambleton Hall had stages and there could be some impact in sweeping the curtains open and saying, 'Here they are, the Beatles.' Presentation is very important.

"You can write your own entry for *Who's Who*, and Paul McCartney has written, 'Made first important appearance as the Beatles at Litherland Town Hall near Liverpool in December 1960.' Mona Best had given them some work at the Casbah but she couldn't sustain them with a residency and I am pleased to say that I got them onto Brian Kelly's circuit. The first booking was on Tuesday 27 December 1960, when they were added to the bill of a BeeKay (Brian Kelly) dance. Brian nearly collapsed when I asked for £8 because he was a tight-wad but most of the promoters were. He offered me £4 and we compromised on £6, which is £1 a man, five Beatles, and £1 for the driver. I didn't take my 10 per cent.

"I had been very enthusiastic to Brian Kelly about them because he told me, 'Oh, I had them on at Lathom Hall and they weren't much good.' I kept telling him how they'd improved, but I was bluffing because it was sight unseen, or rather sound unheard, for me. I hoped they'd improved but I didn't know for sure. In deference to me, he put them on. They were doing half an hour as an extra to the bill and, quite honestly, I wondered if they would even turn up that night, but they did honour the booking.

"They were billed as 'Direct from Hamburg' but too much has been made of this. There wasn't any deceit in trying to present them as a German group, although I did mention they'd been playing in Hamburg when I announced them. It was an amazing night. When I did hear the Beatles, I was fab-ergasted. Other groups were playing what was in the charts - they felt reassured that way. The Beatles liked obscure R&B stuff. They were only on stage for 30 minutes, but they put everything into their performance and rocked the joint.

"People went crazy for their closing number which was Ray Charles' 'What'd I Say'. Paul took the mike off the stand, shed his guitar and did fantastic antics all over the stage. They were all stomping like hell, and the audience went mad. I've never cared for the song, but this was fantastic. You might say, then, that Paul was the leader of the band because he was the guy upfront with the mike - and that, I suppose, is the way he thought of himself.

"The Beatles' impact was tremendous and everyone was taken by surprise. Brian Kelly posted a bouncer on the door which led backstage to stop any other promoters getting to them first. He'd seen Dave Forshaw and he knew others could be there as well as not much else was happening on a Tuesday night. There was lots of rivalry then - Ivemar Promotions was Jim McIver and Doug Martin and when I went to St Luke's Hall in Crosby one day, they looked very suspiciously at me because they regarded me as part of the opposition with Brian Kelly. They thought I had come to spy on them, to count heads.

"Indeed, Brian Kelly wanted to sign up the Beatles before I could get to them as he knew I promoted some dances and I might also tell Ray McFall at the Cavern about them. He got his diary out and immediately signed them for a string of dates at £7.10s (£7.50) or 30 bob (£1.50) a man. I was talking with Dave Forshaw in the coffee-bar upstairs and he was equally impressed. He gave them some bookings at St. John's Hall in Bootle."

Bob took the opportunity to get some regular work for himself: "I asked Brian Kelly, 'Who does your stage management and who announces the records?', and he said, 'No-one.' Someone looked after the stage by opening the curtains but the records were placed on a autochanger, and that was it. I brought some structure to his dances, and I would ask the groups to plug his other venues, 'We will be at Lathom Hall on the 19th,' and so on. It was my job to imbue these evenings with a sense of zest, so that it wasn't just another Saturday night.

"The equipment was primitive. We only had one turntable at Litherland Town Hall and if the amps were dropped onto the floor, the needle would jump. I was constantly saying, 'Watch it, watch it.' Anyone who had pretentions to be a disc jockey could forget it. You were not enclosed in a little private room with twin turntables and headphones. You had to use an autochange, you had to make announcements, you had to hustle a band off and the next one on. It was more stage management than anything else. And I didn't have a car. I used to travel round with my little wooden box made by the joiners at Garston Docks. It contained my 45s and I would smoke Senior Service, the same brand of cigarettes as George Harrison, on the top deck of the bus. I'd get a bus back or get a lift in one of the group's vans.

"None of the equipment was properly checked and I was nearly electrocuted by Ty Brien from Rory Storm and the Hurricanes at Hambleton Hall. I gestured by moving my arm and it went over the neck of his guitar and I was like Johnny Kidd, shaking all over. Ty realised that electricity was going through me, and he wrenched his guitar away to break the chain. I was in a terrible state, and I stumbled off the stage, and Rory went, 'Big hand for Bob.' I staggered into the kitchen and had excruciating pains across my back for days.

"For the BeeKay dances, the Beatles were given the prime time, the middle spot around 9.30pm. The dance would start at 7.30pm and the first group would be on at 8 o'clock, so for the first half-hour I would be playing records and getting the first group organised. If there were three groups on, the Beatles would be the middle group, not as one might think the last group because that was 'tail-home time' (an expression I learned in Garston, a sexual reference meaning 'Are you getting your tail home?') People would be drifting off and so that wouldn't be the right spot for the peak group."

71

Bob Wooler never saw the Beatles perform in Hamburg and he always wondered about its mythical status. "Was it Hamburg that transformed the Beatles? If Hamburg is so magical that it transforms groups, then how come it didn't transform the Big Three, Rory Storm and the Hurricanes, Derry and the Seniors, Kingsize Taylor and the Dominoes, Gerry and the Pacemakers and all the other groups that went there? I saw these groups before they went and I saw them when they returned and I would see no great difference. However, it was a strange environment, a strange people, a strange language, long working hours and exploitation. Hamburg gave the Beatles the awareness and the importance of working as a team - maybe that was the most significant factor.

"When I asked the Beatles what Hamburg was like, they owned up to the wild nights and told me much more than the Pacemakers ever did. They did work long hours, but they would elongate numbers and add guitar breaks, so that a three-minute number could last six minutes and so on.

"I mustn't overlook Tony Sheridan, who was already playing in the Hamburg clubs when the Beatles arrived. He'd been on Jack Good's *Oh Boy!*, but he burned his bridges with Jack Good and Larry Parnes because he was a wild, uninhibited character. The groups loved the way he could jam on stage and took songs from his repertoire like 'Hallelujah I Love Her So', which he had got in turn from Ray Charles. Both John Lennon and Tony Jackson adopted his stance, 'watching the crotch' I call it, and Gerry Marsden started to put his guitar armpit high. Sometime later, around 1963, I met Tony Sheridan when he was appearing at the Liverpool Odeon in a beat show. After his appearance, he came down to the Cavern, but he was as high as a kite. Gerry and the Pacemakers were on stage and said, 'Bring him on', but he was terrible and I couldn't get him off. We could have done with a pantomime hook that night."

Allan Williams: "I always say that it was not Liverpool that made the Beatles, but Hamburg. Bob Wooler would say to me, 'Okay, smart arse, if it did that for the Beatles, why didn't it do it for Gerry and the Pacemakers, Rory Storm and the Hurricanes, and Howie Casey and the Seniors?' The answer is that they were all established acts before they went. The Beatles were known as a bum group. They hadn't got their act together and this is where they learnt their trade. I had enough confidence in the Beatles to know that they were good enough to go, and history has proved me right. Working all those outrageous hours would make or break a group, and it made the Beatles."

In my view, the Beatles picked up a rock'n'roll attitude in Hamburg. They had swagger, they became cool, and Gerry and the Pacemakers in their monogrammed blazers could never hope to do that. I think that explains why Stuart Sutcliffe was tolerated by the other Beatles: look at the pictures of him with the band, he looks right.

Stuart Sutcliffe returned to Liverpool in January 1961. Bob Wooler: "The Sutcliffes lived rather grandly in a flat in a big house at the end of Aigburth Drive, near the boating lake, but when Stu brought his girlfriend, the photographer Astrid Kirchherr, to Liverpool early in '61, they didn't stay in the flat. I asked him about this and he told me his mother hated Germans. Many people who had gone through the war years were like that, and it is quite understandable.

"During the first three months of 1961, Stu did about fifty shows with the Beatles, and I hosted all but about half-a-dozen of them. I got to know him pretty well and his party piece was 'Love Me Tender' with George embroidering the melody. At no time did I see Stu play with his back to the audience. Although I talked to him about art, I never heard him mention Eduardo Paolozzi, but he might not have known him at the time. When they went to Hamburg for the second time in March 1961, Stuart stayed there to study under Paolozzi and I never saw him alive again.

"I saw the first signs of adoration for Pete Best. I particularly remember the Valentine's Day dance at Litherland Town Hall in 1961. Some girls had made satin hearts for the Beatles and they were wearing them on stage. A lot of girls were standing by the footlights and looking beyond the front line to the drummer, Pete Best. I got him to come to the front to take a bow. He was no Dave Clark as he didn't want his drums in the footlights. Johnny Hutch of the Big Three wanted to be in the footlights with the others flanking him and he wanted to do the singing. Chris Curtis of the Searchers used to play the drums standing up, and he was saying, 'Notice me, notice me.' Pete Best was shy and there was an obvious attraction. There was a charisma about him which I found fascinating.

"The Beatles were getting some shrieks at these performances but it was nothing like the way it's been portrayed in some books and films. The best place to see the Beatles was Litherland Town Hall where the stage was quite high. That was better than Hambleton Hall or Lathom Hall, but the Cavern wasn't much good unless you were in the centre tunnel. Also, the Cavern stage was only 18 inches high, so you couldn't see much from the back."

In December 1960, the Cavern was a jazz and country and western venue and its new owner, Ray McFall, was looking for change. Bob Wooler: "The country and western brigade regarded rock'n'roll groups as a novelty, while jazz bands poured contempt on them. I got a hell of a bad name for encouraging rock'n'roll to be played at the Cavern.

The Cavern was a jazz cellar and the followers didn't want rock'n'roll groups coming in. The beat groups were cheaper than the jazz bands, and I'm sure that had a lot to do with the changeover."

The Cavern with its stone walls and wooden stage was best suited for the acoustic instruments of the jazz bands, but the music was losing its popularity. The Swinging Blue Jeans was something of a hybrid in both repertoire and instrumentation, being not quite a jazz group and not quite a rock'n'roll band. This made them unique amongst the Liverpool bands. Ray Ennis, the leader of the Swinging Blue Jeans, recalls: "Bob Wooler was very important. He came in when jazz was on the wane. Bob brought polish and continuity to the shows. He called us the Swinging Blue Geniuses and so we were highly flattered."

Bob Wooler: "It was inevitable that the Beatles would be performing at the Cavern and they made their debut on the Swinging Blue Jeans guest night in March 1961. The Blue Jeans played a mixture of pop and traditional jazz tunes then, and they were very popular. Indeed, I was most impressed with the Swinging Blue Jeans as a jazz band. They had an upright, string bass and they played at a lower volume than they did later. There was none of the stridency of 'Good Golly Miss Molly' when they performed 'Down By The Riverside'.

"Ray McFall allowed them to choose whomever they wanted for their Tuesday guest nights and they invited Dale Roberts and the Jaywalkers, the Remo Four and the Four Jays - groups that wouldn't clash or be more popular than themselves. One night Ray McFall put the Beatles on with them, a good move for the Cavern, but the Beatles' fans swamped the Blue Jeans' fans. The Blue Jeans were not happy and there were altercations between their leader, Ray Ennis and Ray McFall at the top of the steps to the Cavern. Ray Ennis said, 'We're not having them on with us again.' Ray McFall liked the Beatles and he was also thinking of his receipts, so shortly afterwards the Blue Jeans went elsewhere.

"There was a short period at the Cavern where beat groups would be billed alongside jazz bands. It was a strange combination and it wasn't clear for whom Ray McFall was catering. Ray would book the jazz bands, who would say it was no use to be on such a bill. The jazz element became disenchanted with the Cavern and so the club turned completely to rock. Most of the jazzmen now say, 'Oh, I knew right away that the Beatles were going to be stars.' Absolute rubbish. I have heard the country singer Hank Walters talking on *Radio Merseyside* about how he enjoying playing alongside the Beatles - more rubbish. His attitude was, 'Do we have to suffer this lot?' Fair-weather friends, or what?"

LEAD, BASS , RHYTHM AND DRUMS

Uncompleted lyric by Bob Wooler

Lead, bass, rhythm and drums
Playing together
Whatever the weather
And no matter what comes,
Believing we're the best
Ahead of the rest
Lead, bass, rhythm and drums.

Bass, drums, rhythm and lead
In tune with the heartbeat,
Hearing the chartbeat,
Filling a need.
Put us to the test,
We're four of the best.
Bass, drums, rhythm and lead.

Drums, lead, rhythm and bass
Giving each venue
The right kind of menu,
And proving we're ace.
No one could sign up
A better line up
Drums, lead, rhythm and bass.

The Ravin' Texans
(Rory Storm & Co.)

(l to r) Dave Gore (TTs), Harry Prytherch (Remo Four), Bob Wooler, Don Andrew (Remo Four)

The Swinging
Blue Jeans, 1961.

Kingsize Taylor
and the Dominoes.

7 THE BLOOD BATHS, PHILIP, THE BLOOD BATHS!
Was Saturday night alright for fighting?

"Hush a bye bye baby"
(Title of gangster's lullaby written by Bob Wooler.
The rest has been lost.)

"There wasn't a phone at the Top Ten so there was no means of calling the cops if trouble broke out," says Bob Wooler of that ill-fated Allan Williams club, "Derek Chang kept a saw there and he said that he would saw people's hands off if there was trouble."

What was a refined and cultured young man like Bob Wooler doing in these rough, tough dance halls? At times Bob shrugged it off and said that the violence was exaggerated, but at other times his reminiscences painted a different picture. "Allan Williams has some very colourful anecdotes about Liverpool gang life. He says, 'The Krays were going to start a protection racket in Liverpool, but we met them at Lime Street Station and they were on the next train back.' Believe that if you will."

Bob's next observation takes the middle ground and is about as accurate as it can be. "Liverpool clubland was placid compared to drug-dealing, violence and rivalry that you experience today, although we thought it was dramatic enough at the time. In one sense, it was like the Mafia or Chicago gangsters, 'Don't encroach on my territory.' I told the promoter Brian Kelly about a hall in the south end of Liverpool and he said, 'No, that's Wally Hill's area, that's his patch.'"

One day Bob brought a photograph to Keith's Wine Bar. "This is a priceless picture of the promoter Wally Hill at Holyoake Hall in Wavertree surrounded by his heavy crew, his bouncers. He had a dozen of them which was ridiculous for a small hall, but at least he didn't have much trouble at his dances. There was some. Once I was at the top of the stairs talking with Wally's wife who was in the box-office, and this bouncer hit a lad and sent him flying down the stone steps. It was sickening as the lad must have been badly hurt. Wally employed an Oriental doorman who had a black belt in judo but, as I never saw him in action, it could have been a con."

The rule of thumb is one bouncer for every 100 patrons, so a dozen bouncers for a hall that held 400 seems excessive. Wally Hill: "When we had a riot and we had a few riots in our time, you needed them, you are protecting yourselves and not just the dance hall.

They took Blair Hall to pieces. Luckily by different methods we managed to hush it as otherwise we would have been thrown out. The odd knife was thrown and we found out what a docker's hook was. There were branches off trees and milk bottles, but you get acclimatised to it and it becomes a way of life. The adrenalin would flow and if we didn't have much trouble, we would think 'It's a bit boring tonight.' It was quite fun and, except for a few occasions, we were in the strongest army."

When wasn't Wally in the 'strongest army'? Wally Hill: "Two guys were having a fight outside, so stupid me or big-headed me, whichever way you think of it, went to break it up. One of the guys goes to the pub and comes back with his mates. We had just closed the dance hall and I was walking down the stairs and they cornered me and they gave me a right going-over, but apart from that, no problems."

From time to time, Bob felt threatened by Wally Hill himself. "I gave him his company's name of Peak Promotions, which matched his surname, but he resented me because I worked for the opposition. He came with his number one bouncer, Bill McGarry, to see me at Hambleton Hall in Huyton about some free tickets that had been distributed and I thought I was going to be beaten up."

Wally Hill: "My wife could have intimidated Bob and I certainly wouldn't have needed to take Bill McGarry round if I was going to duff him up - I'd have done it myself! No, there was no thought of beating Bob up, but he was doing something wrong. He was giving out free tickets for a dance when we were doing something the same night."

Bob Wooler: "I have seen terrible fights at Hambleton Hall in Huyton. The lights would go up when there was trouble so that the bouncers could pinpoint the trouble, and I saw two gangs booting hell out of each other. Once, when the Beatles were on Hambleton Hall, the troublemakers were throwing things at the stage. I said, 'I'm not having artists being treated in this way.' This was the scoutmaster talking, and I must have been fortified. The Beatles were highly amused by this. Then the lights went on and everything was sorted out."

Wally Hill: "Bob Evans and the Five Shillings were a popular group and they asked us if we had used the Beatles yet. We said no and we asked what they were like. Bob Evans said, 'Don't touch them, they don't wash their hair and there's a fight every night.' There was a fight every night anyway, so that didn't mean anything. We wrote to them in Hamburg and they signed an agreement that they would play for us every Saturday and Sunday at a tenner a night, which was big money then. They played a few times and we increased it to £12 and then one night they came along to Blair Hall, Walton, and Paul said, 'We are not going on unless we get £15.' There was a bit of haggling and in the end we decided that they weren't worth it. (Laughs) We parted company. They didn't play that night and the kids were disappointed and we never had them again. I think I made a mistake there."

Bob Wooler: "The chairs at the Aintree Institute were batoned into fours so that they could not be thrown at the stage, but the odd ones were certainly thrown. I used to close the curtains as I wanted to protect the instruments. Once, they carried on fighting from the hall to a grass verge, and this lad got tetanus in his wound, so that was a fraught occasion. There was trouble at Aintree Institute one Saturday night when Rory Storm and the Hurricanes were on and I got the lad to close the curtains quickly, and the bouncers sorted out the trouble. Rory went in the dressing room and when he went back on stage, he did a Long John Silver act with a brush and a bandage as though he had been hit. It was very amusing if you could be amused by something that was very threatening. There was violence in these dance halls and you accepted that it might flare up at any time. The Galvinisers carry a 'murder bag' with their equipment, which were socks filled with sand and indeed, Les Hurst made me a present of a cosh."

Dave May of the Silhouettes recalls how an accidental manoeuvre could cause a scuffle. "We were playing on stage at St. Luke's Hall in Crosby, and all of a sudden a feller goes down in the middle of the dance floor. The other guys piled on top of him and soon they're laying into each other. The whole floor erupted until the police came with the dogs. We found out later what had caused it. A guy was dancing and he had dislocated his knee. He fell down on one knee and the guy next to him immediately hit him because he thought he wanted a fight."

Harry Prytherch, drummer with the Remo Four, recalls, "Wilson Hall, which was near the docks in Garston and opposite the baths, was the most notorious club that we ever played. All the sailors would come to the dance hall and line up along one side of the hall. The girls would be on the floor dancing and their boyfriends would be on the other side. Around half past ten, everybody would pile in and it would be a free-for-all. The club was run by a lovely man called Charlie McBain and he had a whistle tied round his neck with a piece of string. If the fighting got out of hand, he would blow his whistle and the policemen, who were in a Landrover outside, would come running into the hall and throw all the troublemakers out. I know the bobbies quite enjoyed it as it gave them some exercise."

Bob Wooler: "Charlie McBain used to cover the baths at Garston during the winter and promote dances there - the swimming baths became the dance floor as it were - and I said to the author, Philip Norman, more or less as a joke, 'The blood baths, Philip, the blood baths', which he put in his book, *Shout! The True Story Of The Beatles*. Allan

Williams liked that phrase and started saying, 'Some of the places they played were terrible, like the blood baths of Garston.' They could be tough, but this was OTT. A 16 year old was killed at the Institute in Neston, but when I went there with Derry and the Seniors it was a nice, countrified place with no signs of continuous violence. The managers of the dance halls were, however, wary of rock'n'roll. I remember wanting to book the Kingsland, a ballroom in Borough Road, Birkenhead and I didn't reveal what it was for. I admitted the dance was for teenagers, and the manager said, 'Well, they must not jive.'

"I'm not sure that the infamous fight took place in which Stu Sutcliffe allegedly suffered the brain damage which was to kill him. He was supposed to have been involved in a brawl at Lathom Hall, but, if he was, it wasn't the exaggerated brawl that is described in Beatle books. If such a fight had taken place, I am sure I would have heard the Beatles discussing it, and I never did. Arthur Ballard, who taught Stu at art school, told me that he was quite aggressive and had done some boxing, so if there had been a fight, it wouldn't have been a walkover."

I asked Bob whom he feared the most. "Well, the most notorious figure on Merseyside was Eddie Palmer, who had been a bouncer at the Top Ten and the Jacaranda. The only person who could control him was his uncle, who ran the Tower Ballroom. Your heart would miss a beat if he came into a pub and you would have to say, 'What are you having, Eddie?' Indeed, if he wanted a drink, you'd buy it. I tried to say no to him once and he pinned me against the wall in the Pink Parrot. He terrorised Rory Storm and would order him to drive him home to the Dingle. Rory told me, and he wasn't joking, that he wanted to run him over. It would not have been a wise move as Rory's pink Zodiac was one of the most recognisable cars in Liverpool."

Billy Butler: "Everybody knew Eddie Palmer. He was a bully and a fearsome man. He once danced on the bonnet of Rory Storm's car and Rory was terrified of him."

Allan Williams: "Eddie also pinned me to the wall at the Pink Parrot and this was because I had barred him from the Blue Angel. I said, 'I don't want you coming into the club because you're a bad influence.' To my amazement, he said, 'You've got balls, Allan, I'll buy you a drink' and I never had trouble with him again. His uncle Tommy McArdle was the manager of the Tower Ballroom when I put on Jerry Lee Lewis and Eddie was one of his bouncers. Sam Leach called his team the Mean Machine. I was very wary about them as I never wanted to use bouncers who might start the trouble."

Bob Wooler: "Another bouncer, Beechy Keatley, made a remark to a girl that Eddie took offence to, and Eddie ran him over. Later on, Beechy drew out a knife outside the Peel

Hall, East and West Toxteth Labour Club, and stabbed him. Exit Eddie Palmer horizontally. Beechy was arrested but, according to Allan Williams, the coppers applauded him at the trial because he'd done such a service to the community. I think John Ford was directing that one, but apparently the judge said, 'It's a wonder that this man wasn't killed before.' The police were certainly glad to see the end of him. Beechy was an okay guy who only served a short time behind bars at the Hornby Road holiday camp. I saw him in Lark Lane only the other day - he always wanted to be an opera singer."

Allan and Bob's anecdotes seemed fanciful but when I got hold of the *Daily Post* and *Liverpool Echo* stories about the end of the "Toxteth Terror" in 1979, I realised it was true. Deaths are normally reported impartially, but the *Echo* wrote: "Drinks were on the house at some South Liverpool pubs when the news broke that Eddie Palmer had been killed. People breathed sighs of relief when they heard that the six foot, ex-bouncer and amateur boxer was dead. For, to many, Eddie Palmer was the most feared man in the city." And Allan was right. There was spontaneous applause when Beechy only received three years and as Allan said, "The judge was close to saying that he had done the people of Liverpool a favour."

Bob Wooler: "It won't be long before those huge underground caverns that were built by the eccentric businessman, Joseph Williamson, will be opened to the public and they will be a great tourist attraction. They were close to where Eddie Palmer lived and so when they started work on them, my immediate thought was 'I wonder if Eddie put any of his victims in here.' If they'd opened them in the 60s, they could have had a real live Cavern Club at Edge Hill but I don't think anyone would have been interested with Eddie Palmer on the doorstep."

Eddie Palmer.
Liverpool Daily Post and Echo

81

MAN!

This poem by Bob Wooler was written with Robert Mitchum in mind.

Man! Don't try to manage me
        I'm okay as I am
Man! Don't try to manipulate me
        Our ideas may just jam
Man! Don't try to manoeuvre me
        I am my own monogram
Man! Don't try to manure me
        I'm wise to all that flimflam
Man! Don't try to manufacture me
        Who needs to be a sham?
Man! Don't try to mantra me
        It might just sound like a scam
Man! Don't try to manacle me
        I'm *me* and not an anagram
Man! Don't try to manhandle me
        As though you don't give a damn
Man, man, man…
        Don't you see, I don't want to be
        Just another cloneman
        I want to feel free, then I can be
        Simply my *own* man.

Robert Mitchum

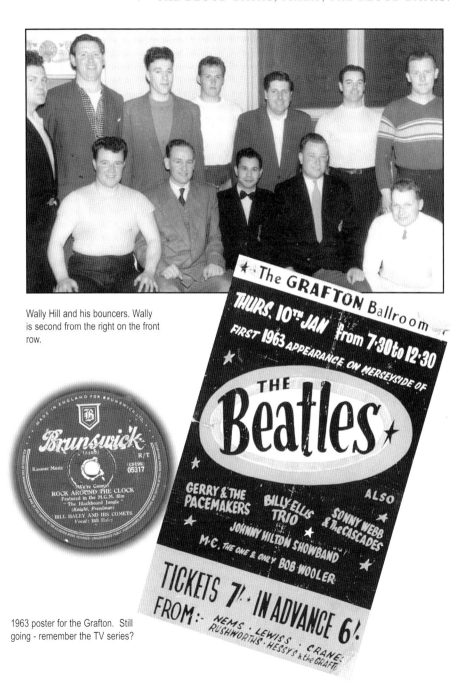

Wally Hill and his bouncers. Wally is second from the right on the front row.

1963 poster for the Grafton. Still going - remember the TV series?

83

8 CLUB CLASS
Rival clubs and clubowners - John Lennon s personality -
The Beatles fan club - Bob s role at the Cavern

*"John Lennon rampaged through Liverpool like some wounded
buffalo, smashing everything that got in his way."*
(Nik Cohn, "Awopbopaloobop Alopbamboom", 1970)

If there was one aspect of the Mersey Beat that Bob Wooler loved talking about, it was his fellow promoters. At times, I felt his autobiography was a means of settling old scores and he would become agitated or angry about minor things that had happened 40 years ago. Undoubtedly, he had a love-hate relationship with Sam Leach. Some days he would praise what he did and others he would show him no mercy. "Sam Leach ran a civic hall in Mossway, around '60 and '61. He was causing havoc, booking groups that I had already booked and always protesting that he had booked them first. When I had the Twisterama at Southport, he booked Gerry and the Pacemakers and the Big Three for the same night at the Tower Ballroom in New Brighton, and it was impossible to have them doubling between Southport and New Brighton. In the end, I had the groups sign statements that I could take to the *Liverpool Echo* saying that they were only booked for Bob Wooler at the Cambridge Hall on such-and-such a date. Sam's ads were printed with gaps where the names should be, and he played hell, blaming everything on me.

"Within a few weeks of me doing my Twisterama night at the Cambridge Hall in Southport, he was doing Twisterama at the Tower Ballroom. I ran an ad at Hambleton Hall for Operation Teen Beat and I had not used the word 'Operation' before. Sam stole the idea for Operation Big Beat, which, to be fair, was a better title, but Sam was a bugger for things like that. There was another situation when Vic Anton, who ran Hambleton Hall, used the Hive of Jive, when there already was a Jive Hive at St. Luke's Hall in Crosby, which is where Rory Storm played. Doug Martin played hell as it was too close to the Jive Hive.

"Sam Leach called himself the Leach Organisation as though he, one man, was like the Grade Organisation or the Rank Organisation. Les Dodd, a very precise person who had the Grosvenor Ballroom, had embossed paper for Paramount Enterprises, which looked very impressive too. Sam was in cahoots with Dick Matthews who was very eccentric but took a hell of a lot of good photographs of the groups. Dick was a civil servant who always looked bewildered, though it didn't alter his focus. Dick Matthews was the only one who was photographing groups on a regular basis. It's a shame no-one was sketching or creating posters - I think of those wonderful posters by Toulouse-Lautrec or the ones they had in San Francisco in the late 60s, but we had nothing like that.

"Dick Matthews was much more affable than Sam, who was always suspicious. Everything was done on the never-never with Sam. He owed the Beatles £19 on one occasion and Epstein told me that Sam had just been into NEMS to see him. He acknowledged he owed the Beatles £19, but he said that he couldn't pay it there and then. He offered to add £19 to the fee for their next booking. That was typical of Sam Leach - there's a bit of the Allan Williams about him, although neither of them will like me saying that. Allan and Sam didn't get on too well, perhaps because they recognised parts of themselves in each other. Even now, I say to Allan, 'Don't go on about Sam Leach because he was there, don't I know it, causing mayhem.' Sam promoted a lot of events outside the city centre so Allan wouldn't have known about them.

"When Allan Williams opened his new club, the Blue Angel, he said to me, 'This is not a rock'n'roll place, I don't want any of your fucking rock'n'rollers in here.' That's the way Allan speaks by the way: there's only one word in his fuckabulary. Later, he transformed the whole place: it went down-market, and became a rock'n'roll club with jazz downstairs. They had Dougie Evans on a piano which Allan had painted white. Dougie wore a tuxedo and Allan thought it was Eddie Duchin and Carmen Cavallaro all over again. It was a make-believe world, and there was Wooler, having survived the cave session, relaxing at the bar with a watered Bacardi.

"The Orrell Park Ballroom, which is still going, was for dance bands and, as a result, the stage was quite low. Ralph Webster was the manager of the OPB and dance bands were his type of music. He reluctantly moved with the times, but he always thought he knew it all and liked to appear authoritative. You could never tell Ralph anything. He never had the Beatles at the OPB because they were a Brian Kelly group, but he had his own Beatles with the Undertakers. Again, they wouldn't thank me for that comparison. Also, I remember Allan Clarke of the Hollies being nasty when I advertised the Hollies as 'Manchester's answer to the Beatles'.

"The Holyoake was a Co-op Ballroom and the manager, John Guise, would play hell about the rock'n'roll dances. He would say over the mike, 'Do you know how long it took to get all the chewing-gum off this floor last time? This place is used as a proper ballroom, it is not just for rock'n'roll.' He might as well have been talking to the wall. He turned puce when Rory Storm jumped on his piano and he told him to get off. I thought of Irving Berlin, 'That's a fine way to treat a Steinway.'

"Dave Forshaw's club at St. John's Hall, Bootle was a good venue. He had to use a name, the Blue Penguin Club, for licensing purposes because he was holding his dances on Sundays. It had a stage with curtains, all important for presenting groups. I used to say to tell them, 'Be tuned up, be ready, don't make any announcements and go straight into the first number.' Most of them went along with that.

"In some books, I'm introducing the Beatles on stage with 'The William Tell Overture', which sounds pretentious - a bit like Elvis with 'Also Sprach Zarathustra'. I didn't use a classical version of 'William Tell' but the Piltdown Men's 'Piltdown Rides Again'. I only used a few seconds and it was simply to command attention. I told them, 'As soon as I take this off, I will say "It's the Beatles", the curtains will open and you go straight into your first number.' The opening number was usually 'Long Tall Sally', which was very suitable as it was a real rocker.

"Sam Leach was not very good at getting the groups on and off stage at the right time. I believed in ten-minute changeovers, four records at the most, as the audience wanted live music. That's why I say being a DJ was far more than presenting records. There was tremendous resentment about going on first or going on last, especially if it was four in the morning on an all-nighter. No-one wanted to be playing while people were coming in, leaving or even falling asleep. Peter Stringfellow used to promote shows in Sheffield and he came to the Cavern one day. He was a nice guy and very flamboyant even then. He said in his book that the DJ at the Cavern didn't sparkle and he wasn't the life and soul of the party. Well, of course the DJ at the Cavern didn't sparkle. He was too busy doing the ads and hustling the groups on and off stage!

"The parents of the groups must have been so glad that the scoutmaster was around to get them into line and encourage them to be punctual. The groups would make excuses like, 'The van broke down', when I'm sure it didn't. Brian Kelly would fine groups if they were late, but my only way of punishing them was to put them on last. Ironically, that was the only time I could sit down and listen to a group as I knew the evening was over. A lot of groups wouldn't start on time. I would say, 'Have you finished tuning up yet?' Gerry was terrible for that, he would be rattling on his brother's drums instead of getting the show under way.

"Once, the Big Three were due on stage at the Cavern, and when I went to see if they were in the White Star or the Grapes, I learnt that they'd gone to the Blue Angel. I had to get one of the groups' drivers to take me there to round them up. I said, 'Don't you know you're on shortly?' They said, 'Don't worry, Bob.' I said, 'If someone doesn't worry, the show doesn't go on properly,'

"When I was booking groups, I had to be very careful with my diary. I didn't want them to see the fees that other groups were getting. I would ask them to move away so that I could look at things properly. Dave Forshaw had a code which was a very good idea. 'A' would be a £5 group, 'B' a £6 one and so on.

"When groups would go to Brian Kelly for more money, he would agonise and say, 'Business is bad.' The groups knew what the attendances were like and could do the arithmetic for themselves. They would ask for more, but they'd be lucky to get it. In Christmas 1961 he put a Christmas tree on stage at the Aintree Institute and this was so unusual that we all remarked: 'Oh, Kelly's laying out money'."

Tony Jackson of the Searchers recalls, "Nearly everything was an audition for Brian Kelly and Sam Leach. It was so difficult to get paid." Nicky Crouch of Faron's Flamingos: "Bob was always saying this is an E.O. booking, which was Expenses Only. Still, I don't hold it against him." Taking early retirement, Ted Knibbs managed Billy Kramer and the Coasters: "Bob asked me to play an audition date at Hambleton Hall and I said, 'We don't do auditions.' He said, 'No, because you're scared they are not good enough.' I said, 'All right, we will do it,' but when I got home, I regretted what I had said and I called the date off. About three weeks later, Ray McFall invited us to the Cavern and I said, 'Do we get paid?', and he said, 'Yes'. Bob was delighted with what he saw so we became regulars then."

Bob Wooler: "Brian Kelly used to say to me about Ray McFall at the Cavern, 'Why don't you tell McFall that he is paying the groups too much? He's spoiling it for us.' Brian Kelly was speaking on behalf of Doug Martin, Wally Hill and Ralph Webster, although they themselves were at each other's throats. Ray was paying the Beatles £15 when they returned from Hamburg for the second time.

"Who can blame the Beatles as they were bringing punters to the venues? They told Brian Kelly that they wanted double money, up from £7.10s (£7.50) to £15. Brian Kelly said, 'No way. The most I pay is £10.' I said, 'You can't ignore the Beatles.' I got them back into Kelly's books at £15, but he resented it terribly and resented me for being the feegotiator. If he hadn't taken them, Ralph Webster would have had them and that would have increased the rivalry. I was once in the kitchen at Aintree Institute and Brian Epstein came in to collect the Beatles' fee. Brian Kelly pushed some bags of coins towards him. Brian wouldn't participate in a plebeian thing like that. He said very haughtily, 'Send me a cheque'.

"Allan Williams used to pay the Escorts very little and say, 'Well, they're only beginners', whereas Ray McFall was much fairer and guided by what he had paid the jazz bands. He didn't pay the groups the same amount but they did get more at the Cavern than elsewhere. The Remo Four and Dale Roberts and the Jaywalkers used to revere Ray as he would pay them double figures, whereas Kelly's payment would be a single figure.

"I have a Woolerism for John Lennon - he went from rage to riches. Sometimes I introduced him as the Singing Rage, which is a name I borrowed from Patti Page, who wasn't outrageous at all. He could hurt with his remarks and observations and the others would laugh in a nervous, apologetic way.

"The first time the Beatles came back from Hamburg they wore leather jackets and jeans, not leather pants. They got those in Hamburg on their second visit and then they performed in full leather. Ray McFall didn't like the Beatles playing in jeans. Jeans spelled trouble in his book and he said to me, 'You know the policy at the Cavern, I don't allow people in with jeans, so they can't play in them.' I groaned as I didn't want to tell them. The Beatles were terrible when they ganged up on you - all of them, Pete Best as well. Their tongues could be savage if you criticised them for arriving late or messing around on stage. I knew that John would say, 'Who the fuck is he to tell us what to wear?' I went back to Ray and asked him to tell them himself. He put on his pained expression, which meant 'Aren't you capable of doing it yourself?'. He went into the dressing-room to see them and I waited for him to come out. There were no four-letter words then as he was the guy with the pay packet."

Ray McFall: "Bob would say to me, 'That's the way they are. Listen to their music.' They were different and they were very well rehearsed because they had come back from three months of torture in Hamburg. The other groups were like Cliff Richard and the Shadows, but their music was so vibrant. As Bob said, 'They had ear and eye appeal.' However, I didn't like them wearing jeans which were taboo in the Cavern. Our doormen would stop anyone wearing jeans. I felt that if people were wearing good, clean clothes they would be more likely to behave themselves as they wouldn't want them getting dirty and damaged. The doormen were very well trained by Paddy Delaney. Even if they had to break up a fight, which only happened occasionally, they were told to separate the combatants and escort them out. They were not to be given the bum's rush."

Bob Wooler: "Paddy Delaney was a very likable, affable person, and still is. He preferred to calm the waters, but there were still some terrible times at the Cavern. Pat brought in Mal Evans from the Post Office in Victoria Street to help him. Mal was a very gentle person but he was big and looked the part. The view was 'I don't think I will tangle with him' and not many people did. He later worked with the Beatles and he was nearly always around as their roadie. You can see him in Magical Mystery Tour and he is handclapping on 'Birthday'. He was shot and killed by the Los Angeles police in 1976 in what has to be an appalling accident. He did write a book about his experiences and I love to know why it has never been published." (The book, *Living The Beatles Legend*, by Mal Evans and John Hoernle, exists, although it has not been seen.)

Bob Wooler: "John Lennon announced one Cavern lunchtime that everyone must behave, which was rich coming from him. Aunt Mimi was coming with a friend and she wanted to see him play. He wouldn't have allowed her to go to a venue in the evening but lunchtime was different. Also, they would perform some quieter or gentler numbers at lunchtime, like 'Over The Rainbow'or 'Falling In Love Again'. I met her there and there was no swearing while she was around, but I don't know what she thought of the place."

I asked Bob if his Woolerisms had ever made John Lennon laugh. "Only once," he said. "Bernard Boyle was the president of the first Beatles fan club, which was started in 1961 with Bobbie Brown as the treasurer and secretary. Bernard was a lapdog for the Beatles. Thalidomide was in the news through the *Sunday Times*' campaigning and once when we were in the bandroom of the Cavern, I said to Bernard, 'Bernie, you're the original thalidomide kid.' Lennon went into tucks of laughter. Bernie wasn't a spastic but he did have some ineptitude, and Lennon thought my remark was hysterical. It shows the type of humour he liked.

"For all his braggadoccio, there are not many instances of John Lennon being violent. Bernie Boyle came into the Cavern one lunchtime and said he had been given a black eye by Johnny Hutch of the Big Three. John said, 'Oh, we'll sort him out', but it was all talk. He would never have taken Hutch on and, if he had, he would have lost. He did go berserk with Nilsson in the 1970s in LA, didn't he, and there were some fisticuffs then.

"Their fan club wasn't very organised, more an act of devotion, but I went to their first event, which also featured the Beatles, at the David Lewis Theatre. When Brian Epstein came to manage the Beatles, he also took over their fan club. Freda Kelly was put in charge. She'd been a fan of theirs for some time, but was withdrawn and didn't want the limelight at all. She subsequently married Brian Norris from Earl Preston's Realms.

"I went full-time at the Cavern in 1962, although I did compère the occasional NEMS show. Brian would say, 'You will be able to do Little Richard at the Tower for me, won't you?' I would ask Brian to see Ray. Ray could be very awkward, but Brian was such a charmer that he would say yes to him. Ray and I developed a close relationship, but one lunchtime session I made a remark about a German Nazi who was about to be executed as I introduced Derry and the Seniors by saying, 'As Adolf Eichmann might say, "This will be a swingin' affair."' The Seniors then went straight into 'A Swingin' Affair', which was an instrumental of the time. Ray came down to the bandroom with that pained look again, and made pyramids with his hands. He said, 'Bob, that was a most unfortunate reference.' It was really as no-one thought it was amusing.

"I was very busy at the Cavern. I had to do the lunchtime sessions, the evening sessions and the all-nighters. I had to write the ads, arrange the tickets, posters and leaflets, and get them distributed. I didn't trust any lad to deliver them as they would dump them in waste-paper bins. You had to find people you could trust or do it yourself. We could only afford to give them free admission, so everything was done on a shoestring. The deadline for the *Liverpool Echo* ads was five o'clock and I would say, 'It's 4.30 and I haven't done those Echo ads yet' If I didn't get the ads in, Ray would be bound to say something. I was a dogsbody, a general factotum really, doing office work before we had an office manager, before we had Billy Butler to help me over lunchtimes, and I was being paid £35 a week. There was a severe consequence of all the work as I started to drink. I found it much easier to keep going when I was fortified and I was able to cope with groups and their tantrums. When it comes to rhythm and booze, I reckon I have paid my dues.

"We didn't have a strong drug scene by any means. Originally, it was just purple hearts, amphetamines, speed or whatever you want to call it. When the Beatles went down south, they sometimes brought back cannabis and gradually the drug scene developed in Liverpool. There was a rare instance of cocaine when Davy Jones, a little coloured rock'n'roll singer who'd been with the Beatles in Hamburg, appeared at the Cavern. He was a Little Richard/Derry Wilkie type, very outgoing and bouncy. His big record was an oldie, 'Amapola', and its lyric about the 'pretty little poppy' must have appealed to him.

"Alan Ross, who was a local compère, brought Davy down to the Cavern, and that was when I had cocaine for the first and only time in my life. I told Davy Jones about my sinuses, and he said, 'This'll clear it.' Alan Ross gave me a smile of approval, I tried it...and nearly hit the roof. There was laughter galore, and I rushed out into Mathew Street, trying to breathe the effects out. I remember Pat Delaney on the door saying, 'What's wrong, Robert?' and I said, 'Nothing. I'm just a bit giddy.' The Beatles welcomed Davy Jones with open arms, so I'm sure the drug-taking didn't stop with me.

That is the common factor with the Beatles - whatever was going, they wanted to be part of it.

"I was so worried about drugs being passed round at the Cavern as there would be trouble if Ray McFall found out about it. He was very strict and a devout Catholic - I'll give you an idea of this. They would serve soup at the Cavern with a cheese roll and it was always tomato soup on a Friday, never a meat soup. This tells you how strict and didactic Ray was. He loved lecturing, and I was often on the receiving end of it.

"Another time I left the table at the Black Rose club one afternoon and when I got back there were two pills floating in my drink. I said, 'What's that?' and Lennon said, 'Oh, give it here' and knocked it back. It was two Preludin tablets and they had brought them back from Germany. Preludin was a slimming tablet really, an amphetamine that suppressed the appetite and you stayed up all night. You became very active, and I did experiment with them. They came in metal tubes and I used to say to them, 'Anyone travelling by tube tonight?'

"When I first took Preludin, I was so full of energy that I couldn't get to sleep and I was so worried as I had a Cavern lunchtime the next day. I did it, and I went to the cinema in the afternoon where sleep came upon me. That was a warning to to be very careful about taking Preludin. Actually, back in the 1950s, one of Kingstrums, who worked at Evans Medical Centre in Speke, said he would get some extra special tablets full of caffeine, Pro-Plus, but they didn't really work.

"My vice was smoking, which was a mug's game. I used to smoke up to sixty a day. At first, Senior Service and then Embassy. The link between smoking and cancer was known well before the official report in 1960 as the Kingstrums used to call cigarettes 'cancer sticks'. It took me a long time to give them up. Occasionally, I have been part of a circle of friends who have passed a joint around and when it has come my way, I have thought, 'Is this going to get me back on the weed?' I have accepted them and unlike Bill Clinton, I did inhale."

Ray McFall: "Bob Wooler was the true friend of all the beat groups from Day One. He knew them well and he lived in the area where so many of them came from. He encouraged and advised them, he found them new members, he suggested songs, he would help them with their bookings and there was no one more competent. He had the most elegant of voices and the most wonderful command of the English language and he was a first class performer. I would have had difficulty in managing the Cavern without him. He could arrange good programmes by putting two or three groups together. He would have got on more himself if he had been more pushy, but that wasn't in his nature."

Allan Williams: "I loved his golden tones. He was so eloquent and he had no trace of a scouse accent. I don't have much of one myself, but that is because my stepmother came from Manchester and she used to hate the way that Liverpool people talked. I had elocution lessons and singing lessons and had a trained voice."

Bob Wooler: "I suppose I was a misfit really, but if I was, then Ray McFall was even more so. We were running the Cavern and we were both oddities. We were promoting a music that was alien to both of us, and I don't think either of us liked all the jealousy amongst the clubowners. Jimmy Ireland hated the success and acclaim the Cavern received and felt that his clubs, the Downbeat and the Mardi Gras, weren't getting the attention they merited. They were being upstaged by a dank and damp cellar. In 1963, he decided to have a piece of the action and managed the Swinging Blue Jeans, the Escorts and Earl Preston. He was badmouthing me to them, but when I had them on at the Cavern, they would still be friendly. He stayed here, and when Epstein moved to London in 1964, he said, 'Right, there's only the Cavern now. Let's see what happens', but it didn't last long. Like a lot of people, he didn't appreciate that the fame had nothing to do with the clubs, and was everything to do with the Beatles. A few years ago the Status Quo songwriter, Bob Young, who was working in Liverpool, told the *Liverpool Echo* that it was not because of the Beatles that the Cavern was famous - it was because of this, that and the other. Total nonsense, and I'm surprised they printed it. The Cavern's fame is down to just one thing - the Beatles".

To D.J. BOB WOOLER

RECORD REQUEST

Dear Bob, Will you please play the following request ;

Title of Record ....

For (Name of Person) ....

From ....

Message (if any) ....

(Pens or pencils not available. Please use your own)
Please hand this completed request to
Disc Jockey BOB WOOLER on the Stage.
He will endeavour to play all requests.

JUST FOR OLD TIMES' SAKE
Song lyric by Bob Wooler

Couldn't we just meet again
And dance and wine and eat again
As we used to do before we knew heartbreak,
Of course it would be
Just for old times' sake.

And we could do a show again
Your laugh I'd like to know again,
Now I've learnt that love consists of give and take
But naturally
Just for old times' sake.

Maybe I'm a sentimental dumb thing
But confidentially do you know something,
I'd so like to light your cigarette again
And see you smile and be in your debt again.

And if we did all this again
P'raps we'd share a goodnight kiss again
For it may not be too late to end my great mistake,
Won't you say you agree
Just for old times' sake.

Bob and Beryl on their wedding day,
1967

Gerry and the Pacemakers (Les Chadwick, Les Maguire) with Bill
Haley at the Star-Club, Hamburg, 1962

BEEKAY PRESENTS

SWING SESSION

TO-NIGHT (Friday), and MONDAY
at LATHOM HALL

7-30 to 11 p.m. — Good Groups — Admission 2/6

Paddy Delaney

SATURDAY JIVE

at LATHOM HALL is best
THIS SATURDAY
SKYLINERS — DELTONES — BLACK HAWKS
, — GUITONES plus Johnnie

8 to 11-45 p.m. — Saturday night at Lathom is the Tops — Admission 4/-

Kansas City Five
at the Odd Spot

BIG BEAT NIGHT

at LITHERLAND TOWN HALL
NEXT WEDNESDAY (Please note day)

7-30 to 11 p.m. — Top Groups as Usual — Admission 2/6

CHRISTMAS EVE ROCK

at LATHOM HALL
REBEL ROUSERS — DELTONES — BLACK HAWKS
— SKYLINERS plus Micky Harkess

8 to 11-45 p.m. ————— TICKETS 4/-
The management accept no reponsibility for the compere's action —
he's nuts

ROCKING INTO SIXTY

NEW YEAR'S EVE — 8 to 12-15
TICKETS 5/-

Advance Tickets for Big Beat, Christmas Eve and Rocking into '60,
from: Continental Cafe, South Rd, 22; 35 Norman Road, 20; or any
Beekay Dance.

94

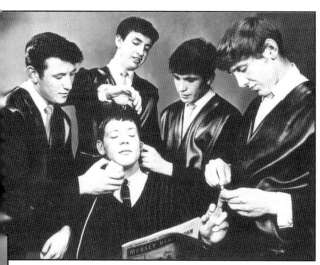

The Merseybeats with Billy Buttler

Gerry and the Pacemakers (Les Maguire on sax)
backing Gene Vincent at the Star-Club,
Hamburg, 1962

9 POLLS APART
The Mersey Beat newspaper

"Liverpool took off like the tango-intoxicated Buenos Aires of the Twenties or the jazz-jumpin' Kansas City of the Thirties or the swingmatized New York of the Forties."
(Albert Goldman, 'The Lives Of John Lennon', 1988)

Bob Wooler recalls, "I met Bill Harry and his wife Virginia Harry one Saturday night in 1960. Wally Hill brought them along to see me. Bill wanted to start a magazine about local music called *Storyville* and it would be mainly jazz. There was no jazz in the suburbs then, only in the city centre, so there wouldn't be too much to write about. There was a jazz magazine for a short while that operated from the Mardi Gras, and maybe that caused him to change his mind. A year later Bill brought out his newspaper but he called it *Mersey Beat*."

The various Beatle books, Bill Harry's included, have Harry inventing the phrase, 'Mersey Beat' (always two words), but Bob thought that Harry was taking credit for something that wasn't his. On at least six occasions, he came to Keith's Wine Bar with yellowing copies of the *Liverpool Echo* from the 1950s. Mersey Beat was the title of a newspaper column which first appeared in *Liverpool Echo* on Saturday 30 November 1957 on the Entertainments Page and it continued until 1959. Disker's column of record reviews, written by Tony Barrow, was on the same page. Mersey Beat was essentially a jazz column written by 'Jazzman', but Bob could never discover who it was. It is only in 2002 that Tony and I have identified 'Jazzman' as the controversial critic, Steve Voce. It is highly ironic that such a hater of rock music should be the first to employ the term, 'Mersey Beat'. The final Echo column appeared on Grand National day, Saturday 21 March 1959. Some two years later (6 July 1961), Bill Harry launched his fortnightly pop paper, *Mersey Beat*.

I well remember the first copies of *Mersey Beat* in 1961. I didn't go to the clubs myself but I was most impressed that there was a publication devoted to local talent. It intrigued me that there was a clique of beat groups on my doorstep. Bob Wooler: "The promoters didn't push *Mersey Beat* as much as they should, even though it was in their interest to do so. After all, they advertised their jive dances in the paper. I would take a supply on the bus to Litherland Town Hall, Aintree Institute and Lathom Hall in Seaforth - all BeeKay weekly dances - and Brian Kelly would say, somewhat resentfully, 'Do I have to sell these?' Allan Williams used to pile them in the corner and made little attempt to sell them. Brian Epstein must be praised for encouraging sales, which he achieved by placing *Mersey Beat* prominently on the counters at his NEMS' stores in the city centre."

As well being a DJ at the Cavern and other Merseyside clubs, as well as organising and compèring events at other venues, Bob Wooler also wrote for the *Mersey Beat* newspaper. "I wrote an occasional column for *Mersey Beat*, which I called The Roving I, and in the fifth issue, I listed what I rated as the ten most popular beat groups on Merseyside - we didn't call them 'bands' then. I excluded the Swinging Blue Jeans, known then as the Bluegenes and not a rock group at the time. According to my column, they were in 'a class of their own': very professional and disciplined. They combined skiffle, folk and jazz styles, sporting a banjo and string bass, although eventually and perhaps inevitably they went the way of all flesh and succumbed to commercial considerations. If you can't beat 'em, join 'em."

So, in October 1961, Bob Wooler listed his Top Ten groups on Merseyside:

1. The Beatles
2. Gerry and the Pacemakers
3. Rory Storm and the Hurricanes
4. The Remo Four
5. The Strangers
6. Johnny Sandon and the Searchers
7. Karl Terry and the Cruisers
8. Mark Peters and the Cyclones
9. Ray and the Del-Renas
10. The Big Three

Bob Wooler: "It proved to be a controversial chart, which I steeled myself to expect, although the positions were decided more by the audience reaction I saw at dances than by my own opinion. The Beatles were top, naturally, with Gerry and the Pacemakers and Rory Storm and the Hurricanes as second and third. The Beatles and Gerry attracted the lads as well as the girls, but Rory didn't attract many male followers. During Beatlemania, there were more girls fans than lads, but it has changed in recent years as more males than females are in evidence at the Beatles Conventions in Liverpool. Indeed, this appeal to both sexes has been one of the crucial reasons for the success of the Beatles. The *Liverpool Echo* was very slow in moving in on the Beatles. I used to say, 'Always the Echo, never the explosion.' They certainly made up for it later by plugging Merseyside bands and running local charts.

"At the time, I used to apply adjectival names to several of the male singers: Rory Storm I would label 'Mr. Showmanship', Earl Preston 'Mr. Magnetism', Gerry Marsden 'Mr. Personality', and Faron 'Mr. Fabulous'. In turn, Rory used to call me 'Mr. Big Beat' and I apologise all these years later to the Philadelphia DJ Alan Freed, who had the name first.

"Faron often wore a white suit, and he was jumping up and down and romping around from an early stage. His rival was Karl Terry who did similar antics. Faron always had a good act and I also called him the 'Panda-footed Prince of Prance'. However, I did not call Karl Terry the 'Sheik of Shake'. That was a Larry Parnes appellation, which he applied to Dickie Pride. I shudder when it is credited to me.

"The Remo Four, at No. 4 in my chart, were very popular as you could put them on and be sure of a good attendance. They featured Colin Manley, whose party piece was the Chet Atkins instrumental, 'Trambone' which called for very tricky fingerwork - he would put a chair on stage, not to sit on but to put his foot on whilst he played. He always got a big round of applause for this number.

"I liked the Strangers very much and I took them under my wing for a time and encouraged them. I gave them the sheet music for 'South American Joe', which came out in the 30s, and Joe Fagin, their lead singer, did it. I also passed them the record of 'The Auctioneer', and Joe managed all that fantastic quick talking. Years later, when I first heard 'That's Living, Alright' on TV, I said, 'I know that voice', but at first, I didn't recognise Joe with his beard. The Strangers were a very good band who could all communicate and it was always fun when they appeared at Aintree Institute, Hambleton Hall or the Cavern.

"Johnny Sandon and the Searchers were at No. 6. Johnny Sandon was the front guy with the Searchers then, although he didn't necessarily call the tune. Mike Pender had a lot to say, Tony Jackson would say it was his group, and Chris would always be asserting himself. The rot had already set in! Johnny Sandon was an excellent singer but he restricted their repertoire as he favoured country and western ballads. He could also sing Ben E. King's songs extremely well. In 1962, he left them to tour American army bases in France with the Remo Four, and then, in 1963, the Searchers had their first chart successes as a four-piece unit - Mike, Tony, Chris and John McNally.

"Karl Terry and the Cruisers performed steam-age rock'n'roll and still do: that's my way of describing the roots of rock which I still have a fondness for. The steam trains disappeared but they kept going. Recently they released a CD, *Cigarettes, Cold Beer, Sexy Ladies*. Look at the titles on it - 'Baby Let's Play House', 'But I Do' 'That's All

Right, Mama' and 'When My Dreamboat Comes Home'. They could have released an album with the same titles 40 years ago. Karl is over 60 now but he still kicks his legs and manages to do the splits on stage. For that reason alone, he commands my respect.

"Mark Peters and the Cyclones, later the Silhouettes, were a popular group with a good-looking lead vocalist who favoured the Brill Building songs. Ray and the Del-Renas were a Garston group and very popular because Ray Walker modelled himself on Roy Orbison. He had the ability to do those high-pitched numbers. They didn't have any national success but they are featured on the *This Is Mersey Beat* LPs, which Oriole issued.

"The Big Three gave me a lot of stick for putting them in tenth place with Mark Peters and the Del-Renas ahead of them. Johnny Hutch said, 'What are we doing here? We don't want to be in your fucking Top 10 if we're only number ten.' Kingsize Taylor was even more annoyed as I didn't include him and his Dominoes in the Top 10 at all. I met with them one Saturday night at Aintree Institute and they were very sore about it. Kingsize lifted me up and said, 'I've got a good mind to throw you out of that window.'" "That is true," says Kingsize now, "but I never would have hurt him."

"Despite all the controversy, it was a fair chart. I would go to these venues and see the reaction when Kingsize Taylor was on stage, and I could see that it was not as strong for them as for some other groups. The mere fact that I could take a seat at the Cavern and watch Kingsize Taylor and the Dominoes was proof that they didn't attract as much attention as other groups. However, this is not to take anything away from them. I thought they were very good and they did a marvellous version of a Gene Vincent album track, 'Why Don't You People Learn To Drive'.

"There are no Earls in the chart but I coined the expression, 'And many an Earl had the girls in a whirl.' Take your choice - was it Earl Preston, Vince Earl or Earl Royce? Actually, that isn't very good - there were only three Earls, so 'many an Earl' is inaccurate. The first time I saw Earl Preston was at the Iron Door when he was working as Gene Day and the Jangobeats. He was so good-looking and he had modelled himself so completely upon Ricky Nelson. He preferred him to Elvis. There was another group called Johnny Tempest and the Tempest Tornados, but Johnny, whose father ran a pub in Green Lane, died when he was 21. The group wanted to perpetuate the name but in the end it was too long for the listings in the Echo and, with Earl Preston, they became Earl Preston and the TTs. The group also featured Cy Tucker, who was an excellent singer. Several of the groups had more than one vocalist, but I don't know if this was unique to Liverpool. It helped with the harmonies, which is part of the so-called Liverpool sound.

"Nearly all the groups played their own instruments, but the Chants were a vocal group who needed instrumental backing. The Beatles sometimes backed them, although Brian Epstein was not happy about that. I also recall the Beatles backing a girl from Manchester, Simone Jackson, who was with the management agency, Kennedy Street Enterprises, but this was Brian's doing as he had done some deal to give her exposure.

"I discovered the Merseybeats rehearsing in a church hall behind the Jacaranda. They were only 16 year old lads and I asked them if they played elsewhere, and they didn't. So I brought them into Aintree Institute and then into the Cavern. They were influenced by the Beatles, and I told them, 'This is what I am going to do, and don't tell the other groups. You're going to get a good spot. I will put you on right before the Beatles and it is up to you to win the crowd round by your performance and your communication.' I did a similar thing with the Escorts and the Dennisons, and it worked each time. I didn't like the Merseybeats' name at the time: they were called the Mavericks, which suggested country and western. I accept now that the Mavericks is a wonderful name! I told Bill Harry that if we changed their name to the Merseybeats, it could be good reciprocal publicity for his paper, and he agreed."

Tony Crane of the Merseybeats recalls how the name change came about: "We were happy with our name, the Mavericks. We dressed in long jackets and boots like the actors on the Maverick TV show. Bob wanted us to do some sessions at the Cavern but he didn't like our name. He asked us to be the Megatons instead and he would guarantee that we would go down a bomb. We didn't like that. He booked us for the Aintree Institute and when we looked in the Echo and saw that this band, the Merseybeats, was topping the bill. We had no idea it was us and we went to the Cavern and complained to Bob that we weren't on the bill. He said, 'That's your new name. Don't you like it?'"

Billy Kinsley, also from the Merseybeats: "Bob loved the name the Merseybeats. It's magic, he would say, magic."

Bob Wooler: "Another group was 'way out' so I called them the Exit. I called one group the Fix and when they went to Decca, they were told that they couldn't be the Fix as that suggests one thing only, which was the reason I gave it to them. They changed the spelling to the Fixx. I also came up with Rip Van Winkle and the Rip It Ups, and Johnny Autumn and the Fall Guys. However, I never really favoured long names as their print would be reduced on the poster, whereas a short name like the Tabs would be in larger letters. I didn't think of the name 'the Beatles', but I wish I had as it is the most marvellous name. Everything is in that name - beat music, a good pun and something akin to the Crickets.

"Rory Storm had a great name and you could announce 'Storm Warning' in the ads. With the Tempest Tornados, you could base a show around the weather forecast. Faron, or Bill Ruffley, lived in a fantasy world like Rory - of all the Merseybeat performers, Faron would have made a convincing actor. He once said to me, 'You never call me Faron. Don't you realise I've changed my name my deed poll to Faron?' I said, 'Does the country star Faron Young know about this?', but he didn't see that as funny.

"One lunchtime session at the Cavern, Freddie Starr came into the bandroom, which led onto the stage, and asked me if he could do a couple of songs with the group. I said, 'Don't let me down, Freddie, as Ray McFall hates it when you're on stage, so please behave yourself.' Gerry and the Pacemakers were on stage and when I indicated that Freddie was in the bandroom, Gerry invited him to do a couple of numbers with the Pacemakers. I went to the snack-bar at the far end of the Cavern for a coffee and all of a sudden there were screams and I thought, 'What's happening?' Freddie worked in the fruit market and he had brought along a kingsize carrot which he was brandishing in one particular place. The girls were going crazy, and the lads were encouraging his ribaldry. I thought, 'If Ray sees this, there's going to be trouble.' I got back to the bandroom and got him off. Freddie was always a law unto himself. His attitude to life was the reverse of what I would expect from a Capricorn.

"I ran an ad in the *New Musical Express* for the Jerry Lee Lewis show at the Tower Ballroom in New Brighton in May 62. The Four Jays were on the bill and, as a result of the ad, which listed the groups appearing, their name was in a national paper. Another group called the Four Jays, who were based elsewhere, protested that they were already established with that name and so, in the circumstances, the Liverpool Four Jays told me that they would have to change their name. The name didn't mean anything to them, as far as I could see - their Christian names weren't Jim, John, Joe and Jerry, for example. I came up with the name, the Four Mosts, which Brian Epstein condensed to the Fourmost, when he signed the group in 1963."

Billy Hatton: "We were called the Four Jays, but the Joe Loss Orchestra used that name for his vocal group, J for Joe obviously. He had registered the name and that group, the Four Jays, had also worked under their own name, backing Billy Fury on The Sound Of Fury. We told Bob that we couldn't use the name anymore and he came up with the Fourmost."

Joey Bower from the Four Jays: "Bob said, 'Why don't you be the Forking L's?' but there was no way we could use that. He then gave us the Four Mosts."

Bob Wooler: "I wore evening dress from time to time and there is a photograph of me in a penguin suit with Jerry Lee Lewis, taken in the Tower's dressing-room alongside the stage. I got £25 for that night, which was more than some of the groups, but I earned every penny. I got there at five o'clock and I had insisted that all the groups got there early to tune up. I told them the running order, and I prevailed upon them to use one set of gear, which they were loath to do. I hear the groups talking now, 'We used to share our gear', but it wasn't that way at all. They would say, 'We sound brilliant with our drums and our amps, we're not going to let somebody else use them.' So we had to ship the amps on and off the stage. I would get everything organised and then change into the monkey suit for the show.

"Rory would say, 'Don't forget to mention in *Mersey Beat* that we have new stage suits', which, trivia buffs might like to know, they bought at Duncan's in London Road in the city centre. Groups made something of appearing in their new suits. For a while, the Escorts sported silver lurex ones for their stage appearances, which were jokingly referred to as their 'tin suits'. Gerry and the Pacemakers had monogrammed blazers and the Beatles favoured black leather. There was a formality to the scene, and the Beatles had been wearing anything to appear different from the other groups. When Mark Peters changed to leathers, well, it wasn't leather but plastic, I told him that he was copying the Beatles. He didn't like me saying that as people like to think of themselves as individuals.

"It is difficult to believe that Epstein didn't know of the Beatles before he went to the Cavern. His ad for NEMS and his reviews of the new releases pieces were on the same page as my article. It is extremely unlikely that he was not aware of the group.

"Contrary to general opinion, I think the Beatles were glad to escape from the black leather to the suits, because everybody else was following them and wanting to be unkempt and devil-may-care. A friend of Brian Epstein's, Beno Dorn, provided the suits, and he was a tailor in Birkenhead with a place in Liverpool. They were not collarless as that innovation came later, from London. Brian said to Ray McFall, 'The Beatles will be wearing suits tonight, and it will be the first time you have seen them wearing suits.' As luck would have it, Ray had just had the stage emulsioned, including the back wall, which had the names of the groups on. Everything looked marvellous but condensation dripped from the ceiling and the emulsion paint got onto their new suits. Brian was furious, livid - I had never seen him so livid - and Ray was full of commiserations. Brian hated the thought of having to have those brand new suits cleaned. Fortunately, it was emulsion paint, so it didn't stain them.

"I had struck up a friendship with Epstein and both *Mersey Beat* and Bill Harry were important to him. He wanted good publicity and Bill bent over backwards to give him that. The other groups got sick and tired of the Beatles dominating *Mersey Beat* during 1962. I agreed and they said it was becoming the Mersey Beatle. It wasn't fair on Faron and Karl Terry and Mark Peters. *Mersey Beat* had its awards night at the Majestic Ballroom in Birkenhead. The results of the second poll in December 1962 were very strange with the Beatles at No. 1 and Lee Curtis at No. 2. Paul McCartney has admitted that they sent in a whole pile of votes for themselves, but that might have been for the paper's first poll. Even if the rules permitted this, it's still cheating. Lee Curtis was probably doing the same, and what if he and his team had sent in more votes than the Beatles? How could Bill Harry have published the results without the Beatles at No. 1?

"I have read a lot of Bill Harry's books and articles. He talks about all his private meetings with Brian Epstein but I feel that anyone can say this and no one can disprove it. Bill likes to give the impression that he controlled the scene and was responsible for lots of changes. There is something godlike about this, but I can't say that it didn't happen. But, I say to Bill, where's your sense of history? If you go to the central library in Liverpool today and ask to see *Mersey Beat*, they only have a few copies and none at all of the rival newspaper, *Combo*. This is terrible. I keep saying to him, 'Give them copies' but he never did."

Although only a regional publication, *Combo* was the first new UK music paper to appear in colour. It started in Crosby but then moved to Slater Street in the city centre. Bob Wooler never wrote for the newspaper and he wouldn't go into its offices in case someone saw him and reported him to Bill Harry.

Bob Wooler: "The population of Merseyside in 1963 was around one and a half million, and yet there were more than 400 groups in the area. Most of these groups were merely makeweight music makers, their longevity measured more by the clock than by the calendar. Here today, gone tomorrow, their fling was quickly flung. There was, however, a much more determined bunch; their staying-power was fuelled and refuelled by the belief that they had the genuine ability to succeed. They looked upon themselves as heirs apparent to the hit parade. They believed that they could soon come good, and that fame, acclaim, and fortune were around the corner, awaiting them with open arms. These stalwarts were not confined to the Liverpool area; they were to be found all over the UK.

"I could name a few dozen Mersey Beat groups who, I feel, had the right mix of ingredients (though who can really say what that is, as the so-called 'experts' know to their embarrassment, often ending up with egg on their faces.) The title of a record by a top Merseyside group of the time has always summed it up for me. The group was the Undertakers and the title of their plea for nationwide recognition was 'What About Us?' That says it all for so many of the also-rans."

103

One day Bob Wooler showed me a photograph of a 60s band and both his filing system and his memory had let him down. "I have no idea who they are or where they are from," said Bob, "I don't remember them and I don't remember being given this photograph, but it portrays a typical mix of insolence, innocence and insouciance. This is just one of thousands of pics I accumulated during the 1960s. They were typical of the countless groups of the time. They had stars in their eyes and dreamed of fame and acclaim awash with dosh. They might as well have been called the Hopefuls. This is the tomb of the unknown pop group, typical of thousands of others who have emerged in the last 40 years of guitar group music."

Johnny Sandon and
the Remo Four.

Freddie Starr and
the Midnighters.

Virginia and Bill Harry.

Kingsize Taylor
and the Dominoes.

Faron's Flamingos.

The Strangers.
L-r: Brian Johnson, Joe Fagin,
Harry Hutchings, George Harker.

And What Is Skiffle ?

Mark Peters

BEST poser of the week came the other night when two members of the Glenn Miller Band asked one of the Steelemen: " What is skiffle? "

This did not quite produce the complexities that emerged when the same Steelemen tried to explain to our American friends what an English pantomime was but it had its difficulties.

I don't know which the Miller boys found the oddest: that an English panto dame is a man or that many performers whose musical knowledge does not go beyond two or three chords are among the highest paid musicians in Britain now.

If the Americans had studied the bill for the fortnightly concert following theirs they would have had a pointer to the times. Two skiffle groups are given top billing over the Squadronaires who, in the early post-war years were one of the biggest-drawing bands in the country. That was long before "The City Ramblers" or "Dickie Bishop and his Sidekicks" were even an idea.

The Ramblers, formed in 1954, were one of the first skiffle groups in the country and may be in the forefront of the latest craze: "Spa, The five men a....

By Jazzman

quarters of the big American cities.

The Ramblers have even managed to take this kind of music to Moscow where they played on TV and were in two colour films.

Dickie Bishop is, of course, the former Chris Barber and Lonnie Donegan man who has now gone out on the road with solo billing.

I dare say that there must be at least three dozen skiffle groups on Merseyside who aspire to this kind of billing. But very few could raise the weekly rent from their playing.

One argument in favour of skiffle is that it is encouraging thousands of youngsters to play instruments instead of being passive listeners. The answer is that very few do learn to play.

This is, of course, a charge that cannot be levied against the top professional groups. They do play with a proper

original place of small house and cellar parties.

IF THE SKIFFLERS AND THEIR FANS DON'T BELIEVE ME I'D LIKE TO HEAR FROM THEM.

Short Trills

★ One skiffler likely to melt even the most hardened critic is pretty, fair-haired GLADYS MARTIN, a ...years-old Everton tailor fronting the Darktown skiffle group at the Majorca Club the other night. She's so loud that the local boys she plays with that she turned down an audition with top-liner CHARLES McDEVITT.

★ Two Merseyside traditional bands are planning to combine for a day into a New Orleans marching band and give the city shoppers a glimpse of the old alchemy that turned brass bands into jazz bands some 70 years ago.

★ Wallasey bassist LEO GREENE was once a square dance caller at the American air bases. Now, he says, he is going to introduce a session of country and western music at the Crofter's Jazz Club.

★ The MERSEYSIPPI BAND got lost in the fog the other night. They arrived at Birmingham for a 9.30 engagement at 11.10.

★ I'm off to tour the small

Tommy Quickly

The Merseybeats.

106

10   MR. RHYTHM S ROCK N ROLL INDEX
Bob Wooler s listing of beat groups

"Group names were rather like the names of baseball teams."
(Bob Wooler, 1975)

Bob Wooler listed 273 rock'n'roll groups in the eighth issue of *Mersey Beat* on 19 October 1961. Bob said that 24 of them were the same groups under different names, and that he had seen 185 of the 249 different acts. He thought that most of them were "destined to play Labour clubs, British Legions and church hall youth club venues, virtually for excitement, experience and expenses, burdened, in some cases, with atrocious hall amplification or none at all, until the groups finally despair and break up. Thus there are likely to be as many casualties with the rock groups as there were with the skiffle groups."

Bob only considered that 125 of the groups were active at the present time, but he points out that in 1958, there were, to his knowledge, seven rock dances a week with four promoters and now there are 57 dances with 32 promoters. Bob describes the Big Beat scene as "the last outpost of rock'n'roll in this country." Surely he should have said the first.

This is Bob's list, and it can be appreciated now as an excellent piece of work as many of these names would otherwise have been lost, though in the case of Foo Foo's Flashy Falcons, Mr. X and the Masks, and Bennie and the Jumpin' Beans, this might have been just as well. Note the plays on the letter 'K' that the Kinks later used to great effect and I am surprised that a group could be named St. Paul and the Angels in 1961 or earlier. Was there any controversy over this name?

When Bob and I looked at the list he said, "Group names were often like the names or nicknames of football teams. Notice how many of these names are of the Cliff Richard and the Shadows variety, and the Beatles were to change that. This list was compiled in October 1961, that is before Central Casting took over as so many of the new bands copied what the Beatles were doing. They would pinch material in the way that young comics do when they can't afford gags or scriptwriters.

"The first band I ever managed was Bob Evans and the Five Shillings. Bob Evans had a flat over a shoe repairers in St. Mary's Road in Garston. I gave their lead singer,

Tommy Thitherington, the name of Tommy Jordan and he was an Elvis-type. I wish I had renamed Danny and the Asteroids, Danny and the Adenoids. Danny had a chain and a talisman round his neck long before such things became fashionable. Rikki and his Red Streaks were a young teenage group from Waterloo who appeared at Litherland Town Hall. They were likeable lads with no stars in their eyes, but they appeared one night with the Beatles. John Lennon remembered the name and referred to it much later on, and then Paul McCartney issued a single for Linda as Suzy and the Red Stripes. The name must have amused them as they were waiting to go on stage, and so Rikki had his 15 minutes of fame."

Pat Clusky, lead singer with Rikki and the Red Streaks: "Bob Wooler suggested that we should be something to do with red streaks and so we got yellow shirts with red flashers on the back. He told the musicians to come out playing with their backs to the audience and then as I came on singing, they would turn around."

Bob Wooler: "Gus Travis was one of the first rock'n'rollers on Merseyside and he was full of antics in Gus and the Thundercaps, which was a play on Gene Vincent's Bluecaps. In that department, Rory really had nothing on him and another group, Johnny Rocco and the Jets.

Alan Stratton of the Kansas City Five: "Bob would say 'Welcome to the best of cellars' at the Cavern, which was a wonderful phrase. His famous 'We've got the hi-fi high and the lights down low' is taken from Elvis Presley's 'I Need Your Love Tonight'. He always had something to say - he once introduced Dave Berry and the Cruisers as 'Sheffield's Hoochie Coochie Men' - and his Echo adverts were amazing, like a Battle of the Bands."

Bob Wooler: "They weren't all good. 'Meet the beat that's reet for the feet' is terrible and so is 'The venue with the menu that's the mostest'. I also had the 'diet of riot', 'a shot of rhythm and news' for *Mersey Beat*, and the Guardian of the Grooves and 'your bringer of the humdingers' for myself."

Kenny Johnson: "He would say, 'A smile and a song with Sonny Webb and the Cascades.'"

Beryl Marsden: "He called me 'the bubbling, bouncing Beryl Marsden' which made me cringe."

There were 273 groups in Bob's list from 1961. Two years later there were over 400 groups playing in Liverpool and its suburbs. Bob Wooler: "I wish I'd named a group, Uncle Tom, because then we could have had Uncle Tom's Cavern."

Ahab and his Lot
Alabamy Coasters
Alamos
Albany 4
Al James and the Tornados
Alligators
Al Quentin and the Rock Pounders
Atlantics
Avalons
Avengers

Back Beats
Beatcombers
Beatles
Belltones
Bennie and the Jumpin' Beans
Bernie and his Tornados
Big Three
Black Cats
Black Diamonds
Black Hawks
Black Knights
Blue Diamonds
Blue Streaks
Bobby and the Be-Bops
Bobby Bell Rockers
Bob Evans and his Five Shillings
Bob's Vegas Five
Broadways
Bruce and the Spiders
Buccaneers

Cal's Combo
Carl Vincent and the Counts
Cascades
Cash and the Cashmen
Cass and the Cassanovas
Casuals
Catalinas
Centurians

Champions
Chee Sydney Group
Clay Ellis and the Raiders
Cliff Roberts and the Rockers
Climbers
Clive Lord Five
Coasters
Comets
Confederates
Conquerors
Corsairs
Crackerjacks
Crescendos
Crestas
Cross Rocks
Crusaders
Cy and the Cimmarons

Dakotas (2)
Dale Roberts and the Jaywalkers
Danny and the Asteroids
Danny and the Hi-Cats
Danny and the Strollers
Dave and the Devil Horde
Dave Bell and the Bell Boys
Dean and the Capitols
Dean Devlin and the Dynamites
Dee and the Dynamites
Dee and the Pontiacs
Dee Fenton and the Silhouettes
Delacardos
Deltics
Deltones
Demons
Derry and the Seniors
Detours
Diablos
Dominators
Dominoes
Drone Tones

Druids
Duke Duval's Rockers
Dynamics
Dynamites
Dynamos (2)

Earl Preston and the TT's
Eddie and the Cadillacs
Eddie and the Earthquakes
Eddie and the Phantoms
Eddie and the Razors
Eddie and the Team Mates
El Diablos

Fahrenheits
Faron and the Flamingos
Faron and the Tempest Tornados
Fenton Weill Five
Firebrands
Fire-Flites
Five Stars
Foo Foo's Flashy Falcons
Four Jays
Frank Knight and the Barons
Freddie and the Fireballs
Freddie and the Rousers

Galvanisers
Gene Day and the Jango Beats
Gerry and the Pacemakers
G Men
Gus and the Thundercaps

Hank's Hoppers
Hi-Tones
Hornets
Hot Rocks
Hot Rods
Huntsmen
Huytones

Ian and the Zodiacs
Irene and the Tall Boys

Jesters
Jet and the Tornados
Jimmy and the Teenbeats
Joey and the Kodaks
Johnny Autumn and the Fall Guys
Johnny Burns and the Renegades
Johnny Paul and the Rockin' DJs
Johnny Rocco and the Jets
Johnny Sandon and the Searchers
Johnny Tempest and the Tornados
Jokers

Karl Terry and the Rockin' Cruisers
Katz
Keenbeats
Ken Dallas and the Silhouettes
Kenny Jordan and the Rousers
Kingfishers
Kingpins
Kingstrums
Kommotions
Konkers

Lawmen
Lee Eddie Five
Les Graham Five
Liam and the Invaders
Liam and the White Brothers
Lidos
Live Jive Five
Lonely Ones

Madcaps
Mailmen
Majestics
Martinis
Mavericks

Mike and the Creoles
Mike and the Thunderbirds
Mike Savage and the Wild Ones
Mohawks
Monarchs
Morockans
Moths
Mr. X and the Masks
Mustangs
Mystics

Neil Olsen and the Four Aces
Night Boppers (2)

Ogi and the Flintstones
Opals

Panthers
Paul Valence and the Tremors
Pegasus Four
Phantom Five
Phantoms (2)
Power House Six
Presidents
Pressmen

Quarrymen
Quiet Ones
Quiet Three

Ramblers
Ravens
Ravin' Texans
Rawhides
Ray Walker and the Delrenas
Rebel Rousers
Rebels (2)
Red Diamonds
Red Mountain Boys

Red River Rockers
Regents
Remo Four
Renegades
Ricky and the Vibrators
Rikki and his Red Streaks
Rip Van Winkle and the Rip It Ups
Rita and the Renegades
Robin and the Ravens
Rockerfellers
Rockin' Clippers
Rockin' Rhythm Coasters
Rockin' Rhythm Quartet
Rory Storm and the Hurricanes
Roy Hepworth and the Hepcats
Roy Hunter and the Falcons
Roy Molloy and the Teenbeats

St. Paul and the Angels
Sapphires (2)
Satan and the Hellcats
Searchers
Senators
Sensations
Sentinels
Silverstones
Skylarks
Skyliners
Sorrals
Spitfires
Sputniks
Stalkers
Statesmen
Steve Bennett and the Syndicate
Steve Day and the Drifters
Steve Day and the Jets
Steve Francis Four
Strangers (2)
Sunnysiders

Teenage Rebels
Teenbeats
Teen Beats
Teentones
Tenabeats
Terry Connor and the Cruisers
Terry and the Tuxedos
Terry and the Zodiacs
Tigers
T.J's
Tommy and the Olympics
Tommy and the Satellites
Tommy and the Teenbeats
Tommy Lowe and the Metronomes
Tony and the Black Shadows
Tony and the Triads
Tony and the Tuxedos
Top Spots
Travellers
Travelons
Trebletones
Tremolos
Tremors
Triumphs
Tuxedos

Undertakers (2)
Unicorns

Valiants
Vanguards
Vermont Quarter
Vikings
Vince and the Hot Rods
Volcanics

Wayfarers
Waysiders
Wild Ones
Wranglers
Wump and his Werbles

Zenet Trio
Zeniths
Zephyrs
Zeros
Zodiacs
Zwinging Coronets

The Fourmost

Cavern Club
Calendar

SALE NOW:

AᵀᵀHE Cᴬᵛᴱᴿᴺ Cᴸᵁᴮ
10 Mathew St., off North John St.

TO-NIGHT:
Tᴴᴱ CᴼᴸᴸᴱGᴵᴬᴺˢ
KᴵᴺGˢᴵᶻᴱ Tᴬʸᴸᴼᴿ & Dᴼᴹᴵᴺᴼᴱˢ
THE
TO-MORROW (SATURDAY):
Rᴱᴰ Rᴵᵛᴱᴿ Jᴬᶻᶻᴹᴱᴺ
Tᴴᴱ Fᴼᵁᴿ Jᴬʸˢ

SUNDAY:
Kᴱᴺ Sᴵᴹˢ
VᴵᴺᵀᴬGᴱ Jᴬᶻᶻ Bᴬᴺᴰ
Plus Tᴴᴱ SᵂᴵᴺGᴵᴺG BᴸᵁᴱGᴱᴺᴱˢ

Lᵁᴺᶜᴴᵀᴵᴹᴱ Sᴱˢˢᴵᴼᴺˢ
NEXT WEEK:
MONDAY, WEDNESDAY, & FRIDAY
Gᴱᴿᴿʸ & THE Pᴬᶜᴱᴹᴬᴷᴱᴿˢ
TUESDAY AND THURSDAY
Pᴱᵀᴱ MᶜLᴬᴵᴺᴱ & Dᴬᴷᴼᵀᴬˢ
THE

DON'T MISS
MAY 14 TO 18:
Jᴼᴴᴺᴺʸ Kᴵᴰᴰ & THE Pᴵᴿᴬᵀᴱˢ
MAY 21 TO 25:
Mᴵᴷᴱ Bᴱᴿᴿʸ & THE Oᵁᵀᴸᴬᵂˢ
APPEARING IN PERSON
LUNCHTIME AND EVENING
AᵀᵀHE Cᴬᵛᴱᴿᴺ
Central 1591.

Kubas

11 STORM WARNING
Rory Storm and the Hurricanes

"Vanity, vanity, all is vanity'- how true. Rory can vouch for that.
In fact, they all can."
(Bob Wooler, 1998)

On one of our first meetings, Bob Wooler said, "Rory Storm deserves a chapter to himself." Bob would introduce him as "Mr. Showmanship" and he said, "I'm sorry that I didn't come up with anything better. It is a not a creative name, but it does say it all. He was not a a brilliant singer, far from it, but then who is in rock'n'roll? It's the image that matters and Rory certainly had that."

For starters, Rory, like Bob, disguised his age. "During the Mersey Beat era, he would give his DOB as 17 July 1940. I thought he might be older than he said, but he was slim and didn't look his age." When I met Rory's sister, Iris, for a radio interview I took the opportunity to question her about this and discovered that he was born on 17 January 1938 - unusually, Rory had even switched the season of his birth. This was deliberate. Rory Storm and the Hurricanes would have summer seasons in holiday camps and it made sense to have his birthday during this period. I conveyed this information to Bob, who was delighted to have his suspicions confirmed. "So he's a Capricorn like me," he mused, "Rory was a Capricorn like me, like Faron, and without being too presumptuous, like Elvis and Jesus. Kris Kristofferson wrote a song called 'Jesus Was A Capricorn', but it was very disappointing as I learnt nothing from it. Capricorns tend to be miserable and are far too precise about things, but this can only be a guide. Faron wasn't like that. Rory was precise, and persistent too. He would wear me down over bookings and I would give him bookings that I had intended for others. When I said, 'At the usual fee', he would say, 'Can't you make it more, Bob?'

"The first time I met Rory was at the Winter Gardens, Hill Street, Garston, when he was still Al Caldwell and the group was Al Caldwell and the Ravin' Texans. He wanted to play some dance halls and as I was handling bookings at the time, I sorted something out for him. They were on that show with Gene Vincent at the Liverpool Stadium in May 1960 and they did very well. That show was a fantastic concept and Allan Williams must be given credit for that.

"Rory Storm was not my cup of glee as he was far more show than substance. He learnt his tricks from watching Elvis Presley and Gene Vincent. He had little originality but was a very good copycat. He would cock his leg over the mike like Gene Vincent and cover his songs like 'Rocky Road Blues'. I will never forget him knocking the Reslo mike over at Holyoake: his foot hit the mike, which was the only one we had. I thought, 'Oh god, I hope he hasn't ruined it', and, fortunately, he hadn't. I told him that he must never do that when we are down to one mike. If you glanced at some of the early photographs of Rory Storm doing tricks with his mike stand, you might think it was a young Rod Stewart.

"One of Rory's group, Lou Walters, had a stronger, deeper voice, but he was a crooner of the old school. When the Hurricanes and the Beatles were together in Hamburg during 1960, Lou cut 'Summertime' in a cheap recording studio with John, Paul and George from the Beatles and Ringo from the Hurricanes. Quite by chance, it happens to be the first recording of the Beatles, as the world knows them, together. I did hear the recording, but I can't remember it now, and no-one knows where the five acetates have gone. Allan Williams had one, but he left it in a pub in London! Whoever has it now has one of the most valuable records in the world."

Wally Hill: "Rory Storm would come in with about 45 followers, all expecting to come in for nothing. We had to sort him out and say he had to curb this. Rory would fill the dance hall anyway. What an entertainer. You would speak to him on the phone and it would take half an hour because he stuttered but on a microphone not one word would he stutter, he could go straight through. The kids would be ten deep at Holyoake watching him."

Bob Wooler: "It's hardly surprising that Rory took two years off his age. That is very showbiz, as is giving yourself a stage name. He was a playboy and did everything with a flourish. He called himself Rory Storm, a curious name for someone who stuttered, and also renamed the members of his group. There was Ty Brien, Lou Walters, Johnny Byrne who became Johnny Guitar, and Richard Starkey who became Ringo Starr. Johnny had taken his name from a film, and like Rory, he inhabited a make-believe world. Ty and Ringo were more down to earth and easy-going, and Ringo remained that way. I loved his remark when he left those antics in India by saying it was 'just like Butlin's'.

"Rory would introduce the Hurricanes rather like that Bonzo Dog record 'The Intro And The Outro', whereby each person in turn would take a solo. It was unusual for a beat group to do this, although it was common with jazz bands. Ringo would also sing something, usually 'Boys', and that was very generous of Rory. Most drummers were usually stuck at the back and were hardly noticed, except by other drummers. Also, like the Beatles, they would count themselves in, but both groups picked that up from Hamburg.

"Rory even asked me to call his mother, Vi, Mrs. Storm, although I changed it to Ma Storm. They lived at 54 Broadgreen Road, Liverpool 13 and most people remember the house as being called Stormsville. It wasn't - it was called Hurricanesville. Rory's father, Ernie, was very quiet. He would sit there dutifully in the living room, reading the paper or poking the fire, and Ma Storm was much more voluble. She would say, 'How's our Rory doing?', and Rory would take me outside to his Cresta. I would say, 'But I've seen it, Rory', and he would reply, 'I've got new wing mirrors', or whatever. He liked flash American cars and if it was pink, so much the better.

"His parents indulged him and I think it was because of his very disabling stammer. He never stuttered on stage, perhaps because he had taken on this persona of Rory Storm. He even wrote a song with 'Red Roses' in the title, and R is a very difficult letter for stammerers. He sang it without any hesitation and yet once he left the stage, the stutter was pronounced. It was much worse than Freddie Starr's.

"I used to hate people mocking Rory Storm behind his back for his stutter. They would say to me, 'Don't you have a sense of humour?' - that is how they would excuse it - and I would say, 'Not of that kind.' His stammer made no difference to me, although, in desperation, and I would try never to betray this, I would say on the telephone, 'Rory, is Ma Storm there?', and he would go and get her. It would be plain sailing then as we would agree the bookings."

Beryl Adams: "Bob was fascinated by Rory Storm. He couldn't believe that anyone with such a terrible stammer could be such an excellent performer. Bob was always intrigued with people's voices and so he admired Rory so much for that. I liked him too, but I didn't go barmy about any of the groups."

Bob Wooler: "Rory was the Golden Boy and he always looked fantastic. He never missed a trick and when he had his photo taken with Billy Fury at the Blue Angel, he looked as much a star as Billy. Most of the Liverpool singers fantasised to a certain extent, they loved looking at themselves in the mirror, but Rory Storm did it more than most. He would practise his movements in front of the mirror. I did write a poem about him, 'Rorytania!', which draws parallels with Narcissus, who fell in love with his own reflection in the pool. Rory had a huge blond quiff and he would draw attention to it by combing it on stage. Vanity, vanity, all is vanity, but Rory Storm is not alone in that.

"He was an excellent athlete, running for Pembroke Harriers and at one stage, running with the Olympic athlete Derek Ibbotson. He had to be a good runner with Eddie Palmer around! There was a 'Beat And Bathe' session at New Brighton Baths in 1963, and Rory said over the mike, 'I'm going to the top board now', and as he went there, he shed his clothes and stripped down to his swimming shorts. The group continued playing and he said, 'Look this way, folks', and did a dive with a proper pike landing. He swam round the baths, came out, dried himself and picked up the mike as though nothing had happened.

"He lived not far from Tuebrook Bowling Alley and started a beat league there. You could always bet on Rory to win, but it was a novelty and it didn't last very long. Everybody was busy in their own way and it petered out through lack of support. More importantly, he was a very good footballer and captain of the Merseybeat XI. I also have a photo of him on the golf links with Howie Casey and Johnny Guitar, so he was always interested in sport."

Promoter Ron Ellis: "Rory would do the Palace Hotel in Southport for £5. He would do two gigs earlier in the evening in Liverpool and come to the Palace for the 1am spot. It was an extra bit for him which is how I got him for £5 instead of £10. If he planned it right, he could do the Cavern first, then St. Luke's Hall in Crosby and then the Palace."

Music fan Chris Beazer recalls that when Rory Storm and the Hurricanes played his school in Childwall, the group decided to have a communal wank before the concert. The headmaster caught them and said, "You will never play here again." Now, supposing Ringo Starr had mentioned this incident to John Lennon, you have, et violà, John's sketch for *Oh Calcutta!*

Bob Wooler: "I considered Rory one of the mainstays of this whole Mersey Beat scene. He was a name that you couldn't escape from, and he always cropped up in conversation. I put him at number three in my Mersey Beat Top 10 in Mersey Beat, thought that didn't reflect my own opinion. His voice was suspect on the recordings from the Rialto on the *This Is Mersey Beat* LPs, although I was intrigued that one of the songs was Stephen Foster's 'Beautiful Dreamer', where his breath control is much better than usual. He didn't have the talent to do well as a recording artist, and I think he knew this, although he hoped to strike lucky. He made very few records but one of his singles, a reworking of 'America' from West Side Story, was produced by Brian Epstein. It seemed a strange choice at the time, but I can see the attraction - he may have been influenced by the balletic-style dancing in *West Side Story*." On talking to the Hurricanes, I can confirm that the lead vocal on "Beautiful Dreamer" is not by Rory Storm but Lu Walters.

"When the bubble burst as it were, he stopped singing and, although he had talked of opening a hairdressing salon, he started a disco. He was still working in front of an audience and, again, there was no trace of a stammer. One of his girlfriends wanted him around in the evenings and he gave up his disco and sold stationery for a while. I admired his courage in doing that, but I do wonder if some people bought the stationery out of pity."

Bob felt that two quotes about Rory summed him up. Cilla Black revealed that she used to sing with Rory Storm and the Hurricanes from time to time. She said, "They could only play in one key, and it certainly wasn't mine." Alvin Stardust, who married Rory's sister Iris, commented, "It's like the Rolling Stones. Listen to them in concert and it's totally exciting. Everybody's moving around and it's incredible. Listen to the tape afterwards, and there's a fair amount that's out of tune."

Bob Wooler also saw something of Rory's girlfriends. "Rory had a lot of girlfriends. One of the first worked at the Jacaranda. She had been going out with Ringo, who had brought her to Liverpool, and she stayed with Audrey, one of the waitresses at the Jacaranda. When the Beatles were about to take off, Ringo didn't want to know her, and Rory carried on. Another was an attractive girl who was a waitress at the Blue Angel. He was dating a hooker at one time so his lovelife was certainly colourful. Personally, and I have no proof of this, I think Rory was ambivalent sexually and I think Ma Storm was aware of it. I would go along to Broadgreen Road and she would say to me, 'Has Rory met any nice girls lately? I do want him to settle down and get married.' But it never happened.

"His father died and he and his mother were in Hurricanesville on their own. I think this plus his stammer plus the fact that he was no longer a success made him disillusioned and depressed. It was 1972 and it seemed to him that his world had fallen to pieces, and his mother may have thought the same way too. No-one knows for certain what happened, but the outcome was that they both died, and it looked as though they had made a suicide pact - Rory in one room, his mother in another. I am certain his failure as Rory Storm the rock'n'roller had a lot to do with it.

"Shortly after his death, there was the new fad called Glam Rock. Shane Fenton became Alvin Stardust, and Paul Raven became Gary Glitter. Many people have suggested that Rory would have done well as a Glam Rocker, but this is questionable. Alvin Stardust, like Dave Berry, had some menace about him, and I don't think Rory could have adopted such techniques.

"Rory Storm is a romantic figure and there have been a couple of musicals about him on Merseyside. One of them was called *The Need For Heroes* and the other, *King Of*

Liverpool - a ridiculous title, although Johnny Guitar did not agree with me on that. Most Liverpudlians regard Bill Shankly as the King of Liverpool, not Rory. I do accept that he may have called himself that as he was egocentric and really did rate himself.

"I was involved in a tribute evening for Rory Storm at the Montrose club in Liverpool in 1992 on the twentieth anniversary of his death. Iris and Alvin, who are divorced, have a son, Adam, and he was there, asking me for tips for getting into the business. Now I find that Adam F, as he is known, is a very popular drum'n'bass artist. I saw the merchandise for sale in his CD booklet and I know Rory would have been very impressed. He would have said, 'We never had this in our day.'" In 2002, Adam F wrote the soundtrack music for the film, *Ali G Indahouse*.

Bob concluded, "Rory Storm is fondly remembered and in 1998, when the *Liverpool Echo* held a telephone poll for the leading Merseyside entertainers, Rory came in at number nine, some 26 years after his death. It's an amazing result as no-one under 45 could have voted for him, never having seen him. Rorytania lives on."

RORYTANIA!
An open letter to Rory Storm (1938-1972), written by Bob Wooler in 1974.

Dear Mister 'Go, Man' Showmanship:
You vainly sought the iceberg's tip.
That so elusive lucky break
That puts the icing on the cake.
To you, just living up a Storm
Was really quite the natural norm.
In dreams you felt that you were blest
With being up there with the best
And not submerged with all the rest.

You were lauded/applauded/feted/elated/
Fantastic/'tanfastic'/athletic/cosmetic
In suits of flamboyant flamingo hue,
There was Johnny, Ty and Lou, and Ringo too.
You left without a single wave goodbye:
In disbelief we could but wonder why,
No more the calls to Number Fifty-Four,
To Hurricanesville's late-night Cresta'd door.
You always wanted headlines, didn't you?
You got them with a headstone, didn't you?
From Rip It Up to R.I.P.
You could not, would not let it be
But that's all past for now at last you're free.

You narcissistic/'carcissistic'/Dean-ager/preenager,
You Hi-diving/Jive Hiving/hair-raising/self-praising
Teen Pan Alley rock'n'roller,
Tenpin alley Beat League bowler.

From far Alaska to Tasmania
You dreamed of worldwide Rorytania.
A fame that was not meant to be
Just one big showbiz fantasy.
You rose above a speech impediment:
You were the wine and not the sediment.
You Wild One, beguiled one, rich in reckless risks:
You golden boy, but alas for you no golden discs.
For the gold your mind refined was merely fools'…
But deep in Life's reflecting pools:
Oh boy. RORYTANIA-Mania really rules.

Rory Storm and Johnny Guitar.

Rory Storm and The Hurricanes

Shane Fenton (later Alvin Stardust)
marries Iris Caldwell, Rory holds a
guitar behind Iris with Duffy Power &
then Johnny Guitar on the left.

12   CUNARD BLANKS
Black influences - Cunard Yanks - American records

"Who Put The Beat In Mersey Beat?"
(Title of Granada TV documentary, 1995)

More than any other, this chapter questions some of the generally accepted wisdom about Mersey Beat. When I started the interviews for this book in 1998, I found that Bob Wooler was still agitated about a documentary, *Who Put The Beat In Mersey Beat?*, which was screened by Granada in 1995. "It went over the top in emphasising the importance of black culture in Liverpool," said Bob, "which is a very PC view to hold. Several people who should know better took part in that programme and subscribed to the theory. In reality, there were very few black musicians among the beat groups - the Chants, Steve Aldo and Derry Wilkie come to mind - and rock'n'roll wasn't being performed in the black clubs around Upper Parliament Street. To say that the black musicians in those clubs despised rock would be the wrong word, but they certainly looked down upon it. They favoured jazz and the 'beat' in Mersey Beat is not to be found there. So where do we look for the 'beat' in Mersey Beat? Liverpool was a busy seaport with regular sailings to New York. Many of the Liverpool musicians had relations who worked on the ships, and a legend has grown up around the so-called 'Cunard Yanks'."

"Bill Harry, in the introduction to his book of reproductions from *Mersey Beat*, wrote about 'the large number of seamen who brought their younger brothers American records unavailable in the British shops.' I think he has been taken in by what commentators have said, and I doubt that he thought that at the time. He didn't, for example, write a feature in *Mersey Beat* about it.

"Bill Harry also said that another reason 'why Liverpool rock'n'roll bands had such a strong repertoire was due to the fact that Bob Wooler played his rare collection of American rock'n'roll discs at many of the venues.' I didn't have a fantastic collection, and I certainly didn't have Cunard Yanks passing me obscure records. Of course, I had some little-known items. I had a 78rpm of Joe Bennett and the Sparkletones' 'Black Slacks', but I couldn't interest anyone in that. I also wanted a local group to cover Webb Pierce's 'Teenage Boogie', because it had a good beat and the lyrics were just right for a dance on a Saturday night, but no-one did. Even now it would suit Kenny Johnson and Northwind, who still work as Sonny Webb and the Cascades on occasion." Maybe not as Kenny is now approaching 60.

Bob Wooler: "I accept that there were hundreds of Cunard Yanks and that, before the War, they brought back dance band records which were unavailable here. There was a society in the Wirral that met to play them. In the 1950s, the Cunard Yanks brought back jazz and country and western records which were not released here, and John McNally of the Searchers got several country records from his seafaring brother. However, there is no evidence, I repeat, no evidence, that the beat groups were performing songs that were brought over from America by the Cunard Yanks. When it comes to the Cunard Yanks, I'm a man from Missouri, and a man from Missouri always says, 'Show me'. Only then will he believe it."

With Bob's thoughts in mind, I thought I would look at every cover version recorded by a Liverpool group. There were almost 400 of them and in almost every case I discovered that the original version had been released in the UK. It would have been easy to order these singles from NEMS, and NEMS was so well-stocked that many would be on the shelves anyway.

On the whole, you can see that the groups liked fairly obscure artists who were not in the UK charts, and to a large extent, the groups were following the Beatles' lead. Arthur Alexander is a good example with 'Anna (Go To Him)', 'A Shot Of Rhythm And Blues', 'Soldier Of Love' and 'You Better Move On'. The Shirelles are another with 'Boys', 'Baby It's You', 'Everybody Loves A Lover' and 'It's Love That Really Counts'.

Bob Wooler: "The Beatles wouldn't do the Shirelles' 'Will You Love Me Tomorrow', which was so well known. They did the other side, 'Boys', instead. There are some backing vocals on 'Boys' and the Beatles used to sing 'Abop Bob Wooler, Abop Bob Wooler'. Ray McFall said to Paul McCartney, 'We thought you'd sing that on the record', and Paul said, 'Oh, I wish we'd thought of it at the time.' 'Boys' was really a girl's song, but that didn't bother the Beatles anymore than Gracie Fields singing 'Sally'. That song was meant to have sexual overtones - the man was singing about Sally because he had her in the alley every night - but there was none of that in her version.

"I don't think the groups improved on the original versions as most of the time, they took the records and did them note for note, tempo for tempo. They didn't slip in a coda or do it differently. The Beatles would slavishly copy the records when Elvis did

'Wooden Heart', he took a breath after 'wood' so Paul did that too. Paul was very Elvis-oriented. Gerry never embroidered things. He did 'You Win Again' and 'Jambalaya' just like Hank Williams and 'Pretend' just like Carl Mann. He got 'I'll Be There' from me playing Bobby Darin's original record at the Cavern. He never credited me with that. Out of cantankerousness if you like, I continued to play Bobby Darin's version." (Bob was cremated to the sound of Bobby Darin singing 'I'll Be There'.)

Bob Wooler: "Paul always liked 'Wooden Heart' from the film, *G.I.Blues*, so that's why he did that one. In later years, Elvis's films were all gloss and dross and he needed a song from the Beatles to get back up there again."

In his anecdotage, Bob liked telling the story of 'Hippy Hippy Shake'. "In 1959, Mike Millward, who was with Bob Evans and the Five Shillings, asked me if I had heard Chan Romero's 'Hippy Hippy Shake', which was mainly falsetto singing. We didn't even know if it was by a guy or a girl. The record had come out on Columbia and I bought it. Mike was very impressed with the song but I don't think he did it either with Bob Evans or later with the Fourmost. I played it at one lunchtime at the Cavern, and Paul McCartney asked me about it as he fancied himself as a high-voiced singer. I lent him the record and the Beatles started doing it. In the summer of '63, following a lunchtime session at the Cavern, I got a call from Brian Linford, the manager of the Mardi Gras club, who asked if he could borrow Chan Romero's 'Hippy Hippy Shake' and return it within the hour, which he did. I thought he wanted the song for the Escorts who were under the Mardi's management. It never occurred to me that he wanted it for the Blue Jeans because they had an upright bass and banjo then. The Blue Jeans were jumping on the bandwagon - a classic case of 'If you can't beat them, join them.'

"I'm not aware of the Beatles picking up on songs that other Liverpool groups had covered first, but they may have done as Kingsize Taylor and the Dominoes and the Big Three favoured the same kind of music and were quick off the mark. I remember Johnny Gus singing Ben E. King's 'Spanish Harlem' with the Big Three before I'd even heard the original. Usually it was the other groups copying the Beatles. Lance Railton told me that Earl Preston and the TT's were reworking their act and weren't ready to come into Liverpool. In reality, they were performing the Beatles' cover versions out of town and doing very nicely, thank you. They didn't dare do those songs in town because fingers would be pointed and people would say, 'You're copying the Beatles' and worse. Ian and the Zodiacs heard the Beatles do the Marvelettes' 'Please Mr. Postman' and found another song of theirs, 'Beechwood 4-5789', which they did very well.

"Freddie Garrity of Freddie and the Dreamers heard the Beatles do 'If You Gotta Make A Fool Of Somebody', which was in three-quarter time which is very unusual for a rock number. He didn't steal it from them, though, as it was up for grabs. Faron goes on and on about Brian Poole stealing 'Do You Love Me' from him, but that is being childish: how can he make a claim on a song that he was covering himself? Even now he says, 'Wait 'til I get him.' Because most groups were doing cover versions, I'm convinced that there was no such thing as a Liverpool sound, except of course when they spoke into the microphones. Like a lot of other cities, we were obsessed by cover versions - the big difference was that we had a lot more groups than the other cities." Jim Turner confirms that there is more substance to Faron's claim: Faron Flamingos did "Do You Love Me" as a recording test for Decca and Brian Poole was on Decca.

"Bill Haley was passé then and very few groups did his songs. Karl Terry stayed true to Bill Haley but he was the only one. Little Richard and Chuck Berry were still popular and I was talking to Brendan McCormack from the Memphis Three the other day. He was one of the few guitarists to emerge as a proper instrumentalist fully capable of reading the dots. He is a classical guitarist now but he still plays Chuck Berry numbers from time to time. Chuck Berry's lyrics made sense, although he was always recycling his melodies. Everly Brothers and Buddy Holly songs were performed by the Escorts, but they were ignored by a lot of groups, which is a pity. Oddly enough, George Harrison was very influenced by Joe Brown and he copied him to a large extent - how he would stand and how he would play, and it was George who inspired the Beatles to wear black leather, which he had also taken from Joe Brown."

I showed Bob a book which referred to the Beatles performing a 70-minute version of Ray Charles' 'What'd I Say' in Hamburg. "I hope not," said Bob, "The song is boring enough as it is. I always felt that the crowd was getting fed up when the Big Three kept the song going by saying 'One more time'. It is the most over-rated song from the period and the lyrics say nothing.

"Some standards were performed by the groups, and I used to encourage Gerry to sing 'You'll Never Walk Alone' as I wanted him to broaden his repertoire. Faron's Flamingos did a good version of 'My Happiness', but Rory Storm's voice was very suspect on 'Beautiful Dreamer'. The Merseybeats got the lyrics wrong when they recorded 'Hello Young Lovers'. Instead of 'not merely by chance', they sing 'not nearly by chance'. Still, I give them top marks for doing it. They change the tune for 'My Heart And I' but you could argue that Billie Holiday didn't sing the tunes properly. I'm a bugger about interpreting the lyrics properly and I wasn't happy when Freddie and the Dreamers did 'Once In A While'. They started it seriously and then they began laughing and made a mockery of it. I would say to Freddie, 'Why do you do it? I revere that song.' He could have found a lesser song to have fun with.

"I liked the Chants' version of Rodgers and Hart's 'I Could Write A Book' very much. They had a contemporary arrangement from Tony Hatch, but it didn't distort the quality of the song. Nothing to do with Mersey Beat, but I even made allowances for the Marcels with their No. 1 record, 'Blue Moon', which was also Rodgers and Hart. However, I wasn't impressed with their follow-up, 'You Are My Sunshine'. I once asked Ian McCulloch of Echo and the Bunnymen why he did 'September Song', which is a very old song. He said, 'I did it because it was my father's favourite', so people often record songs for very personal reasons. It is like dedicating a book to someone. Whether their parents would like the way they do the songs is a different matter.

"A set list given to me by a Beatles fan, who followed them around Merseyside, is printed here. They took 'Red Sails In The Sunset' from Ray Sharpe, and they used to call 'Besame Mucho' 'Besammy Leacho' for Sam Leach the promoter. They got 'Falling In Love Again' from Hamburg and Paul got some songs from his father. Stu Sutcliffe would do 'Love Me Tender' and he would stand at the front of the stage and croon the song, with George adding a few chords. There is an instrumental, 'Beatle Bob', on the list - the Beatles used to call themselves the Big Beat Boppin' Beatles, so the title might really be 'Beatle Bop'. Spencer says it could be the Collins Kids' 'Beetle Bug Bop', a 1955 country record by two American youngsters, but I don't recall that record at all.

"There are over 90 songs on the list and only a handful are self-penned, usually by Paul, and they are 'Love Of The Loved', which was performed from an early stage, 'Hello Little Girl', 'I Call Your Name', 'Like Dreamers Do', 'Tip Of My Tongue', 'Pinwheel Twist' and possibly 'Beatle Bob'. Even if they could write, groups hardly ever did their own songs because they were too preoccupied covering the songs that American groups were doing. I shall return to this theme in *I Blame The Beatles!*

"John and Paul shared the lead vocals with 35 and 37 namechecks, respectively. George has 20 namechecks and his repertoire is different from the others - there are several songs associated with Joe Brown - 'The Darktown Strutters Ball', 'I'm Henry The Eighth', 'A Picture Of You','The Sheik Of Araby', 'Shine' and 'What A Crazy World We're Living In'. Later on George and Joe lived close to each other and became good friends. Paul favours a few standards, while John appreciates Chuck Berry's lyrics - and that's revealing, isn't it? - Paul going for the melodies and John for the words. The early rock'n'roll artists like Arthur Alexander, the Coasters, Chuck Berry, Little Richard, Carl

Perkins, Elvis Presley and Larry Williams dominate the Beatles' list with a few standards, Brill Building and Motown songs added for good measure.

"There are a few songs that can't be identified for sure. 'Dream' could be 'All I Have To Do Is Dream', 'Open' could be Buddy Knox's song, 'Open Your Lovin' Arms', and 'Time' could be the Craig Douglas hit. The list finishes around October 1962 because by then the Beatles would have been performing their first single, 'Love Me Do', which is not on the list."

CAVERN CUTS

This list of songs from the Beatles' early repertoire was given to Bob Wooler by a girl who was a Cavern regular in the early 1960s. The lead vocalist was noted on most occasions.

Ain't She Sweet (John)
Anna (John)
Baby It's You (John)
Beatle Bob (Instrumental)
Beautiful Dreamer (Paul)
Besame Mucho (Paul)
Boys (Ringo)
Chains (George)
Clarabella (Paul)
Claudette (Paul)
The Darktown Strutters Ball (George)
Don't Ever Change (George / Paul)
Dream (George)
Dream Baby (Paul)
Falling In Love Again (Paul)
Glad All Over (Paul)
Hello Little Girl (John)
Hey Baby! (Paul)
Hey Good Lookin' (George)
Hey Hey Hey Hey (Paul)
Hippy Hippy Shake (Paul)
The Honeymoon Song (Paul)
Hully Gully (John)
I Call Your Name (John)

I Forgot To Remember To Forget (George)
If You Gotta Make A Fool Of Somebody (John / Paul)
I'm A Hog For You Baby (Paul / John)
I'm Gonna Sit Right Down And Cry (John)
I'm Henry The Eighth (George)
I'm Talkin' About You (John)
I Remember You (Paul)
It's Now Or Never (Paul)
Johnny B.Goode (John)
Kansas City (Paul)
Keep Your Hands Off My Baby (John)
Lend Me Your Comb (John)
Like Dreamers Do (Paul)
The Locomotion (John)
Long Tall Sally (Paul)
Love Me Tender (Stuart)
Love Of The Loved (Paul)
Loving You (Paul)
Lucille (Paul)
Matchbox (Pete or Ringo)
Maybellene (John)

Memphis (John)
Money (John)
Mr.Moonlight (John)
My Bonnie
Nothin' Shakin' (George)
Ooh! My Soul (Paul)
Open (George)
Over The Rainbow (Paul)
A Picture Of You (George)
Pinwheel Twist
Please Mr.Postman (John)
Quarter To Three (Paul / John)
Rip It Up (Paul)
Red Hot (George)
Red Sails In The Sunset (Paul)
Roll Over Beethoven (George)
Save The Last Dance For Me
The Sheik Of Araby (George)
Sheila (George)
Shimmy Shimmy (John)
Shine (George)
A Shot Of Rhythm And Blues
(John / Paul)
Slow Down (John)

Soldier Of Love (John)
Some Other Guy (John / Paul)
Stand By Me (John)
Sure To Fall (Paul)
Sweet Little Sixteen (John)
A Taste Of Honey (Paul)
Three Cool Cats (George)
Till There Was You (Paul)
Time (George)
Tip Of My Tongue (Paul)
To Know Her Is To Love Her (John)
Too Much Monkey Business (John)
Tutti Frutti (Paul)
Twist And Shout (John)
What A Crazy World We're Living In
(George)
What'd I Say (Paul)
What's Your Name (John)
When The Saints Go Marching In
Where Have You Been (John)
Wooden Heart (Paul)
Yakety Yak (George / John)
You Better Move On (John)
Young Blood (George)
Your Feet's Too Big (John / Paul)

Paul McCartney at The Odd Spot, 1963.

The Searchers.

13   TOO MUCH MONKEY BUSINESS
Songs covered by Mersey Beat acts up to 1967
Compiled by Spencer Leigh for Record Collector (February 1999) and reprinted with permission.

"I always loved hearing Bob Wooler at the Cavern. He wouldn't say very much when he played the records but he would have fascinating little snippets about the records he played. He'd tell you where it was in the American charts rather than just saying, 'Here is such a thing by so and so.'"
(Billy Butler, 2002)

The Liverpool-dominated beat boom of the early 60s was, and still is, the most exciting thing that ever happened to British popular music. Its reverberations are still heard today as each new successful British band is hailed as the latest Beatles and each new songwriter as the new Lennon or McCartney. But, in the early stages at least, the Liverpool music was decidedly second-hand. Every group, including the Beatles, covered American rock'n'roll and R&B songs. Much of this repertoire was recorded by the Liverpool bands, which means we can identify the performers who influenced them the most.

I once asked Pete Best where the Beatles' repertoire came from: "We heard records on *Radio Luxembourg* and got some things from the seamen, and we found some on the juke-boxes in Germany. When we got back to Liverpool, we found that everybody was collecting records and we tried to hear the new ones in NEMS before anybody else. We didn't buy many of them - we could listen to them two or three times and then play them - we would scribble the words down or with a bit of luck, Bob Wooler may have bought them." I don't like to dispute what is said by someone who was there, but I suspect his memory has been clouded by what he has read in books.

For this survey, I have taken every song that was covered and recorded by a Liverpool band up to the release of *Sgt Pepper's Lonely Hearts Club Band* in 1967, although the performances may not have been issued until later (e.g. *The Beatles Live At The BBC*). This ruling omits John Lennon's *Rock'n'Roll* album and Paul McCartney's Russian album, but, if I included them, I would also have to include Gerry Marsden's *Fifty Non-Stop Party Hits,* which would distort the results. Also, there would be vintage rock'n'roll songs that the performers mightn't have heard during the Merseybeat era. George Harrison had a Top 10 hit in 1987 with James Ray's 'Got My Mind Set On You', but the original was so obscure that I doubt that any Liverpool group knew it at the time.

And so to the survey of over 350 cover versions. 60% of the artists covered are black and 30% are white US pop or rock'n'roll artists. There are also some standards (was Cilla thinking of the Mersey when she recorded 'Ol' Man River'?), and some folk and country material, but only two Bob Dylan songs. The most popular artists covered by Merseybeat acts are as follows:

American artist	Songs covered	Total cover versions
Chuck Berry	14	20
Little Richard	12	18
Drifters	11	13
Larry Williams	7	13
Coasters	10	12
Carl Perkins	9	12
Ray Charles	6	11
Arthur Alexander	6	10
Everly Brothers	8	9
Shirelles	5	9

The chart is dominated by black artists - 8 out of 10 - with Chuck Berry and Little Richard way out in front. However, if you add Ben E. King to his former group, the Drifters, you get 16 songs covered and 20 covers in all. In style, Larry Williams was simply a continuation of Little Richard and their combined results give 19 different songs and 31 covers in all. Burt Bacharach is a key songwriter with compositions for himself, Jerry Butler, Lou Johnson, the Shirelles and Dionne Warwick. Bill Haley was out of favour so the lack of covers is unsurprising, but the rating for Buddy Holly is much lower than I expected - only five songs and five covers for a premier singer-songwriter, whose publishing catalogue was bought by Paul McCartney.

In addition, several performers wrote new songs in the style of their favourite performers - the Beatles' 'I'm Down' and the Merseybeats' 'Jumpin' Jonah' are Little Richard revisited. The most distinctive feature of Gerry Marsden's ballad, 'Don't Let The Sun Catch You Cryin'', was its title and yet it came from a Ray Charles record. Gerry regards this an unfortunate coincidence but whatever the truth of the matter, 25% of the royalties had to be passed over. This, in itself, is interesting as you cannot copyright a title and there are many songs with the same title, no matter how distinctive. So, why did he have to give up some of his royalties?

Spare a thought for Sonny Webb and the Cascades - they were booked to tour Ireland by a promoter who assumed that they were the American group, the Cascades, of 'Rhythm Of The Rain' fame. When he discovered that they weren't the same group, he said, "You'd better know the song by tonight if you want to get paid."

What can we conclude from the list? Simply this. Nearly every Beatle book tells you of the importance of the Cunard Yanks - the Liverpool sailors who went to New York and came back with American records. The Liverpool groups sang these songs and so got an edge on bands from other cities. Well, it didn't happen. Many of the songs were obscure, but nearly all the originals were released in the UK and could be bought or ordered from NEMS.

It is possible that the Cunard Yanks brought some of these records back from the US before they were released in the UK, but the time-delay was rarely more than six weeks. The Ribbons' 'Ain't Gonna Kiss Ya' didn't have a UK release, but the Searchers found that song among some demos at Pye Records. So it's official - the Cunard Yanks existed but they had no impact on the repertoire of the Liverpool bands.

The listing includes the most likely original source for a particular song. For example, Paul Anka recorded a beat version of 'Hello Young Lovers' before the Merseybeats and Ray Charles was the first to rock up 'My Bonnie'. Songs where there is not an obvious source - for example, Kingsize Taylor's 'The Skye Boat Song' and the Mojos' 'Goodbye Dolly Gray' - have been omitted.

Bob Wooler was very excited by this list as he felt it demonstrated what he had known all along - the Cunard Yanks are not a part of the Mersey Beat story.

Artist	Title	Covers
Addrisi Brothers	Cherry Stones	Searchers
Arthur Alexander	Anna (Go To Him)	Beatles
Arthur Alexander	A Shot Of Rhythm And Blues	Beatles, Cilla Black, Lee Curtis, Gerry & Pacemakers
Arthur Alexander	Soldier Of Love	Beatles
Arthur Alexander	Where Have You Been All My Life	Gerry & Pacemakers, Searchers
Arthur Alexander	You Better Move On	Dennisons
Arthur Alexander	You're The Reason	Gerry & Pacemakers
Paul Anka	Hello Young Lovers	Merseybeats
Ann-Margret	I Just Don't Understand	Beatles
Louis Armstrong	Ol' Man Mose	Swinging Blue Jeans
Burt Bacharach	Trains And Boats And Planes	Billy J Kramer
LaVern Baker	Bumble Bee	Searchers

The Best Of Fellas - The Story Of Bob Wooler.

Artist	Title	Covers
Richie Barrett	Some Other Guy	Beatles, Big Three, Searchers
Richie Barrett	Tricky Dicky	Searchers, Denny Seyton
Len Barry	One Two Three	Cilla Black
Chuck Berry	Around And Around	Swinging Blue Jeans
Chuck Berry	Broken Arrow	Kingsize Taylor
Chuck Berry	Bye Bye Johnny	Searchers
Chuck Berry	Carol	Beatles
Chuck Berry	I Got To Find My Baby	Beatles
Chuck Berry	I'm Talkin' About You	Beatles, Faron's Flamingos
Chuck Berry	Johnny B. Goode	Beatles
Chuck Berry	Maybellene	Gerry & Pacemakers
Chuck Berry	Memphis, Tennessee	Beatles, Lee Curtis, Kingsize Taylor
Chuck Berry	Reelin' And Rockin'	Big Three, Gerry & Pacemakers
Chuck Berry	Rock And Roll Music	Beatles
Chuck Berry	Roll Over Beethoven	Beatles
Chuck Berry	Sweet Little Sixteen	Beatles, Searchers, Kingsize Taylor
Chuck Berry	Too Much Monkey Business	Beatles
Dave Berry	The Crying Game	Ian & Zodiacs
Bob B Soxx & the Blue Jeans	Zip A Dee Doo Dah	Big Three
Booker T & the MG's	Green Onions	Kingsize Taylor
James Brown	Good Good Lovin'	Merseybeats
James Brown	I Go Crazy	Tommy Quickly
James Brown	I Love You Yes I Do	Merseybeats
James Brown	Think	Undertakers
Joe Brown	The Sheik Of Araby	Beatles
Gus Backus	Short On Love	Kingsize Taylor
Solomon Burke	Down In The Valley	Kingsize Taylor
Solomon Burke	Somebody's Always Tryin'	Kingsize Taylor
Solomon Burke	Stupidity	Lee Curtis, Kingsize Taylor, Undertakers
Johnny Burnette	Lonesome Tears In My Eyes	Beatles
Jerry Butler	He Will Break Your Heart	Merseybeats

134

Artist	Title	Covers
Jerry Butler	Make It Easy On Yourself	Cilla Black, Ian & Zodiacs
Butterflies	Goodnight Baby	Searchers
Capitols	Cool Jerk	Ian & Zodiacs
Carter-Lewis & Southerners	Here's Hoping	Gerry & Pacemakers
Johnny Cash	Guess Things Happen That Way	Earl Royce & Olympics
Ray Charles	Hallelujah I Love Her So	Gerry & Pacemakers, Quarry Men, Derry Wilkie, Beatles
Ray Charles	I Got A Woman	Beatles
Ray Charles	My Bonnie	Beatles
Ray Charles	This Little Girl Of Mine	Tony Jackson
Ray Charles	Unchain My Heart	Kingsize Taylor
Ray Charles	What'd I Say	Big Three, Gerry & Pacemakers, Searchers
Buzz Clifford	Babysitting Boogie	Fourmost
Clovers	Love Potion Number Nine	Searchers, Tony Jackson
Coasters	Ain't That Just Like Me	Searchers
Coasters	Besame Mucho	Beatles
Coasters	Girls, Girls, Girls	Fourmost
Coasters	Little Egypt	Cyclones, Lee Curtis
Coasters	Searchin'	Beatles
Coasters	Three Cool Cats	Beatles, Nocturnes
Coasters	Thumbin' A Ride	Earl Preston
Coasters	What About Us	The Undertakers
Coasters	Yakety Yak	Fourmost
Coasters	Young Blood	Beatles
Eddie Cochran	Boll Weevil Song	Howie Casey
Eddie Cochran	Hey Teresa	Paddy Klaus & Gibson
Nat 'King' Cole	Let True Love Begin	Big Three
Nat 'King' Cole	Nature Boy	Ian & Zodiacs
Nat 'King' Cole	When I Fall In Love	Cilla Black
Bobby Comstock	Let's Stomp	Lee Curtis
Bobby Comstock	Shimmy Shimmy	Searchers, Beatles
Contours	Do You Love Me	Faron's Flamingos
Contours	Shake Sherry	Faron's Flamingos

Artist	Title	Covers
Don Covay	See-Saw	Ian & Zodiacs
Sam Cooke	Bring It On Home To Me	Big Three, Merseybeats
Sam Cooke	Tennessee Waltz	Billy J.Kramer
Cookies	Chains	Beatles
Crickets	Doncha Know	Searchers
Crickets	Don't Ever Change	Beatles
Crickets	When You Ask About Love	Billy J.Kramer
Crystals	Da Doo Ron Ron	Billy J.Kramer, Searchers
Bobby Darin	I'll Be There	Gerry & Pacemakers
Bobby Darin	Irresistible You	Lee Curtis, Billy J.Kramer
Bobby Darin	When I Get Home	Searchers
Bobby Day	Rockin' Robin	Ian & Zodiacs
Doris Day	Que Sera Sera	Earl Royce
Doris Day	Secret Love	Ian & Zodiacs
Del-Vikings	Come Go With Me	The Chants
Sugar Pie DeSanto	Soulful Dress	Ian & Zodiacs
Jackie De Shannon	Break-a-way	Beryl Marsden
Jackie De Shannon	Each Time	Searchers
Jackie De Shannon	Needles And Pins	Searchers
Jackie De Shannon	Til You Say You'll Be Mine	Searchers
Jackie De Shannon	When You Walk In The Room	Billy J.Kramer, Searchers
Marlene Dietrich	Falling In Love Again	Beatles
Fats Domino	Domino Twist	Kingsize Taylor
Fats Domino	I'm Ready	Searchers
Fats Domino	My Girl Josephine	Lee Curtis, Kingsize Taylor
Fats Domino	When The Saints Go Marching In	Searchers
Fats Domino	Whole Lotta Lovin'	Kingsize Taylor
Donays	Devil In Her Heart	Beatles
Lonnie Donegan	Seven Daffodils	Mojos
Dr. Feelgood & Interns	Dr. Feelgood	Rory Storm, Kingsize Taylor
Dr. Feelgood & Interns	Mr. Moonlight	Beatles, Merseybeats
Lee Dorsey	Get Out Of My Life, Woman	Ian & Zodiacs
Lee Dorsey	Ride Your Pony	Ian & Zodiacs
Lee Dorsey	Working In The Coalmine	Ian & Zodiacs

Artist	Title	Covers
Drifters	Dance With Me	Billy J.Kramer
Drifters	I Count The Tears	Searchers
Drifters	I Don't Want To Go On Without You	Escorts, Searchers
Drifters	If You Don't Come Back	Undertakers
Drifters	I'll Take You Home	Ian & Zodiacs
Drifters	Nobody But Me	Swinging Blue Jeans
Drifters	Please Stay	Cryin' Shames
Drifters	Save The Last Dance For Me	Swinging Blue Jeans
Drifters	Some Kind Of Wonderful	Fourmost, Johnny Sandon
Drifters	Sweets For My Sweet	Searchers
Drifters	Under The Boardwalk	Billy J.Kramer
Bob Dylan	Blowin' In The Wind	Searchers
Bob Dylan	She Belongs To Me	Masterminds
Duane Eddy	Peter Gunn	Remo Four, Freddie Starr
Betty Everett	It's In His Kiss	Searchers
Betty Everett	You're No Good	Swinging Blue Jeans
Everly Brothers	Let It Be Me	Escorts
Everly Brothers	Nashville Blues	Del Renas
Everly Brothers	Sigh, Cry, Almost Die	Del Renas
Everly Brothers	Since You Broke My Heart	Searchers, Rory Storm
Everly Brothers	So How Come	Beatles
Everly Brothers	Some Sweet Day	Swinging Blue Jeans
Everly Brothers	Walk Right Back	Mark and John
Everly Brothers	When Will I Be Loved	Del Renas
Fiestas	So Fine	Faron's Flamingos
Toni Fisher	Hurt	Cy Tucker
Five Americans	Western Union	Searchers
Eddie Fontaine	Nothin' Shakin'	Beatles
Tennessee Ernie Ford	Sixteen Tons	Johnny Sandon
Four Pennies	My Block	Fourmost
Four Seasons	Sherry	Kingsize Taylor
Four Tops	Baby I Need Your Loving	Fourmost, Ian & Zodiacs
Marvin Gaye	Can I Get A Witness	Steve Aldo
Marvin Gaye	I'll Be Doggone	Searchers, B.J Kramer

Artist	Title	Covers
Marvin Gaye	You're A Wonderful One	Trends
Barbara George	I Know	Beryl Marsden
Don Gibson	Legend In My Time	Johnny Sandon
Don Gibson	Sea Of Heartbreak	Searchers
Roscoe Gordon	Just A Little Bit	Undertakers
Grass Roots	Take Me For What I'm Worth	Searchers
Grandisons	Alright	Searchers
Dobie Gray	The In Crowd	Ian & Zodiacs
Bill Haley	Skinny Minnie	Gerry & Pacemakers, Lee Curtis
Ronnie Hawkins	One Of These Days	Searchers
Eddie Hodges	I'm Gonna Knock On Your Door	Pete Best
Brenda Holloway	Every Little Bit Hurts	Cilla Black
Buddy Holly	Crying Waiting Hoping	Beatles
Buddy Holly	Listen To Me	Searchers
Buddy Holly	Reminiscing	Beatles
Buddy Holly	That'll Be The Day	Quarry Men
Buddy Holly	Words Of Love	Beatles
Buddy Holly	You've Got Love	Swinging Blue Jeans
Hollywood Argyles	Sho' Know A Lot About Love	Searchers
Jimmy Hughes	Goodbye My Love	Searchers
Tommy Hunt	Gonna Send You Back To Georgia	Searchers, Ian & Zodiacs
Ivory Joe Hunter	A Tear Fell	Searchers
Ian and Sylvia	Four Strong Winds	Searchers
Frank Ifield	I Remember You	Beatles
Impressions	It's All Right	Ian & Zodiacs
Isley Brothers	Nobody But Me	Mojos
Isley Brothers	Respectable	Fourmost
Isley Brothers	Shout	Beatles
Isley Brothers	Twist And Shout	Beatles, Searchers, Kingsize Taylor
Chuck Jackson	Any Day Now	Ian & Zodiacs
Jaynettes	Sally Go Round The Roses	Remo Four
Jodimars	Clarabella	Beatles, Ian & Zodiacs, Kingsize Taylor
Lou Johnson	Magic Potion	Searchers, Kubas, Johnny Sandon

Artist	Title	Covers
Lou Johnson	Message To Martha	Ian & Zodiacs
George Jones	Who Shot Sam	Sonny Webb
Johnny Kidd & Pirates	Hungry For Love	Searchers
Johnny Kidd & Pirates	I Can Tell	Rory Storm, Kingsize Taylor
Ben E. King	Ecstasy	Lee Curtis
Ben E. King	I (Who Have Nothing)	Searchers
Ben E. King	On The Horizon	Johnny Sandon
Ben E. King	Stand By Me	Lee Curtis, Searchers
Ben E. King	Yes	Billy J. Kramer, Johnny Sandon
Kingsmen	Louie Louie	Rhythm And Blues Inc
Kingston Trio	All My Sorrows	Searchers
Kingston Trio	Where Have All The Flowers Gone	Lee Curtis, Searchers
Major Lance	Um Um Um Um Um Um	Lee Curtis
Brenda Lee	Sweet Nuthin's	Searchers
Peggy Lee	Fever	Cilla Black
Peggy Lee	Till There Was You	Beatles
Ketty Lester	Love Letters	Cilla Black
Ketty Lester	You Can't Lie To A Liar	Searchers
Lettermen	The Way You Look Tonight	Denny Seyton
Barbara Lewis	Baby I'm Yours	Cilla Black
Barbara Lewis	Someday We're Gonna Love Again	Searchers
Ramsey Lewis	Wade In The Water	Ian & Zodiacs
Jerry Lee Lewis	Fools Like Me	Merseybeats
Jerry Lee Lewis	Great Balls Of Fire	Billy J. Kramer
Jerry Lee Lewis	High School Confidential	Big Three
Jerry Lee Lewis	It'll Be Me	Gerry & Pacemakers
Jerry Lee Lewis	Livin' Lovin' Wreck	Ian & Zodiacs, Searchers
Jerry Lee Lewis	When I Get Paid	Lee Curtis
Jerry Lee Lewis	Whole Lotta Shakin' Goin' On	Gerry & Pacemakers
Little Anthony & Imperials	Goin' Out Of My Head	Cilla Black
Little Anthony & Imperials	Tears On My Pillow	Dimensions
Little Eva	Keep Your Hands Off My Baby	Beatles
Little Eva	Let's Turkey Trot	Ian & Zodiacs

Artist	Title	Covers
Little Richard	All Around The World	Earl Preston, Kingsize Taylor
Little Richard	The Girl Can't Help It	Fourmost
Little Richard	Good Golly Miss Molly	Swinging Blue Jeans
Little Richard	Heebie Jeebies	Fourmost, Kingsize Taylor
Little Richard	Kansas City/Hey Hey Hey Hey	Beatles
Little Richard	Long Tall Sally	Swinging Blue Jeans, Beatles, Searchers, Kingsize Taylor
Little Richard	Lucille	Beatles
Little Richard	Ooh! My Soul	Beatles
Little Richard	Ready Teddy	Swinging Blue Jeans
Little Richard	Rip It Up	Gerry & Pacemakers, Valkryies
Little Richard	Slippin' And Slidin'	Kingsize Taylor
Little Richard	Tutti Frutti	Swinging Blue Jeans
Little Willie John	Leave My Kitten Alone	Beatles
Hank Locklin	Border Of The Blues	Sonny Webb
Bob Luman	You've Got Everything	Sonny Webb
Frankie Lymon & Teenagers	Why Do Fools Fall In Love	Fourmost
Carl Mann	Pretend	Gerry & Pacemakers
Marathons	Peanut Butter	Big Three
Marino Marini	Honeymoon Song	Beatles
Martha & Vandellas	Dancing In The Street	Cilla Black
Martha & Vandellas	Love Is Like A Heatwave	Cilla Black
Tony Martin	Walk Hand In Hand	Gerry & Pacemakers
Marvelettes	Beechwood 4-5789	Ian & Zodiacs
Marvelettes	Please Mr. Postman	Beatles
Johnny Mathis	The Twelfth Of Never	Billy J.Kramer
Mighty Avengers	So Much In Love	Ian & Zodiacs
Roger Miller	Chug-A-Lug	Swinging Blue Jeans
Miracles	Going To A Go-Go	Ian & Zodiacs
Miracles	Mickey's Monkey	Lee Curtis
Miracles	The Way You Do The Things You Do	Trends
Miracles	You Really Got a Hold On Me	Beatles

Artist	Title	Covers
Chris Montez	Let's Dance	Kingsize Taylor
Moody & The Deltas	Everybody Come Clap Your Hands	Searchers
Ricky Nelson	It's Up To You	Billy J. Kramer
Ricky Nelson	I've Got My Eyes On You	Lee Curtis
Ricky Nelson	Mad Mad World	Escorts, Billy J. Kramer
Ricky Nelson	My Babe	Lee Curtis, Gerry & Pacemakers
Tony Orlando	Beautiful Dreamer	Beatles, Billy J.Kramer
Tony Orlando	Chills	Gerry & Pacemakers
Orlons	Don't Throw Your Love Away	Searchers
Orlons	The Wah-Watusi	Kingsize Taylor
Buck Owens	Act Naturally	Beatles
Buck Owens	Excuse Me	Sonny Webb
Bobby Parker	Watch Your Step	Tony Jackson, Earl Preston
Lance Percival	Shame And Scandal In The Family	Lee Curtis
Carl Perkins	Blue Suede Shoes	Lee Curtis
Carl Perkins	Boppin' The Blues	Lee Curtis
Carl Perkins	Everybody's Tryin' To Be My Baby Now	Beatles
Carl Perkins	Glad All Over	Beatles, Searchers
Carl Perkins	Honey Don't	Beatles, Rhythm And Blues Inc
Carl Perkins	Lend Me Your Comb	Beatles
Carl Perkins	Matchbox	Beatles
Carl Perkins	Sure To Fall	Beatles, Fourmost
Carl Perkins	The Wrong Yo-Yo	Gerry & Pacemakers
Gene Pitney	Donna Means Heartbreak	Johnny Sandon
Platters	My Prayer	Cy Tucker
Platters	Twilight Time	Billy J. Kramer
Premiers	Farmer John	Searchers
Elvis Presley	Anything That's Part Of You	Billy J. Kramer
Elvis Presley	Can't Help Falling In Love	Lee Curtis
Elvis Presley	I Forgot To Remember To Forget	Beatles
Elvis Presley	I'm Gonna Sit Right Down & Cry	Beatles, Merseybeats
Elvis Presley	A Mess Of Blues	Lee Curtis
Elvis Presley	One Night	Lee Curtis
Elvis Presley	That's All Right	Beatles

Artist	Title	Covers
Lloyd Price	Lawdy Miss Clawdy	Swinging Blue Jeans
Otis Redding	Respect	Ian & Zodiacs
Jimmy Reed	Baby What Do You Want Me To Do	Steve Aldo, Denny Seyton
Jimmy Reed	Shame Shame Shame	Searchers
Jim Reeves	The Blizzard	Johnny Sandon
Malvina Reynolds	What Have They Done To The Rain	Searchers
Ribbons	Ain't Gonna Kiss Ya	Searchers
Charlie Rich	Mohair Sam	Lee Curtis
Righteous Brothers	Little Latin Lupe Lu	Dennisons
Righteous Brothers	You've Lost That Loving Feeling	Cilla Black
Marty Robbins	Ruby Ann	Kingsize Taylor
Paul Robeson	Ol' Man River	Cilla Black
Alvin Robinson	Something You Got Baby	Searchers
Rolling Stones	Take It Or Leave It	Searchers
Chan Romero	The Hippy Hippy Shake	Swinging Blue Jeans, Beatles, Kingsize Taylor
Billy Joe Royal	Down In The Boondocks	Billy J. Kramer
Ruby & Romantics	Our Day Will Come	Merseybeats
Mitch Ryder	Jenny Take A Ride	Searchers
Sam The Sham & the Pharaohs	Wooly Bully	Lee Curtis
Del Shannon	Kelly	Lee Curtis
Shirelles	Baby It's You	Beatles, Cilla Black
Shirelles	Boys	Beatles, Lee Curtis, Jeannie & Big Guys
Shirelles	Don't Let It Happen To Us	Merseybeats
Shirelles	Everybody Loves A Lover	Undertakers, Beryl Marsden
Shirelles	It's Love That Really Counts	Merseybeats
Shirley & Lee	Let The Good Times Roll	Searchers
Simon & Garfunkel	The Big Bright Green Pleasure Machine	Gerry & Pacemakers
Frank Sinatra	I Could Write A Book	The Chants
Frank Sinatra	You'd Be So Nice To Come Home To	Cilla Black
Benny Spellman	Fortune Teller	Tony Jackson, Merseybeats, Kingsize Taylor

142

Artist	Title	Covers
Barrett Strong	Money (That's What I Want)	Beatles, Searchers, Kingsize Taylor, Undertakers
Supremes	When The Lovelight Starts Shinin' Through His Eyes	Beryl Marsden
Teddy Bears	To Know Her Is To Love Her	Beatles
Rufus Thomas	Jump Back	Ian & Zodiacs
Rufus Thomas	Walking The Dog	Dennisons
Hank Thompson	Wild Side Of Life	Tommy Quickly
Toys	A Lover's Concerto	Cilla Black
Doris Troy	Whacha Gonna Do About It	Cilla Black
Tommy Tucker	Hi-Heel Sneakers	Searchers
Joe Turner	Lipstick Powder And Paint	Kingsize Taylor
Joe Turner	Shake Rattle And Roll	Swinging Blue Jeans
Titus Turner	Sticks and Stones	Lee Curtis, Jeannie & Big Guys
Conway Twitty	It's Only Make Believe	Lee Curtis
Conway Twitty	Make Me Know You're Mine	Swinging Blue Jeans
Conway Twitty	You'll Never Walk Alone	Gerry & Pacemakers
Philip Upchurch Combo	You Can't Sit Down	Kingsize Taylor
Bobby Vee	Someday	Mark Peters
Gene Vincent	Ain't She Sweet	Beatles
Gene Vincent	Be Bop A Lula	Beatles
Gene Vincent	Summertime	Gerry & Pacemakers
Junior Walker	Shotgun	Cilla Black
Fats Waller	Your Feet's Too Big	Beatles
Dionne Warwick	Anyone Who Had A Heart	Cilla Black
Dionne Warwick	Don't Make Me Over	Swinging Blue Jeans
Dionne Warwick	This Empty Place	Cilla Black, Ian & Zodiacs, Searchers
Dionne Warwick	Wishin' And Hopin'	Merseybeats
Muddy Waters	Got My Mojo Working	Mojos
Lenny Welch	A Taste Of Honey	Beatles
Mary Wells	Bye Bye Baby	Tony Jackson
Mary Wells	The One Who Really Loves You	Mojos
Mary Wells	You Beat Me To The Punch	Tony Jackson
Marty Wilde	Jezebel	Lee Curtis
Marty Wilde	My Heart And I	Merseybeats

Artist	*Title*	*Covers*
Hank Williams	Jambalaya	Gerry & Pacemakers
Hank Williams	You Win Again	Gerry & Pacemakers
Larry Williams	Bad Boy	Beatles, Kingsize Taylor
Larry Williams	Bony Moronie	Howie Casey
Larry Williams	Dizzy Miss Lizzy	Beatles, Escorts, Gerry & Pacemakers, Kingsize Taylor
Larry Williams	High School Dance	Cy Tucker
Larry Williams	She Said Yeah	Kingsize Taylor
Larry Williams	Short Fat Fannie	Denny Seyton
Larry Williams	Slow Down	Beatles, Lee Curtis, Kingsize Taylor
Sonny Boy Williamson	Good Morning Little Schoolgirl	Ian & Zodiacs
Kathy Young & Innocents	A Thousand Stars	The Chants
Timi Yuro	Hurt	Cy Tucker
Timi Yuro	I Apologise	Cy Tucker
Timi Yuro	Let Me Call You Sweetheart	Cy Tucker

Denny Seyton & the Sabres

144

Billy Kinsley and Tony Crane of the
Merseybeats

Jim Turner at the Odd Spot, 1963

Ian & The Zodiacs

14 MIX ME A MANAGER
Managers in Liverpool

"You Don't Own Me"
(Lesley Gore US hit song, 1964)

In 1961 Brian Epstein was not interested in beat music in Liverpool clubs, so why was he able to enter that world and steal the Beatles from under the noses of the promoters and club owners who had been around for years? Why didn't Ray McFall, Bill Harry or even Bob Wooler manage the Beatles as all of them had recognised the Beatles potential before Eppy?

Bob Wooler: "Since the Beatles' appearance at Litherland Town Hall in December 1960, I had wanted to write about them, but writing takes me ages. Eventually, in August 1961, I wrote about the Beatles for Bill Harry's *Mersey Beat* newspaper. People were always asking me about this group, and I knew that they were remarkable, magic even. I tried to encapsulate that in an article full of soundbites, to use a contemporary expression. I culled the famous last words of Humphrey Bogart from *The Maltese Falcon*. When he is asked about the black bird by Ward Bond, he replies, 'It is the stuff that dreams are made of.' I paraphrased that as 'the stuff that screams are made of'.

"Pete Best is the only Beatle mentioned by name in that article, but there is a simple explanation for this. The poster for Jane Russell in *The Outlaw* described her as 'mean, moody and magnificent', and I wanted an excuse to use it. Pete Best was moody and he looked mean and magnificent like James Dean. He was mostly unsmiling, although he did have a winning smile, and this would intrigue the girls. He wasn't a communicator but the girls loved him. Sam Leach called him the Atom Beat Drummer, which seemed appropriate, although I've no idea what he meant."

Pete Best: "The first time I read Bob's article I started laughing. I didn't think I was mean and moody at at all and I certainly didn't try and look like Jeff Chandler. I would put my head down and flail away but I don't think anyone would say I was mean and moody personally. Still, if that's how he saw me, okay."

146

Bob Wooler: "I closed the article by saying the Beatles were so fantastic that I didn't think anything like them would happen again. Quite honestly, if I'd been in a position to manage them, I would have done so. The Beatles wanted someone who could further their career in a very positive way: they wanted somebody with nous, somebody with clout and somebody with cash, and they wanted somebody who drove a car. I had a bit of nous, no clout outside Liverpool, no cash and no car.

"I did think that Allan Williams might patch up his differences with the Beatles and manage them. He fell out with the Beatles when they went back to the Top Ten Club in Hamburg in 1961. They told me that they had got the booking themselves while they were over there. Paul said, 'I suppose you're going to tell your mate about this.' I said, 'Too bloody true.' After all, Allan had secured the first booking and one depended on the other. I did tell Allan and he was fuming about this. They went to Hamburg and Allan got a letter from Stuart Sutcliffe saying that they were not going to pay him the 10% and he said, 'You'll never work in Liverpool again.' He told me not to have anything more to do with them, and I said, 'Too late, I am already totally Beatleised. It's impossible, Allan.'

"I kept on saying to Allan, 'The Beatles are fantastic, you should see what they're doing to people, they're transforming the whole scene.' Allan was mobile, he could have jumped in his Jaguar, and I said, 'I will tell you exactly when they will be on, so you don't even have to wait around in the hall.' I would leave his name at the door and I would ask the doormen afterwards, 'Did Allan Williams come in?' 'No, he's not been.' Afterwards, I would go to the Blue Angel, and I would say, 'You didn't go, did you, Allan? When are you going to go? You didn't go to Litherland, you didn't go to Lathom, you didn't go to Aintree, you didn't go to Hambleton Hall.' I invited him to a lunchtime session at the Cavern and he never appeared. His theme song could be 'Who Wants To Be A Millionaire?' and it's completely his own fault that he never made a million.

"Allan Williams didn't want to know them, but Ray McFall, Bill Harry and Sam Leach all toyed with the idea of managing them. Ray knew they needed someone to manage them, but his personality was very different from theirs and he wouldn't have tolerated their behaviour. I remember him saying to me, 'The Beatles really need a manager,' and I thought, 'Then you'll find out how awkward the sods can be.'"

"Bill Harry was too preoccupied with *Mersey Beat*, and I think they would have fallen out with Sam. I don't know about Mona Best but she was looking after their bookings at the time and recognised their potential - or at least, Pete's potential!. I don't think the other three would have accepted her as she would have been furthering Pete's career

147

rather than the group's. I wonder if Paul McCartney considered doing it himself. After Brian Epstein died, he took over their management for *Magical Mystery Tour*, and I wonder if he could have done it earlier.

"Brian Epstein was obviously the right choice for the Beatles, and, following his lead, so many managers sprang up around Merseyside. In 1961 Adam Faith starred in a film called *Mix Me A Person* and I did think of writing an article for *Mersey Beat* called Mix Me A Manager. The three managers were to be Brian Epstein, Joe Flannery and Ted Knibbs, but to be honest, Brian Epstein was so far ahead of everyone.

"Ted Knibbs was a married man whose wife had died and he had grown up kids. He was a boilerman by trade, and William Ashton, who became Billy J. Kramer, lived nearby in Bootle. Ted had many contacts in social clubs and British Legions and was able to get Billy some bookings with his group, the Coasters. He spotted his potential and he retired early to look after him. He was shrewd but not shrewd enough to appreciate the consequences of giving up his pension rights.

"Ted didn't know the jive halls but Bill Harry and I helped him out and I got to know Ted very well. Ted and I would watch Billy and the Coasters on stage from the small balcony at Aintree Institute, and Billy was a very hesitant performer. Ted took away his guitar and put him into the foreground with a gold lamé suit, which was the done thing then. He was a very good-looking lad and very Elvis-oriented. If it wasn't for the fact that Ted had highlighted him, he would never have come into the orbit of BE. I can't blame Billy for signing with Brian as Ted would have been lost in London dealing with the big-time agents."

Beryl Adams: "Ted Knibbs was a very pleasant feller and he and Bob did a lot to try and build up Billy's confidence. He was a nice old guy who never did anybody any harm. Ted knew that he couldn't have done for Billy what Brian did."

Ted Knibbs died some years ago but he told me in 1982: "I think Billy would have made it with me if I'd had a couple of hundred pounds. I could always see the possibilities in Billy so long as he stuck to ballads. I was 60 then and I was the only one who was able to bridge the gap between their generation and mine. I was getting a bit tired and I said to Brian, 'I'll let you have Billy but it will cost you £50.' He said, 'I'll be delighted.' I got £25 of it and I'm still waiting for the rest."

Bob Wooler: "Another manager, Joe Flannery, is writing his autobiography at the moment, and I met him through Frank Knight and the Barons at the Tuebrook Bowling Alley. He had a flat at the back of the bowling alley and he ran a mobile fruit and veg shop. He admits to being gay and so it was more fruit than veg, I suppose. He was also looking after his brother, Peter Flannery or Lee Curtis, who had based his name on the American singer, Curtis Lee, who did 'Under The Moon Of Love'. I introduced Joe to Bill Harry and told him about the venues. He was very influenced by Brian Epstein and he liked to be called the Colonel. I said, 'It's not terribly original, Joe.' Full of airs and graces, he said, 'It is in this country, Bob. Call me the Colonel.'

"Joe and Peter came from a very close-knit family. His other brother, Ted, managed a group called the Young Ones, but everyone was signing on the dotted line in 1963. Pat Delaney, the doorman at the Cavern, had the Nomads for a while. Alan G. Cheetham (what a wonderful name!) from Manchester was nice, plausible and affable. He was in shirts and that's all the Merseybeats got out of him - those frilly shirts."

One would-be impresario, Frankie Martino, sent a letter to all the Liverpool groups asking them to sign up with him. He probably didn't plan to do anything with them, but no doubt would have collected his 10 per cent when something happened. Bob criticised him in *Mersey Beat* and Martino's solicitors contacted the printers and demanded an apology. Bob refused to apologise and Bill Harry had to insert an apology on his behalf in order to get the next issue printed.

Bob Wooler referred to Brian Epstein as the Nemperor and Ted Knibbs enjoyed expanding the joke by calling Bob the Nemperor's Vassall, a reference to the homosexual spy scandal at the time. Bob Wooler: "I was always on Brian Epstein's side, but he wasn't always right. Brian Epstein took the Chants on because the Beatles favoured them. He put them on a kind of a retainer but he wasn't paying them money. It was more a promise and they were in suspended animation. I found out that Joe Flannery was making in-roads on the Chants and instead of saying, 'Go ahead, Joe', I went and reported it to Brian. I felt that they would be better with him if only he would do something for them. I said, ' If you don't do something soon, Joe will move in.' He didn't like the idea of having a rival, especially Joe, whom he didn't really go for. In the end, the Chants went to Ted Ross in Manchester.

"There is no doubt in my mind that Brian was in a different league to the other managers, and he felt he had the whiphand as he had the Beatles. Or did he? He never signed the management contract with them and I think that was because he had reservations about whether he would be able to do something for them. He felt he was on trial and if he hadn't landed that record contract with Parlophone and George Martin, maybe he would have returned to the family store."

I am convinced that a key reason for the Beatles' success is that they had a manager they could trust, which left them free to concentrate on their work. Over the years, I have met many musicians who ran into trouble with their managers - the Animals, the Kinks, the Rolling Stones, the Searchers, the Troggs and the Zombies, among them - and this must have affected their work. Brian Epstein's secretary Beryl Adams agrees, "I will never have anything said against Brian. I loved working for him and he was a perfect gentleman. He was so honest and he was totally straight with the Beatles from Day One."

Billy J. Kramer

JAZZ

" GREAT BALLS OF FIRE !"
BOB WOOLER presents his
" ROCKERSCOPE '62 "
In two weeks' time, Thursday May 17,
at TOWER BALLROOM, New Brighton.
ONLY MERSEYSIDE APPEARANCE OF
JERRY LEE LEWIS
AMERICA'S No. 1 ROCK SHOWMAN.
Plus 12. Yes 12. Star Groups.
1. THE ECHOES of TV and Disc fame.
2. The Big Three. 3. The Pressmen.
4. The Undertakers. 5. The Strangers.
6. Kingsize Taylor and The Dominoes.
7. Billy Kramer with The Coasters.
8. Lee Curtis and The Detours.
9. Lee Castle and The Barons.
10. Rip Van Winkle and The Rip It Ups.
11. Steve Day and The Drifters.
12. Vincent Earl and The Zeros.
NORTH'S BIGGEST EVER ROCK SHOW !
MAN! THIS IS CRAZY
All This For Just 5/-.
Tickets are selling like hot cakes!
HURRY! Get yours now from:—
Nems, Rushworth's, Lewis's, Cranes,
Top Hat, Strothers, Tower, &c., plus
Coffee Clubs and Local Record Shops.
Read all about it in "MERSEY BEAT"
on sale NOW, price 3d.
HOT NEWS!
Negotiations are in hand with Jerry Lee's
agents for this Terrific Show to be filmed
for Coast to Coast TV screening in
America.
DON'T MISS THIS BIG. BIG NIGHT!

John Lennon and George Harrison being presented with
two imported Gibson guitars by James Rushworth, 1962.

151

15 B.E.
NEMS - My Bonnie - Raymond Jones - Brian Epstein sees the Beatles -
Brian s personality - Brian s homosexuality

Roy Plomley: "Were you born in Liverpool?"
Brian Epstein: "Yes, I'd say it was essential."
("Desert Island Discs", BBC, 1964)

Bob Wooler was very affectionate when he spoke of Brian Epstein. He admired him enormously and this comes over in everything he says: "Several promoters on the Mersey Beat scene were thinking about managing the Beatles, but they foolishly delayed their decisions. Enter Brian Epstein, who had no connections with the beat clubs at all. He was the manager of NEMS and he wrote record reviews for *Mersey Beat.* To be honest, he wasn't much of a record reviewer. He was more intent on telling you the price of the record and the fact that you could buy it from NEMS. He didn't miss a trick. My article about the Beatles appeared just before his article, so he must have noticed it when he was looking through *Mersey Beat* for his own work.

"NEMS stands for the North-End Music Stores. Albert Goldman in *The Lives Of John Lennon* has NEMS standing for the Northern England Music and Electric Industries - he must be confusing it with EMI and, anyway, that would be NEMEI. If someone is writing a book, he should try and be as accurate as possible. Then again, Goldman couldn't even spell Mathew Street correctly.

"BE had a naked bulb over his desk in his Liverpool office. He said it reminded him of his humble beginnings and I said, 'Brian, you didn't have humble beginnings.' He said, 'No, but my family did.' He came from a Jewish family and he was very proud of his Jewishness, but I don't know how he avoided observing the Sabbath. I didn't see any signs of him doing that and he thought the cash registers were more important. He spoke beautifully and his voice was one of his assets. He compèred the *Hullabaloo* shows for American TV in his polite Leslie Howard voice and that's what Americans particularly like about the English.

"The Epstein's flagship was a big shop in Walton Road in the North End of Liverpool, which was run by Brian's father, Harry Epstein. In 1962 Harry told me to take down a poster advertising Little Richard, which was Brian's first promotion, as I had stuck it on the outside wall of his store. Brian told me I had been over-zealous, and I said, 'It's keeping it in the family.' He said, 'Pater doesn't want to know about NEMS Enterprises.' His family didn't approve of it and were alarmed by his involvement. This is why he had to get his younger brother, Clive on his side. Clive became a partner in NEMS Enterprises, the entrepreneurial spinoff of NEMS Ltd, and with Clive on board, he could present a united front to his parents, particularly his father. They were constantly telling him to give it up - at least, they did until he struck gold."

Beryl Adams: "Brian's parents were very nice, lovely people, but they weren't happy when he started NEMS Enterprises. It was very unusual for Brian to do this. Both Bob and Brian would mull things over before they did anything and they were both very cautious. The only thing that Brian wasn't cautious about was taking on the Beatles and that must be because they impressed him so much."

Bob Wooler: "Brian's own shop was in the centre of Liverpool in Whitechapel, and Clive's was in Great Charlotte Street, close to Lewis's and the Adelphi. Brian was the elder brother and got the bigger shop. They sold washing machines and vacuum cleaners as well as records in Whitechapel, and Brian was responsible for the lot. Peter Brown was the manager of the pop section in the basement.

"Every week Brian would put the NEMS Top Ten in his window and this was reprinted in the *Liverpool Echo*, which was clever marketing. I'm not sure that it reflected the likes of the people in Liverpool as it was purely the sales in NEMS. It could have been manipulated too as he could have included records that he wanted to shift.

"I didn't know Brian at the time, but I bought my records from NEMS because they gave me a 10% discount as I told them I was a disc-jockey. Otherwise, I would have bought them from Rushworth and Dreaper's, which was also in Whitechapel. In return for the discount, I told them that I would mention that I was playing a record that I had bought from NEMS in Whitechapel. He was getting an advertisement for less than one shilling (5p)! We got no promotional copies from the record companies. They were my own records because if they had belonged to the Cavern, I couldn't take them and play them at Aintree Institute or Litherland Town Hall. Ray McFall bought some too, mostly jazz like Kenny Ball's 'Midnight In Moscow', and he also liked Anthony Newley's 'Why', which I would dutifully play."

While the Beatles had been in Germany, they had recorded a single with Tony Sheridan of 'My Bonnie' for the Polydor label. It made No. 32 on the German charts in December 1961 and so can be regarded as the Beatles' first chart entry. Pete Best: "If my memory serves me correct, we gave a copy of 'My Bonnie' to Bob Wooler and asked him to play it, either at the Aintree Institute or Litherland Town Hall. It sounded good to hear our record coming out of the speakers alongside the American stuff." Local fans would hear the record - and want to own it. A key factor in the Beatles' story is that an 18 year old lad called Raymond Jones went into NEMS in Whitechapel in October 1961 and asked for 'My Bonnie', which would have to be imported from Germany. There are conflicting stories about what happened.

Bob Wooler: "Alistair Taylor worked for Brian Epstein at NEMS as his personal assistant. He has already written his autobiography (*Yesterday - The Beatles Remembered,* Sidgwick And Jackson, 1988) and he doesn't identify himself as Raymond Jones in that. In 1997 I went, somewhat reluctantly, to the Penny Lane Beatles Festival. Raymond Jones was listed as one of the guests, and who should stand up but Alistair Taylor and say, 'I am Raymond Jones'. It reminded me of Spartacus as I thought of standing up and saying the same thing myself. Alistair has said this publicly on several occasions since, notably on the Brian Epstein Arena special. According to Alistair, Cavernites were asking for 'My Bonnie' but Brian wouldn't order it until he had a definite order in the stock-book. Alistair said, 'It was me. I ordered the Beatles' record for Brian' and I thought, 'My god, this is getting out of hand.' Pinocchio-time, I'm afraid, and I think Alistair says it to appear more important.

"You see, I have an address book from 1963 with the entry, 'Raymond Jones, 48 Stonefield Road, Liverpool 14.' He worked at KB Print, Central 1207. I made another entry in April 1975 - 'Raymond Jones, teenage boy about 18 who in 1961 asked BE at NEMS for 'My Bonnie'.' I started another book in the late 70s and this says, 'Raymond Jones drinks in the Bull and Dog, a Greenall's pub in Ormskirk.' Liz and Jim Hughes had him as a guest when they were running the first Beatles Conventions. I met him there and I can assure you that it was not Alistair Taylor I was talking to.

"I am raking out the bones of Raymond Jones because he is a vital cog in the wheel. He got Brian Epstein interested in the Beatles. I've been in touch with Raymond Jones recently. He is married with a family and lives in a farmhouse in Spain, and he gave me a photograph of himself when he was about 18. Leather jacket, tight jeans and Beatle boots - is it any wonder that BE was enchanted by him? He was an attractive boy and I'm sure that had the record been requested by a girl, Brian would not have been interested. Nothing transpired between them, of course, but it made Brian want to seek out the group that Raymond Jones liked so much.

"In his letter to me, Raymond Jones wrote, 'The Beatles gave me so much pleasure in those days and I saw no reason to say anything derogatory against them as some of the members of the press wanted me to. Many years ago I took the decision not to take any recognition for what I did and it makes me mad to hear that other people are telling lies.' By the way, Raymond Jones should not be confused with another Raymond Jones, the Manchester boy, who played with the Dakotas."

Following Bob's revelations, I spoke to Raymond Jones myself and had him on my programme on *BBC Radio Merseyside*. He was not interested in taking part in Beatle Conventions, but he was unhappy that Alistair was claiming to be him. (To be fair, Alistair, who heard the programme, doubted his authenticity and wondered if I had set it up.) Ray owned a printing press in Burscough, which is now run by his son and daughter, and as further confirmation, they sent me a copy of a letter from NEMS in September 1964 in which Brian's secretary, Diana Vero, was writing to one of Raymond's friends for his address so that he could be sent Brian's book.

Raymond Jones has seen a feature in the *Mail On Sunday* based on Sam Leach's memoirs. Sam Leach claimed he was the one who told Brian about the Beatles, but Brian didn't want to acknowledge Sam's presence. Sam says,"If I was the reason Brian went to see the lads for the first time, he would never have admitted it. He would invent a fictitious character instead and my own opinion is that Raymond Jones was a figment of Brian's imagination."

Raymond Jones: "I saw them every dinnertime at the Cavern and they were fantastic. I had never heard anything like them. Everybody had been listening to Lonnie Donegan and Cliff Richard and they were so different. A friend of mine, Ron Billingsley, had a motorbike and we would follow them all over the place - Hambleton Hall, Aintree Institute and Knotty Ash Village Hall."

And how did he come to be talking to Brian Epstein? "I used to go to NEMS every Saturday and I would be buying records by Carl Perkins and Fats Domino because I heard the Beatles playing their songs. My sister's ex-husband, Kenny Johnson, who played with Mark Peters and the Cyclones, told me that the Beatles had made a record and so I went to NEMS to get it. Brian Epstein said to me, 'Who are they?' and I said, 'They are the most fantastic group you will ever hear.' No one will take away from me that it was me who spoke to Brian Epstein and then he went to the Cavern to see them for himself. I didn't make them famous, but Brian Epstein made them famous and things might have been different without me."

Bob Wooler: "Brian Epstein learnt that the Beatles were playing close to his shop in Whitechapel. He was intrigued to see what they were like and he phoned Bill Harry at *Mersey Beat* and asked him to smooth his entrance into the Cavern. Bill arranged this with Ray McFall and with Pat Delaney on the door. On 9 November 1961, Brian took his PA, Alistair Taylor, along for support and they stood at the back of the crowd and heard John, Paul, George and Pete on stage, although they can't have seen much. Nevertheless, Brian was bowled over by them.

"It was very fortunate that when Brian saw the Beatles for the first time, they gave a good performance in friendly surroundings at the Cavern. Only a couple of weeks earlier, I went with the Beatles to the Albany Cinema in Maghull for a charity show for St. John's Ambulance Brigade. It was cold as Leslie Blond had no heating in the cinema and the bill consisted of tenors, ventriloquists and jugglers, with Ken Dodd at the top of the bill. The Beatles were out of place and should never have been there, and Paul McCartney later admitted to Ken Dodd that they were dreadful that day. The show was organised by Jim Gretty who worked across the road from NEMS at the instrument store, Frank Hessy's. He was the kingpin at Hessy's and he would demonstrate 'Guitar Boogie Shuffle' in the shop to all budding guitarists. Jim might easily have given Brian tickets for the show and, if he had, his views on the Beatles would have been quite different.

"A few days after that concert, I'd been drinking with the Beatles in the afternoon and we got to Litherland Town Hall, where Gerry and the Pacemakers were also on. Gerry had had a few as well and everybody was in a merry, outgoing mood. I thought, 'Ah, we've got the Beatles, we've got the Pacemakers, we should have the Beatmakers.' It was a wide stage and it could have worked well but they larked around too much. They did a few numbers like 'Hit The Road Jack', swopping instruments and the like. John Lennon was on Les Maguire's sax and at one stage, he was lying on his back under the piano. Brian Kelly was fraught with anxiety over it, but the audience liked it. It was a bit of a shambles really, so I lowered the curtain on the proceedings."

The fact that the Beatles and the Pacemakers never repeated their Beatmakers combination suggests that Bob is correct in calling it a shambles, but Gerry Marsden disagrees, "You sometimes do something spontaneously and you know it won't work if you do it again. It worked very well as we all knew the same songs and all played the same songs. Paul, John and I took turns on the piano and Les played the sax. We did 'Roll Over Beethoven', 'Johnny B. Goode', 'Great Balls Of Fire', 'Pretend', 'Blueberry Hill', 'I'm Walkin'' and 'Sweet Little Sixteen', probably some others too. We didn't pay PRS on the songs though. I don't remember filling in many forms in those days."

Bob Wooler: "It was fortunate that Brian saw a good performance when he came down to the Cavern that lunchtime. He knew straight away that he wanted to manage them, but he didn't rush in as he needed a getting-to-know-you period first. He went to a couple of other venues to see what they were like and how they behaved, and he found them very animalistic. They were unkempt, they didn't comb their hair - and, most importantly, they were lithe and physically attractive."

Paddy Delaney, the doorman at the Cavern: "I remember Brian Epstein coming down to the Cavern to a lunchtime session. He was very well-groomed in a smart, dark blue suit and looked out of place. When it was all over, he was still hanging about, so I approached him and said, 'It's all over now, sir.' He said, 'It's all right, I'm going to meet the Beatles.'"

Bob Wooler: "After one lunchtime session, the Beatles and I repaired to the Grapes - it was three o'clock closing then - and they told me that Brian Epstein wanted to see them with a view to securing a recording contract and even managing them, but they were very dubious. People had said to them over the years, 'I will manage you and do this, that and the other', and it was all promises, promises. They asked me to go with them to NEMS to suss him out. It was very embarrassing because we were late and it was half-day closing. They knocked on the glass door and it looked as though he had gone, but he came up from the basement and unlocked the door. The introductions were made at the Classical counter on the ground floor. I should have done the intros but I didn't because I felt uncomfortable as I was only there as an advisor. John came to the rescue and said, 'This is me dad', which I resented, by the way. I was older than him, but surely I didn't look that much older. Epstein was bewildered by all this and he didn't want to say anything about management whilst this outsider was there. He was very nice and very polite, but he arranged another meeting when 'Dad' wouldn't be there. At that first meeting, he asked about 'My Bonnie', and said he was in a position to import copies if he was sure it would sell enough to be worthwhile.

"Brian Epstein made the Beatles PR conscious: he would say, 'Don't smoke on stage' and things like that. I was very pleased that they stopped smoking on stage as I didn't like it myself. He had no difficulty persuading Paul as he knew instinctively how a band should behave on stage, but John was a rebel and George could be difficult. I did my bit. I shall never forget the Sunday night that followed an abortive night in Aldershot for Sam Leach in December 1961. They had lost heart because there were only a dozen people in Aldershot to see them and I blame Sam Leach for not promoting it vigorously. If you haven't got the organisation to promote something 200 miles away, then it is better not to do it at all. I had them booked at Hambleton Hall the following night, and where the hell were they? They did finally turn up and played the last 15 minutes before the dance ended. They still got paid their £15, but I did lambast them in the dressing-room. I said, 'You mustn't do things like this, you mustn't allow one booking to affect another.'

"The Beatles got more bookings as a result of their association with Brian Epstein. I was DJ'ing at the Majestic in Conway Street in Birkenhead which opened in Easter '62. Bill Marsden was the manager and I told him that he should have the Beatles. Brian drove me across and they retired to the Conway Arms pub right opposite the Majestic and then I went and joined them. Bill said, 'What a charming guy. I didn't expect a rock'n'roll person to be like this.' What Brian had learnt at RADA was coming to the fore and he knew how to present himself to get business. The Beatles went into the Majestic and did fantastic business.

"Brian Epstein was fond of giving away bottles of Johnnie Walker whisky. He gave one to the journalist, George Harrison of the Over The Mersey Wall column in the *Liverpool Echo*, to secure a mention of the Beatles, and George accepted it gladly it as it was Operation Elbow with him. Of course, George milked having the same name as a Beatle for all it was worth. When Brian came out with a bottle for the manager of the Queen's Hall, Widnes, the manager's face dropped and he said, 'I'm sorry, I can't accept this. This is a Methodist Hall, and we restrict all alcohol on the premises. I hope there is no liquor backstage on your presentations.' To his credit, Brian made a very quick recovery, 'No, of course not. There's nothing like that.' Brian said afterwards, 'What do you think of that?', and I said, 'It's a pity to waste Johnnie Walker.' He said, rather like a naughty schoolboy, 'Then we'll have one backstage.'

"BE hired the Cavern on a Tuesday night in April 1962 and it was for the Beatles to thank their fans and they had the Four Jays as their guests. Because it was a special night, they asked me to sing with them and I said no. On the other hand, Ray McFall did two songs with them - the Elvis song, 'Can't Help Falling In Love', and the title song of the film, *Tender Is The Night*, which had been recorded by Vic Damone. The Beatles played a few chords behind him and the audience dutifully applauded. He had a good voice and he did well." I asked Ray McFall about this, "I don't think that this has ever been mentioned before, but it's true. It was good fun but I should have stuck to the one song that they knew. The second song was an unwise choice, but how could they refuse me? I owned the club."

Bob Wooler: "Brian was always testing the water. Barry Miles' *The Beatles - A Diary* has this entry: '25th July 1962 - Cabaret Club, Liverpool. A failed attempt by Brian Epstein to get the Beatles into the lounge club circuit. The audience hated the Beatles. The Beatles hated the audience.' That's not true. Brian Epstein was trying out a scene which wasn't really the Beatles' scene. The club featured a quartet who could read music and accompany acts like Shirley Bassey, Danny Williams and the Southlanders, but the patrons didn't complain or throw things at the Beatles. The Beatles bowed at the end, and true, it wasn't rapturous applause, but I wouldn't regard it as a failure.

"Brian Epstein's main objective was to get the Beatles a recording contract. He felt that if he could do that, everything else would follow. He didn't have much luck at first and the Beatles were impatient. This impatience for overnight success was typical of all the groups. I remember phoning the Who's management in London called New Action, only to be greeted by someone announcing No Action. They all wanted things to happen instantly.

"I was the shoulder, as it were, for Brian Epstein to lament on. Following a Cavern midday session, he would invite me for lunch to the Peacock in nearby Hackins Hey, and he would say, 'What am I doing wrong? Why aren't the record companies responding?' All I could say was, 'I can't believe it, Brian. They should come and see what the Beatles are doing to audiences.' In those days, the A&R men didn't hurry to a provincial town to see a group. It was different once the Beatles happened - we had a rush of Artistes & Repertoire men, that is, the record producers, up here. Brian was so disappointed but he was persistent and determined to make a breakthrough.

"Brian realised that he had to prove his worth by securing a proper contract for the group with a major label which could guarantee national distribution. John lost his patience with him from time to time, which didn't help matters. Then he made in-roads with Dick James and George Martin. To get the Beatles on EMI with a recording manager who was prepared to promote them was a tremendous achievement.

"Small-time hicksville local labels are okay for a group's ego, enabling them to say that they are a recording act, but so what? The record is seldom heard in London where it needs to be heard by media people. I often impressed upon groups the vital need for a record to get as much exposure as possible - there wasn't even local radio in Liverpool until 1967. In respect of promoting unknown and regional groups, John Peel has been particularly outstanding. So many beginners owe him a lot of gratitude for his help and encouragement.

"People talk about Dick Rowe at Decca missing the boat but I can understand it. He was of a certain generation and he was at heart resentful of rock'n'roll groups. Jack Baverstock at Fontana was the same. When the Beatles happened, Dick Rowe rescued the situation by signing the Rolling Stones. It must have hurt him immensely to sign a group that was more outrageous than the Beatles. By then the Beatles were cosy people due to the Epstein influence.

"Dick Rowe wasn't the only one to turn down the Beatles as Epstein had been desperate to get them a recording contract, and Decca did at least arrange an audition. What about the music publishers, Ardmore and Beechwood, who missed the boat through indifference? They published the Beatles' first single, 'Love Me Do' / 'P.S. I Love You', which only dented the charts. That was sufficient to encourage George Martin to persevere with them, and then Dick James moved in. He was the sole publisher of the next record and the next one was a Northern song, which was a company set up by the two of them, Dick James and Brian Epstein. To make matters worse, Ardmore and Beechwood was an EMI company, so they missed out on a fortune.

Brian Epstein was responsible for many of the changes in the Beatles and yet, oddly, he encouraged them to use their normal accents - indeed, they played up their Scouse diction on occasion. Bob Wooler: "Brian Epstein never spoke to me about their accents. He gave them their head in that regard, although I'm sure he didn't say, 'Pile on the accent, you're doing great.' Cilla Black came from Scotland Road and I do remember him saying, ''We'll have to improve her appearance and the way she talks.' In the end, her accent has been her key to success. Cilla's mother had a stall in Paddy's Market in Great Homer Street and, once she was successful, Cilla relocated her to millionaire's row in Woolton, so I wonder if she was happy there. She was very down to earth and didn't want to lose her friends from Scotland Road. She would chastise Cilla if she stayed out late. A parent wouldn't dare do that now.

"Anyway, as soon as the Beatles started singing, everything was Americanised: listen to the way Paul sings the word 'half' in 'I'm not half the man I used to be', which is not the way he spoke. The 'Can't' in 'Can't Buy Me Love', is another example.

"Brian put the Beatles into suits and he liked the idea of a Beatle haircut. Joe Flannery carries a photograph of his mother and says, 'Look at her haircut. John liked my mother and copied her hairstyle.' It's not impossible, but you could just as easily say it came from watching the *Three Stooges*. My theory is that Stu and Astrid saw the Peter Pan statue by George Frampton in Sefton Park. This was erected in 1928 and Peter Pan has a Beatle haircut, a Beatle bob if you like. She gave Stu that haircut and the rest followed on from that. That is certainly as tenable as Joe's theory. I think it is Joe, and not Alice, who is in Wonderland.

"Brian could never fully control John and I would love to know the full story of his marriage to Cynthia. Cynthia was pregnant and it would have been very bad publicity for the group if John had fathered an illegitimate child. They did get married and I suspect that it was Aunt Mimi insisting John did the right thing. Cynthia came from Hoylake and I never met her parents but if they were of the same mind, John would have found it hard to refuse. When they got married, Brian let them use his flat in Falkner Street, which curtailed his own activities.

"Let me give an example of John's behaviour, or rather misbehaviour. The setting is the Blue Angel and Paul McCartney is upstairs talking to some press people, while in the basement is John Lennon shooting his mouth off, well away with drink or whatever. He said, 'Hitler should have finished the job', meaning that the gas ovens should have been more active than they were. Brian was Jewish and I prevailed upon him to be quiet because the press were upstairs but he didn't take any notice of me. I told Paul that John was shooting his mouth off and that the press must not get wind of it. That was an example of John's indifference. He enjoyed the danger associated with his remarks, and later on he did say 'We're more popular than Jesus now.' It's on the cards that he made the Hitler remark to Brian's face as John was quite merciless about other people's feelings. He had no diplomacy, he left that to Paul, and he would come straight out with what he wanted to say. Oddly enough, I found that one of the more likeable things about John, and it's difficult not to agree with his remark about being more popular than Jesus."

I wanted to know about Brian's personality - his anger, his gambling, his drug-taking and his homsexuality. It took some time to get information from Bob, at times he felt he was betraying a confidence, but I have been able to piece something together. Often the best insights into the Epstein family were his anecdotes of their everday life. "The Epsteins had a luxurious detached house in Queen's Drive and when I had a Sunday lunch with him and Clive once, they had a maid waiting on them. I had always been taught to eat quietly and I was on my best behaviour. I also knew that from watching films that you spooned the soup away from yourself. I am not saying they were using a labourer's technique but I noticed that they were very noisy eaters. The main course was oxtail, and they chomped away at it. The meal was very nice indeed. I am sure that they discussed my table manners when I left."

But first, Brian's anger. "Brian wasn't always polite and I have seen him very angry. I saw him livid, foaming at the mouth, as it were, with one of his employees, Peter Brown, in his office in NEMS. I felt very uncomfortable, but Brian didn't tell me to leave. Brown said he wanted another meeting with Clive present as well, someone to arbitrate as it were, but I don't know what the row was all about. Peter Brown flounced off, and he was like Brian in that respect. They were both RADA flouncers.

"Brian was a considerable gambler: there was not much of a gambling scene in Liverpool then, but he was often in the Odd Spot. I can't tell you much about this as he knew I didn't approve of gambling. He gambled a lot, but always within his means. I don't want to make him sound like the Cincinnati Kid.

"Also, I don't want to give the impression that Brian was a drug addict, but, as he became more involved in the business, he was popping Prellies, Purple Hearts and God knows what else. He'd take anything, especially if the Beatles had them. They'd say, 'Come on, Bri, be one of the lads, you're too stuffy.' The pills didn't make him incapable but sometimes you could see the lesions in his eyes. Still, the drug scene was comparatively low-key in Liverpool, and was nothing like what he experienced in London. Later on, I'm sure Brian took cocaine, LSD and heroin because he wanted to be seen as 'one of the lads'.

Brian Epstein's gayness is undoubtedly a factor in the attraction of the Beatles. "The fact that he was on the opposite side of the street was very important when it came to signing the Beatles and other artists to his empire. I'm sure Brian was attracted to the Beatles physically when he first saw them, and then he became aware of the music. Their vocal harmonies were fantastic and McCartney was the outstanding bass player on Merseyside - Paul admitted that Johnny Gustafson of the Big Three had the edge on him, but they both were exceptional. Initially though, it was those four figures on stage that captivated him. I will never forget him being transfixed at the New Brighton Tower as he looked at John Lennon singing 'Baby It's You': I was talking with him but he wasn't listening, he was on Cloud Nine. It was both the message of the song and the person that attracted him.

"I also remember Brian being in one of his transfixed states when Tommy Quickly was on stage at the Queen's Hall, Widnes. He said, 'Isn't he marvellous, Bob?' and although I couldn't see that ingredient myself, I dutifully said yes. 'I think I'll manage him', said the Nemperor, and out went Tommy's twin sister, Pat, and his group, the Challengers. Nothing must interfere with Tommy, and he put him on Beatles tours backed by the Remo Four. Tommy got into the charts with a country song, 'The Wild Side Of Life' and how prophetic that turned out to be as he went on the wild side of life. Tommy was given some marvellous exposure but it was to no avail, and Brian dropped him because he hated failure."

Paddy Delaney, the doorman at the Cavern, seized the opportunity whilst Bob was with Epstein: "I learned a lot from Bob, just by watching him, but there came a time when he was so wrapped up with Brian Epstein that Bob would ask me to change the groups over for him. That is, take one group from the stage, play a couple of records, and announce the next group. I became quite adept at this and I used to enjoy Bob's disappearing act. Bob had been Ray McFall's general - he did the graft and he had the brainwork and the know-how - and now he was doing the same for Brian Epstein."

Bob Wooler: "BE said he was intrigued about Mark Peters because of what I'd written about him in *Mersey Beat*. I had written that Mark Peters could succeed on looks alone, so Brian said, 'Any chance of seeing him? Where does he play?', and I thought, 'Oh my god, he's thinking of another conquest.' As far as I know, he only had one homosexual among his artists. He was one of the Midnighters and they got on so badly together that the group left him very quickly.

"The Beatles never complained about Brian's behaviour and I am in two minds as to whether there was a physical side to the John Lennon and Brian Epstein relationship. George Harrison told me this story in all innocence and yet there was a dark side to the whole thing. Epstein had taken George to the detached house his family had just past Childwall Five Ways in Queen's Drive. There was just the two of them and he was showing him round the house: 'And this, George, is the bedroom' and so on. He wasn't showing off but he was saying, 'This is what I want for you, George. I want you to have a standard of living that you and the other Beatles have never had in your council houses.' It wasn't to get George, attractive George, into the bedroom etc etc etc. Well, Clive Epstein arrives unexpectedly and there was absolute hell because there was only one thing that occurred to Clive. The Beatles hadn't taken off and here was Brian with a boy in a house on his own. It was raised voices and slammed doors, and the Nemperor, who was shaking all over, got into his car and sped away with George alongside him - George couldn't drive at that time - he was the first of the Beatles to drive by the way, no doubt his father, being a bus driver, showed him how. The payoff line is amusing. George said, 'He shouldn't have said those things to you, Brian. After all, he is younger than you.' At that time, and I don't think it applies now, a younger brother respected an older brother. George was the younger brother in his family and he showed his brothers some respect. But the argument had nothing to do with the fact that Clive was younger than Brian, it was as though Brian had been caught in flagrante delicto, it was though he had bedded him, 'What are you doing bringing boys home?' Brian did have a reputation that the Epsteins had to live down."

Unknown to his family, Brian had a flat in Falkner Street for his conquests. "Homosexuality was illegal and you could go to prison and worse;" said Joe Flannery in the Arena documentary, you might be carted off to the 'loony bin', as he put it, at Rainhill. Bob Wooler: "The dangerous element must have had some appeal to BE, and I do remember a banner headline in the *Daily Express* about a young Lord who owned vintage cars down south being on a 'serious charge' with a couple of boy scouts. Cliff Richard made a film called *Serious Charge* in 1959 and the nature of the serious charge, which was homosexuality, was never explicitly mentioned in the film.

"*Victim* in 1961 was one of the first British films to deal properly and thoughtfully with the subject. Dirk Bogarde welcomed the opportunity to play the homosexual barrister, and there were some very tense scenes between him and his wife, Sylvia Syms. In one scene, Dirk Bogarde lifts his garage door at the back of the mews to discover that someone has painted graffiti about him on the wall. The Beatles were sitting together at a Cavern lunchtime session and John Lennon, who was talking to Paul and George, was making biting remarks about *Victim*, which was on at the Odeon. I knew by then that Brian was what he was, and I thought, 'Well, I am surprised at John, who is 21 and a young man of the world.' He was making such nasty, puritanical observations, but I never said anything as they didn't know that I was listening.

"I didn't see much of this side of Brian Epstein's life myself as I didn't move in his circle of friends, which was the Liverpool Playhouse crowd. Brian used to go to the Cavern with a girl, but she was a smokescreen as Brian wasn't interested in having a relationship with her. I'm sure that Brian was much more outrageous with the Playhouse crowd, and they gravitated to the Magic Clock, which was a pub opposite the Royal Court, and the other pubs around Williamson Square, where the fruit market was. I went into the Magic Clock once, and I was very nervous and hoped I wasn't going to be seen. It was very difficult, as I was dealing with teenagers at the Cavern and it wouldn't have looked right to be there. It was known affectionately as the Magic Cock and it was run by a woman whose boyfriend was a copper, who must have known it was a liaison place for homosexuals.

"Brian liked the theatre and I remember him recommending *Chips With Everything* at the Royal Court to me, but I was too tied up with the Cavern at the time. He told me that the Arnold Wesker play was fantastic, but it wasn't the chips that Brian was interested in - it was the chaps. The play was about young men in the RAF.

"Brian never discussed his sexuality with me, but I should add a proviso here. He did tell me once that he was in a limousine in New York with a TV in it: that was nothing to New Yorkers, but it was quite something for us. He said, 'I saw you on television in this limo', and I groaned as I hate anyone to talk about my appearances. I had featured in a documentary film for Jewel's Power production in Liverpool called *The Rockin' City* and it was terrible, I didn't like it at all. I don't know how long he was in the car, but he said, 'They also showed *The Leather Boys*'. That was a British film made in 1963 with Rita Tushingham and Colin Campbell. Colin Campbell befriends a merchant seaman who had fallen in love with him and right at the end there's a dénouement. He goes into the pub full of queens, and he walks out in a state of disillusionment. There are no fisticuffs, no beating up of the people in the pub which is what John Wayne would do. It was a marvellous sad ending, which reminded me of Tchaikovsky's Pathetiqué. Brian brought this up, he didn't know that I had seen the film and I thought, 'That's the nearest you've ever got to talk with me about homosexuality.' It was an example, as Oscar Wilde put it, of a love that cannot speak its name. When Brian Epstein went to London, the *New Musical Express* made a reference on its Alley Cat back page to his autobiography and called it *A Cellarful Of Boys* instead of *A Cellarful Of Noise*, which can't have pleased him. Considering some of the the things he says in that book, *A Cellarful Of Salt* would have been a better title. Considering the number of times, I had to turn down requests from groups to appear at the Cavern, I should call mine *A Cellarful Of No's*."

Bob admired BE's commercial mind. "BE's favourite Beatles record was always their latest release. He was a very shrewd businessman who never missed giving his artists a plug. He had the ability to become a Richard Branson if he had set his mind to it, but he didn't. He had his demons. Most of us have demons that prevent us doing all we want to do in life. Brian Epstein's career can be seen as a huge success story, the red carpet came out for him everywhere, but he could have done so much more without his demon. And his demon was semen."

The Peter Pan statue in Sefton Park

Raymond Jones (1962) above and
Alistair Taylor (1996) below.

Bob with artist Tony Brown at the unveiling of Tony's portrait of Brian Epstein. Neptune Theatre, Liverpool, 1999.

Presenting . . . .
KINGSIZE TAYLOR
AND THE DOMINOES
WITH SWINGING CILLA

S. K. HARDIE   GRE 2363.
D. LOVELADY   WAT 4538.

J. DULGARN,
61 GLASSONBY CRESCENT,
WEST DERBY, LIVERPOOL 11.

Portrait of Brian Epstein by Tony Brown, 1999

NEMS Enterprises present
LITTLE RICHARD AT THE TOWER
Friday 12 October 1962

1 The Merey Beats
2 The Four Jays
3 Billy Kramer with the Coasters
4 The Big Three
5 Lee Curtis with the All Stars
6 THE BEATLES
7 LITTLE RICHARD
8 Pete Maclaine with the Dakotas
9 The Undertakers
10 Rory Storm and The Hurricanes
11 Gus Travis and the Midnighters

& The groups will be introduced, and the entire stage presentation by BOB WOOLER

16 ODD MAN - OUT
Sacking of Pete Best - The new drummer - First Parlophone single -
Merseyside bookings

*"Bestie on the drums was the big attraction. He was such a good-
looking bloke that the girls would go crazy about him."*
(Wally Hill, promoter, 2002)

Because Bob Wooler was so close to all parties in the drama, I suspected that he had
unique and invaluable views on the sacking of Pete Best. Bob Wooler: "During 1962,
Brian got them onto the BBC's Light Programme, which was a big achievement at the
time although it seems paltry and routine in relation to what happened later. NEMS
even organised a coach trip to Manchester for the recording. And then came the
contract with EMI. And the sacking of Pete Best."

Bob saw some of the tension between Pete Best and the rest of the Beatles. "The
Beatles used to play the Cavern at lunchtimes and sometimes they would stay behind
and rehearse, and just myself and the cleaners would hear them. One day I came back
from the Grapes about ten past three and the Beatles were rehearsing. Paul was showing
Pete Best how he wanted the drums to be played for a certain tune and I thought, 'That's
pushing it a bit.' At times Pete would be like a zombie on the drums: it was as though
he was saying, 'Do I have to do this?', and that went against him with Paul McCartney,
who was all for communication. Pete had no show about him - he always looked bored
- but he certainly came alive for photo sessions as he was very photogenic."

I wondered what Bob Wooler knew of the events of 16 August 1962, the day on which
Pete Best was sacked. "The Beatles had a recording contract at last, but George Martin
had expressed some doubts about Pete Best's ability and that, I think, was the deciding
factor - an important voice in the record industry didn't rate him. On 15 August, the
night before it happened, Brian Epstein told me that Pete Best was going to be sacked.
I could imagine it with someone who was constantly late or giving him problems, but
Pete Best was not awkward and he didn't step out of line. I was most indignant and I
said, 'Why are you doing this?' but I didn't get an answer.

"It was very wrong of the Beatles to suggest on the *Anthology* video that Pete Best was
unreliable - well, they didn't suggest it, they stated it and it is absolute rubbish to say
that. The most unreliable Beatle was Paul McCartney, who had the worst punctuality
record, although he was not consistently late for engagements. I saw him on TV saying

that Stevie Wonder was unreliable, he turned up late for the recording of 'Ebony And Ivory', and I thought, 'Look who's talking.' I would say to Paul at Aintree Institute, 'You've missed the middle spot and you'll have to go on last', which is going home time. He'd say, 'Sorry, I was busy writing a song.' That didn't impress me at the time as I had a show to put on. John, surprisingly, was quite dutiful. Maybe Aunt Mimi was the one behind him, telling him to get out of the house.

"The relationship between Brian Epstein and Pete's mother, Mona, is also a factor. I am reminded of Neil Kinnock and Margaret Thatcher and how they clashed in the 80s. Kinnock would say in despair, 'Oh, that woman' after an encounter with her. Brian Epstein would do the same, he would say, 'That woman', meaning Mona Best, 'She's driving me crazy', and they never got on well. She was very strong and he was also strong, and she felt that Pete wasn't getting a fair crack of the whip. For one thing, she felt he should be given more vocals."

What about the accusation that Pete Best was a poor drummer? "Well, it makes you wonder who is a good drummer as Ringo Starr wasn't used on the first record. Pete was with them for two years and although I saw Paul instructing him that time, I never heard them complaining about him. It is difficult to comment further as I was an outsider looking in."

Nevertheless, Bob wanted to write about the split in *Mersey Beat.* "I was having drinks with Brian and Ted Knibbs, who managed Billy Kramer, at the New Cabaret Club and I told BE that I was going to tell the whole story in Mersey Beat. Brian got very annoyed and walked out. Ted, who was older and wiser than me, said that I should make it up with him. He said, 'You've made your Declaration of Independence, and that's enough.' I was going to write an article called Odd Man - Out but it never materialised and I regret that very much. The piece that appeared in *Mersey Beat*, and not written by me but Bill Harry, said it was an amicable split, which shows the influence that Brian Epstein was having on the scene. Brian was manipulating him. I don't think he would have threatened Bill with taking his ads away, but none of us liked offending Brian. We were all charmed by him.

"BE felt guilty about firing Pete Best when it wasn't really his doing, but he was not prepared to sacrifice a recording contract with a major company for the sake of keeping Pete in the group, so he went along with it. He felt so guilty that he offered Best a role with another group under his auspices, the Merseybeats. Pete Best and his mother were so inflamed by what had happened that they wanted nothing more to do with him, which is what Brian was probably counting on. That is when Joe Flannery stepped in and put Pete with Joe's brother in Lee Curtis and the All Stars, which was a very good move on his part.

"The Beatles didn't want a new drummer who would be a force to be reckoned with and hence, Johnny Hutchinson of the Big Three didn't stand a chance. Trevor Morais of Faron's Flamingos was also considered but he was a centre of attraction and front-line singers like Faron didn't care for his showmanship. He later had chart success with a very good jazz-rock trio, the Peddlers. Also in the running were Bill Buck from Dale Roberts and the Jaywalkers, Bobby Graham from Joe Brown's Bruvvers, and Tony Mansfield from the Dakotas - Tony is also of the faith so maybe he was Brian's suggestion. Apparently, there was another name in the frame, one that was certainly news to me. When Mike McCartney was interviewed by Libby Purves on *BBC Radio 4* in 1992, he said he would have become the Beatles' new drummer if only he hadn't broken his arm. I'd never heard that one before and I suspect he is doing an Alistair.

"I'm making it sound as though there were lots of drummers in the frame but that isn't true as so many of them would have been unacceptable. So many of the groups had drummers who would hammer on the drums and I would say, 'Haven't you heard of light and shade?' I would tell them that Gene Krupa drummed on a matchbox in one of the films.

"Most drummers are bombastic and certainly Johnny Hutch put the frighteners up BE. Ritchie Galvin was temperamental too and he would argue over anything with Lance Railton in the TT's. The rest of the group would laugh about them. On the other hand, both Aynsley Dunbar and Roy Dyke were shy and retiring. Aynsley became a very respected avant-garde drummer with Frank Zappa, but he hadn't got those peculiarities when I knew him.

"The Beatles wanted a very good drummer who would not intrude and Ringo played that role very well indeed. No-one notices the finer points of drumming technique as you're falling for the voice or the image, because that is what it's all about. AIM - Attitude, Image, Music - and in that order. AIM is the name of the game, as far as I can see.

"Ringo was playing with Rory Storm and the Hurricanes in Skegness so he wasn't available straightaway. The Beatles did a show with me at the Riverpark Ballroom in Chester with Johnny Hutch sitting in as their drummer, and they were all so quiet - Hutch knew why he was there and they knew how I felt about it as I was very disgruntled. They came to life when the mikes were on but my memories of that night are dire. They didn't explain what had gone on - those who knew them would assume that Pete was indisposed."

Beryl Adams worked as Brian Epstein's secretary: "I had no idea that Pete was going to be sacked - nothing had been building up as far as I could see - and I was shocked to come back from holiday and find out what had been happening. I had called in the shop on the Saturday and Brian said, 'Beryl, are you doing anything tonight?' and he invited me for a meal and said that we would then go and see the Beatles with Ringo at Hulme Hall in Port Sunlight. It was his first appearance with them and it was amazing to watch - half the girls were crying hysterically and half of them were happy because it was Ringo. Bob was very upset about it because he was very fond of Pete."

Bob Wooler: "When Ringo joined them, George got a black eye from a disgruntled fan at the Cavern. They recorded two numbers at the Cavern for Granada TV on 22 August 1962. The sound engineer ran me off an acetate of 'Some Other Guy' and 'Kansas City', and he gave another to Ray McFall and a couple to Brian Epstein. I kept mine in my box of records and I should have been more careful. When the Beatles became famous, the record disappeared. In 1993, a copy turned up at Christie's and was sold for £15,000, but I don't know if it was my copy and anyway, I couldn't prove it if it was.

"The Beatles were asked to record a Mitch Murray song, 'How Do You Do It' for their first single. I've heard their demo and Lennon does it very well. Maybe they rejected it because they hadn't got a piece of the songwriting action, but Epstein must have felt confident in allowing them to turn it down. George Martin and Dick James were pushing for the Mitch Murray song, and Epstein told them that he had signed a perky personality à la Tommy Steele, who was perfect for the song. 'How Do You Do It' was thrust upon Gerry, who, initially at least, was easier to handle than the Beatles, who were very strong-minded. He was the perfect choice for the song and it was a No. 1 record.

"A&R men are very powerful so George Martin could have put his foot down and insisted that the Beatles did 'How Do You Do It' for their first single. Wasn't it remarkable that he gave them their head, and the Beatles then blossomed under his guidance? George had simply wanted rock'n'rollers, Parlophone's answer to Columbia's Cliff Richard, and he got so much more instead.

"Brian Epstein signed the Beatles at the end of 1961 and 'Love Me Do', their own composition, was released in October 1962. We know now that John and Paul were writing a lot of songs, if not performing them on stage, and I did see something of that. One day in 1961 the Beatles did the Cavern lunchtime session and afterwards we went to drink at the Mandolin which was an old cinema in Windsor Street, just outside the city centre, run by Harry the Pole. John sat on a settee with a girl in the club, and Paul went over to the upright piano on stage and played a song. When he came across to where I was sitting, he said it was called 'Suicide', and I told him that was a strange and uncommercial title for a song." (*In Many Years From Now*, Paul McCartney recalls how Frank Sinatra asked him for a song and he sent him 'Suicide'. "He thought it was an almighty piss-take," Paul recalls, "I think he sent the demo back.")

"Incidentally, the first single credits the songs to 'McCartney - Lennon'. McCartney's name came first and I can't see him surrendering to Lennon all that easily. Was he resentful when it became 'Lennon - McCartney', how did Brian sell it to him, and why? Certainly 'Lennon - McCartney' sounds better than 'McCartney - Lennon', although Paul wouldn't agree with that.

"If Lennon and McCartney had not been songwriters, they would have been little more than just another group. They would have been an exceptional group but they would not have enjoyed such fame. It's down to those two really, and this must have rankled George. Ringo just regarded himself as lucky - and he was really. They allowed an outsider to come in at a late stage and he received the same cut as them for their performances, which was very generous.

"Ringo would run me home to Garston after a session at the Blue Angel as he was one of the few people to have a car, although I don't think he had a licence! Freddie Starr certainly drove around without a licence, but lots of people did then. Most of Rory Storm's groups had cars, and I used to talk to Ringo a lot when he was with the Hurricanes. When he joined the Beatles, he couldn't believe that a manager was setting up the dates for them. The drummers usually had the worst lot, they would be packing up their gear while the others were at the pub and I'd be telling them to move quickly for the changeover. I wanted it all done in ten minutes or four records.

"When 'Love Me Do' was released, no-one in the media knew anything about the Beatles. EMI issued a monthly newspaper, *Record Mail*, to promote their products and they ran a story on the Beatles based on my article in *Mersey Beat*. Brian Epstein had given them that article. They described me as 'a Liverpool critic', and quoted certain parts of it. For the next single, 'Please Please Me', EMI asked Brian Matthew to write something as they were more established then.

"Brian Kelly told me that Epstein had bought 'Love Me Do' into the charts. He was biting and nasty about it but then he wasn't a very affable person. He said that Eppy had bought 10,000 records and he added, 'They're upstairs in NEMS in those vacant offices.' I said, 'Really? Next time I go there, I must do a bit of spying.' I didn't see them but that doesn't mean he didn't do that. If you study the charts, that single yo-yoed, 17 from nowhere and then it disappeared quickly. It was a bewildering movement, which gives support to Kelly's theory. We know that there was jiggery-pokery with the charts around that time as it all came out later, and BE could have been part of it. Over the years, I have been an innocent saying, 'Oh no, that can't be right', but Epstein may have been manipulating things.

"In order to push the single, Brian promoted a concert through NEMS Enterprises with Ray McFall at the Liverpool Empire on Sunday 28 October 1962. Neil Brooks, the manager of the Empire, was very much against it. He said, 'I don't make my hall available to any Tom, Dick or Harry.' Brian added Little Richard, Craig Douglas and Sounds Incorporated to the bill and he changed his mind. The Beatles had to back Craig Douglas but that didn't bother them as they sometimes performed 'Take Good Care Of My Baby' and 'I Remember You', and Craig Douglas' hits weren't much different.

"We had decent audiences, but I don't know how much Brian papered the house. When you've two houses, you can't allow the show to overrun and it is a tight schedule. Sounds Incorporated, who were backing Little Richard, wanted to do their own spot, and Brian said to me, 'Sort it out, but the Beatles have got to do 12 minutes.' I could hardly tell Little Richard to do four minutes' less, and why should Sounds Incorporated give up their time for an unknown group?

"Neil Brooks, the manager of the Empire, was laying down the law. Because of the Lord's Day Observance Society, he told Little Richard that he wasn't to wear makeup. People think that David Bowie and Sweet were the first rock artists to wear makeup, but Little Richard was doing it back in 1957. Neil Brooks went to the London Palladium and subsequently had the audacity to say, 'I put the Beatles on at the Empire in their early days. I knew they were going to be stars.' He'd never heard of them at the time and he didn't think that on the night.

"George Harrison was the baby of the group and he was given the job of opening the Beatles' set. He didn't like the idea of the curtains opening on him singing 'Glad All Over' and he was shaking all over. He was, after all, playing the Empire, the biggest theatre in Liverpool. Two thousand people at the Empire didn't bother John as he couldn't see them. He didn't wear his spectacles on stage and he didn't switch to contact lenses, so in many respects he was a traditionalist. He became more adventurous as the years went by. He thought, 'What the hell? Does it really matter if people see me in glasses?'"

Like Brian Epstein, Bob Wooler felt that something was happening. "I told Brian that he should always include the year on his posters and his tickets and he always did that. Allan Williams left '1962' off the poster for his Jerry Lee Lewis night at the Tower

Ballroom and he told me, 'Everyone knows it's 1962.' I said, 'I like to think that these events will be talked about and remembered for years to come.'

"There was one occasion where they were due to appear at a university dance which Brian Epstein had arranged, and they didn't do it. Brian said to me, 'If the university gets in touch with you about this, will you confirm that Paul has been knocked down by a taxi?' I said, 'Has he?' He said, 'No, no, but that's what I'm telling them as to why they can't do it.'

"In December 1962, the folksingers from the *Tonight* programme, Robin Hall and Jimmie MacGregor, were booked to appear with the Beatles at the Cavern. I went on stage and said, 'I have got some dreadful news for you. Because of this terrible weather, one of the acts is not able to appear tonight.' There were gasps, I was milking it of course, and when I named the act that couldn't make it, Robin Hall and Jimmie MacGregor, everyone applauded.."

Bob Wooler revealed that Brian Epstein had plans for a club in Liverpool devoted to the Beatles. "Leslie Blond had a building, which is now the Everyman Theatre, and it had originally been a church and then a cinema. He had a bar in it and he wanted to open the top part as a club. He approached Brian with a view to taking it on. Brian knew it would be opposition to the Cavern, but he discussed it with me as he thought I might become a part of it. Brian had seen the Star-Club in Hamburg and he visualised something similar with the Beatles as the resident group. I did think about it, and I did give him a name for it, Route 66. It wasn't on a Route 66 bus route and it wasn't 1966 but it was a well- known phrase. I was lukewarm about the concept as I knew it could be the death knell for the Cavern. The crowds went wherever the Beatles played, and Sam Leach knew this only too well at the Iron Door. I was telling the Beatles, 'Don't go with Sam, you've got to stay where you are. We'll give you lots of bookings.' Route 66 could have been a beat venue with a vengeance, but this was too parochial as Brian had plans for the Beatles that went far beyond performing in an old church in Hope Street. At the time, Brian said that the Beatles would be bigger than Elvis. I thought it was just managers' hype, but as it turned out, he was quite correct."

B.E.A.T.L.E.S.

This was written by Bob Wooler for the Liverpool Beatles Convention, 1977

B.E.A.T.L.E.S.
That spells 'Beatles', yeah, yeah, yes!
George and Ringo, Paul and John,
The mop top pop top phenomenon.

F.O.U.R F.A.B.
Four fab fellas, yes siree!
They made music effervesce
While other groups cried, 'S.O.S.'

From Elpool, England to L.A.
It's Beatles! Beatles! all the way
They sang their songs, the whole world shook
And put their names in the Guinness Book.

B.E.A.T.L.E.S.
That spells 'Beatles', yeah, yeah, yes!'
Shout it loudly, 'Beatles rule!'
Superstars from Liverpool.

They gave hope to worldwide youth
By singing songs that told the truth,
So carve a Rushmore monument
They're nothing less than heaven sent.

All you need is love, my friend,
To know that they're the living end,
Beatles, they can do no wrong,
Let's all sing a Northern song.

The Beatles 'Anthology 1'

B is for the biggest and B is for best
E is for ever like Mount Everest
A is for ageless and also for always
T is for talent, terrific in tall ways
L is for Liverpool, love, life and laughter
E is for evergreen, and ever after
S is for seven letters spelling success:
B.E.A.T.L.E.S!

The Beatles with Pete Best photographed at the Cavern

Ticket Price 5/- for The Rhythm & Blues Spectacular

'Thank Your Lucky Stars'

Staged in the **TOWER BALLROOM** New Brighton
Thursday 17th May, 1962 7-30 p.m. to Midnight
Late Transport   Licensed Bars & Buffet

Starring "Mr. Rock 'N' Roll" Himself

The Fabulous **JERRY LEE LEWIS** and the Echoes

Plus a Galaxy of Ten Star Groups

The Big Three	Billy Kramer with The Coasters
The Pressmen	Lee Castle & The Barons
The Undertakers	Kingsize Taylor & The Dominoes
The Strangers	Steve Day & The Drifters
Vincent Earl & The Zeros	Rip Van Winkle & The Rip It Ups

Britain's Mightiest Ever Non-Stop Big Beat Show Dance!
A Bob Wooler Rockerscope '62 Presentation
Read all about it in "Mersey Beat" — Out 2nd May

17 AND THE REST IS HYSTERIA
Billy J. Kramer - NEMS Enterprises - Rise of Beatles

"Everyone in Britain knows how fab they are."
(From "We Love The Beatles" by the Vernons Girls, 1964)

If Brian Epstein thought the Beatles would rival Elvis Presley, you might wonder why he bothered to sign anybody else. I suspect that he wanted to control the scene and he certainly admired the pop impresario Larry Parnes with his stable of artists. It made good economic sense as he could fill an evening with his own acts. Bob Wooler recalls him signing Billy Kramer and the Coasters: "I put Billy Kramer on the Jerry Lee Lewis show at the Tower Ballroom in May 1962 while the Beatles were in Hamburg. Brian Epstein came across to the show and that was when he first saw him. To employ a Johnny Burke title, he thought 'That's For Me' - one line in that song is 'The lighthearted gay kind of charm you display, That's for me.' Billy wasn't gay but BE saw Billy and he was transfixed, he went overboard. He wanted to manage Billy and his manager, Ted Knibbs, saw that Brian could do more for Billy than he ever could. He sold Billy's contract to BE for £50, which was hardly a good business deal.

"However, the Nemperor mightn't have signed Billy at all as he also went overboard about another lad. The scene is the Majestic, Birkenhead in July 1962 and the Nemperor was there to see someone else. Clay Ellis and the Raiders came on and BE went into one of his transfixed states. Clay Ellis was an 18 year old lad and he said to me, 'Are you going to come fishing with me?', adding that I would find it very restful. He then went home and BE asked me if I knew him well and if I knew where he lived. I said, 'Bromborough', and he said, 'Is there any chance of meeting him?' 'Tonight?' 'Tonight.' It was 11.30pm, the end of the dance, and I agreed to take him. The Nemperor stayed in the car while I knocked on the door of an ordinary council house. His mother said he was in bed, he had a day job and had to be up for work in the morning. When I did see him again, he said, 'I wish I hadn't gone to bed.' and I thought, 'Just as well you did. God knows what would have happened in the back seat of the Nemperor's car. Brian wasn't only interested in your tonsils.' Brian did have ideas for signing the lad but it would have been instead of Billy J. and the lad kept asking me about it. The Nemperor said, 'I am in a dilemma, I want to sign Billy Kramer, he has great potential and so what can I do for Clay Ellis? I would like to take the

Bromborough lad on but I can't have two similar solo artists.' It was head or tails between Billy J. Kramer and Clay Ellis, and Billy won.

"Clay Ellis and the Raiders operated mostly on the Wirral, but I did get them some bookings at the Cavern and also at Aintree Institute and Litherland Town Hall with Brian Kelly. Brian Kelly would ask me just three questions about a group - Are they good? Are there any problems with them? And, most importantly, how much? Clay Ellis became disillusioned that the Nemperor didn't follow this up and he stopped performing. He died about a year ago.

"The Coasters were not happy with Billy signing with BE and they didn't join him. I don't think it was a question of them not being willing to pack their jobs in, all the lads wanted to escape from the routine and none of them had important jobs. It was a case of 'We'll stand by you, Ted, you haven't lost us.' Brian, the charmer that he was, couldn't persuade them. That must have annoyed him because he liked his own way and usually knew how to manipulate people. The Coasters became very resentful of Billy Kramer for deserting Ted Knibbs, but you can't blame Billy because Epstein was Mr. Big with everything happening, and Ted was not in that category.

"Brian placed Billy with the Dakotas, who were an excellent band from Manchester. They had a good singer in Pete Maclaine, but they deserted him. Pete was very irate about this and with good reason, and there was to be a lot of tension between the Dakotas and Billy. However, it was a good move as the Dakotas were much more professional than most of the Liverpool groups.

"Even to this day, there is a problem with Billy's nerves, although he was very good when I saw him recently with the Dakotas at *BBC Radio Merseyside*. He was always very vulnerable because he knew he wasn't outstanding. It got worse when he heard other musicians say, 'He's not much of a singer.' John Lennon gave him songs, but I wonder if he also taunted him about his voice. I doubt if he could resist it. Billy was booked for the Prince of Wales Theatre one Sunday night on live TV to promote his new record, 'I'll Keep You Satisfied' and he was in a terrible state. I can sympathise with him as I have been that way myself. I'm sure that Brian tried to pacify him but he was absolutely terrible that night, so bad that the record dropped down the charts. Brian didn't desert him though, he perservered and Billy had further hits.

"John and Paul gave him songs, chiefly because of Brian's requests, but usually they only gave away songs that they didn't want or didn't have time for. 'I Wanna Be Your Man' is a terrible song and I am not fooled by the fact that it is by Lennon and McCartney and recorded by the Rolling Stones. That song put the Stones on the map but it is so repetitious. If it took John and Paul longer than ten minutes, I would be surprised. Billy J. Kramer says he turned down 'Yesterday' but I can't accept that. Do you really think Paul McCartney offered him a song as good as that? I doubt it. 'Yesterday' was far too precious for McCartney to give away."

Brian Epstein signed the Beatles, Gerry and the Pacemakers, Billy J. Kramer with the Dakotas, Cilla Black, the Fourmost and Tommy Quickly, but he missed the Searchers, the Swinging Blue Jeans and, because they left him after a few weeks, the Merseybeats. Bob Wooler: "Brian wanted the Searchers but they were not prepared to play second fiddle to the Beatles, and Brian wouldn't have anyone vying with the Beatles. He also missed out on Beryl Marsden and I preferred her to Cilla Black as a singer. Cilla was a belter, a girl with a big voice à la Della Reese or Bette Midler. Beryl was managed by Joe Flannery and she did okay, but if Brian had taken Beryl, she would have been a big seller as she had the talent and the personality. However, BE had got one girl singer with Cilla and that was enough. He was influenced by Larry Parnes and his stable of stars including Marty Wilde and Billy Fury. Larry Parnes only had one girl on his books, Sally Kelly, so Brian did the same.

"BE was a mother hen, he took on a hell of a lot and they became too hot to handle all at once. I told him about Earl Preston and when he saw him, he said, 'I can understand how you feel about Earl Preston, he's very good.' He asked me to manage him under the NEMS umbrella. I delayed the decision, just like everything in my life, and I never did.

"Brian knew that 'the boys' were in a league above all his other performers. He was very proud of everything they did. I remember being at the Casino Ballroom in Leigh in February 1963 and Brian played me the acetate of their next single, 'From Me To You'. I was as excited as he was. I was exhilarated by the pace of it, by the brilliance of it and, yes, by the shortness of it as well. I don't like records that go on and on and on."

Dave Williams of Group One: "We did 'From Me To You' at the Cavern and Bob said, 'You did that better than the Beatles.' That was very flattering and I think he really liked the way we played and the way we dressed."

Dave Peacock of the Wigan group, the Nightboppers: "We played with the Beatles and Bob said to us, 'You had them worried.'"

Bob Wooler: "I often wonder why the Beatles were so important and so far ahead of all the bands of the 60s. There must have been something initially about the Beatles to attract attention, to get people talking about them, and I am not sure that applied to the

Beach Boys, who didn't look all that attractive and were initially a vocal group like the Four Freshmen. The Beatles had everything right - and the Byrds are simply as a result of the Beatles - look at the mere fact that their name is misspelt, Beatlewise. I do like them though - you can hear the words with the Byrds. The Beatles were four young guys, looking innocent and angelic, and no wonder they were popular with people of all ages. They were humorous, well-spoken, physically attractive and parents would say, 'Oh, I hope my son grows up just like them and writes all these beautiful songs like 'All My Loving'.'

"Those tax exiles on main street, the Rolling Stones didn't have that appeal. The Beatles were originally rebellious like the Stones, and through their manager Andrew Loog Oldham, the Stones played up their outrageousness in order to be contrasted with the Beatles. They wanted to be offensive, but their protests would be regarded as mild today. They refused to go on the roundabout at the end of *Sunday Night At The London Palladium*. I'm sure the Beatles would think it was ridiculous but they would do it. They were ostensibly so nice. The Rolling Stones had a large, teenage audience but the Beatles were tamed and publicity-conscious and loved by everyone. We can thank Brian Epstein for that."

LIKE A LIGATURE

Bob Wooler: "The first line is taken from a Dorothy Fields song and the second from a Sammy Cahn. This challenged me to come up with something entirely different and entirely original. Merged letters like æ are known as ligatures, hence this fragment of unfinished lyric."

'Close as pages in a book'
'Closer than a kiss'
These expressions only go half the way
To convey what you mean to me
Just how close we are.

Our love is like a ligature
Ever binding, always finding
New ways of saying 'I love you'.

Our love is more precious than the Mona Lisa
You're as close to me
As the 'a' to the 'e'
In Julius Cæsar.

Stringfellow Bros.
| (DANCE & SHOW PROMOTIONS)

47 Kingston Street,
Sheffield 4.

ST. AIDANS
CITY ROAD

DANCES
TUESDAY & FRIDAY NIGHTS

ROCK - TWIST - RHYTHM
and BLUES

Dear Bob. Sorry about thursday but as I explained in T-gram, I had a slight misshap, with a lorry, nothing serious though. However I'm coming on Sunday now. The vacant dates for April and May for the Skeletons are as follows.

April the 5th at the "Starrkass Club".

APRIL 9th - 11th - 16th - 21st - 23rd - 25th - 30th

MAY 2 - 7 - 9 - 10 - 14 - 16 - 17 - 19 - 21 - 23
24 - 26 - 28 - 30 - 31.

As it stands now thats it. I'm holding all further bookings up until I see you. Yours Truly Pete.

FRID 15 MARCH 63

Letter to Bob Wooler from Peter Stringfellow.

Joe Flannery.
1999

Earl Preston

18 PUNCH DRUNK
The fighting side of John Lennon

"If I was with Bob in the company of someone else and they asked him about the fight, he would say, 'It's for me to know and for you not to know.' Sometimes he might say, 'And what do you think happened?' but he would never reveal anything himself."
(Billy Butler, 2002)

John Lennon, described by Bob Wooler as going 'from rage to riches', was argumentative and sarcastic, but he was not regularly getting into scraps and fights. Even at school. One day I arrived at Keith's Wine Bar early to interview Bob and found myself talking to Mal Perry, who released a few singles in the 1950s. "I was younger than John Lennon," he said, "but I was still able to beat him up when he was at Quarry Bank." Mal, incidentally, was part of that 1960 Liverpool Stadium show with Gene Vincent and when he heard that Lennon had called his group the Beatles, he said, "You'll never get anywhere with a name like that."

Bill Smith, the first washboard player with the Quarry Men, recalls, "John did funny things, which could be cruel. At the Pier Head one day there was an old man who had fallen asleep reading a newspaper. John got a match, lit it and shouted, 'Wake up'. He thought it was very funny to watch the old man putting the newspaper out."

It is significant that John Lennon is the one Beatle who is often referred to by his surname alone. It has an aggressive sound to it. Bob Wooler: "John Lennon was a hard knock with a soft centre really. But most of the time he would portray his hardness, because for one thing it was fashionable to appear mean - the meanness that was coming across from rock'n'roll - which is part of its image. He commanded the stage with the way he stared and stood. His legs would be wide apart, that was one of his trademarks, and it was regarded as being very sexual and very aggressive. The girls up front would be looking up his legs, keeping a watch on the crotch, as it were. I can't think of any of the rock'n'rollers of the 1950s who had that particular stance. I always thought it was unique to Lennon."

If you ask Mersey Beat musicians about Freddie Starr's zaniness, nearly everyone has a different story as there are so many examples. Ask them though about John Lennon's violence and you get the same story over and over, that is, John punching Bob Wooler at Paul McCartney's twenty-first party. This suggests that John Lennon was not fighting all and sundry and, indeed, I don't know of any other fights in Liverpool, and nor did Bob.

Paul McCartney was born on 18 June 1942 and he had his twenty-first birthday party at his Auntie Jin's house, 147 Dinas Lane, Huyton on 18 June 1963. Many of his fellow NEMS artists including Billy J. Kramer, the Dakotas and the Fourmost had been invited as well as their new friends, the Shadows, and some old ones including Bob Wooler. To accommodate the numbers, a marquee was erected in the back garden.

Bill Heckle, one of the directors of Cavern City Tours, says, "Auntie Gin no longer had the Beatles' first LP as she had given it to a fan. She wanted one for the party and so she asked my auntie for the loan of hers. She brought it along and they played one of the sides. As they were turning it over, Paul said, 'That's not the album I gave you, it's a different pressing.' The story came out and Paul signed my aunt's LP with the message, 'Thanks for the loan.'"

At the end of April 1963, John Lennon had taken a short holiday in Spain with Brian Epstein. They had returned early in May and the Beatles had then undertaken three weeks of touring around the UK. In-between some recording sessions for the BBC in London, they returned to Liverpool for Paul McCartney's twenty-first. John Lennon went with his wife Cynthia and such was the rivalry between the two Beatles that he might have resented Paul being the centre of attention. Dave Lovelady, the drummer with the Fourmost, told me that John was paying little attention to Cynthia.

At one stage, Bob, John and Brian Epstein found themselves going through the back door into the garden. And, as they say in TV panel games, what happened next?

"John Lennon had little to eat and too much to drink at the party. Bob Wooler said something to John about his visit to Spain with Epstein. John laid into Wooler with a ferocity that landed the disc jockey in hospital with a black eye, bruised ribs and torn knuckles. Brian Epstein drove Bob Wooler to the hospital. The party broke up in disarray. Cynthia, who left with John, recalls, 'John said, 'He called me a queer so I battered his bloody ribs in.'"
(John Winston Lennon, Ray Coleman, 1984)

"John Lennon beats up the Beatles' old disc jockey friend Bob Wooler after Wooler insinuates that Lennon is homosexual."
(The Beatles: 25 Years In The Life, Mark Lewisohn, 1987)

The incident was a sticking point between Bob Wooler and myself. Bob did not want to discuss it. Every week I would ask him if he wanted to talk about it, and every week he declined. I told him that people who paid good money for a book deserved a full account, but he said, "No, they will understand that I don't want to talk about it." I lent him *Walk Right Back*, a book about the Everly Brothers, by Roger White. I said, "This is an excellent book but Don and Phil are determined not to discuss their break-up." Bob borrowed the book and passed it back a few weeks later. "I admire them for this," he said, "They don't want to discuss it and nothing will make them. It doesn't diminish the book in any way. I respect them for not discussing it." I kept persevering. I received a few snippets here and there, but I never got the full story. "And no one else can tell it," he would say, "Only John Lennon, Brian Epstein and myself know what happened. Nobody else was near us at the time. I pooh-pooh all these accounts. I would just ask the authors, 'Were you there?' and they weren't."

Was there anything to tell? That is what I don't know. At times, Bob thought he had a story that was worth £20,000. "I have fought shy of talking about this," he said, "but if you get me a deal for £20,000 from the *News Of The World* or *National Enquirer*, I will change my mind."

The story would have to be very dramatic to be worth £20,000. I showed Bob Wooler Albert Goldman's account and asked if he was along the right lines.

"Bob Wooler came up to Lennon and said, 'How was the honeymoon, John?'. Taking Wooler's remark as an insulting reference to the recent trip to Spain, John doubled up his fist and smashed the little disc jockey on the nose. Then, seizing a shovel that was lying in the yard, Lennon began to beat Wooler to death. Blow after blow came smashing down on the defenceless man lying on the ground. It would have ended in murder if John had not suddenly realised, 'If I hit him one more time, I'll kill him!' Making an enormous effort of will, Lennon restrained himself. At that instant, three men seized him and disarmed him. An ambulance was called for Wooler, who had suffered a broken nose, a cracked collarbone and three broken ribs. Lennon had broken a finger."
(The Lives Of John Lennon, Albert Goldman, 1988)

Bob exploded when he saw this: "This is preposterous," he said, "Absolute nonsense. Goldman sees that the party was in the garden and rushes to the conclusion that all the garden implements are to hand. He'll have me buried in the rose bushes next."

Was Goldman extracting revenge because Wooler hadn't come clean? "But why should I? Goldman never offered me anything to come clean. I was living in Grove Park, recovering from a stroke, and I sat with his researcher, Ron Ellis, in the lounge. I said, 'There is no money being offered here. I am not obsessed with money but all I know is that he must be doing it for money, otherwise why the hell is he doing it, and you are doing your research for money.'"

"One of Bob's traits was to make cutting remarks, not intended maliciously, but rather out of fondness for word-play. He made some reference to John's recent short holiday break in Spain with Brian Epstein, obviously couched in some way to contain a double-meaning. To a Lennon who'd drunk too many beers and wasn't interested in the subtle cleverness, it was like a red rag to a bull. He leapt on to Bob and battered him to the ground, giving him a black eye, bruised ribs and torn knuckles, which Bob sustained when he'd tried to protect his face from John's foot as he was being kicked. Members of the Fourmost pulled John off and Brian drove Bob to hospital."
(The Beatles Encyclopedia, Bill Harry, 2000)

That is, I think, getting close to the truth, but Bill Harry backtracks when questioned about his account of the fight: "I don't think that John Lennon liked fighting. At the Rosebery Street parade, John fled from some thugs, and after a Quarry Men gig at Wilson Hall, he hid downstairs on a bus to avoid a fight. It wasn't a proper fight with Bob. John was being drunk and offensive."

It wasn't a fight because Bob was no match for John Lennon. Beryl Adams: "From what I know of Bob, I think it was some trivial remark that upset John. John snapped and he found it hard to cope with Paul being the centre of attention. He was a strange person but he had had a lot to cope with in his life."

Billy Hatton of the Fourmost: "We had just signed for NEMS Enterprises. There was a marquee in the back garden and we were doing a show for the folks at the party. The word came down that John Lennon was drunk and had beaten up Bob Wooler. Bob couldn't punch a hole through a wet Echo and he was just a nice man. John Lennon wasn't a nice guy when he was pissed, he wasn't Mr. Love And Peace, he was vicious when he was drunk. He had picked on an easy target. This is what he was like, matey. He came staggering down to the marquee where I was, and Billy J. Kramer was there with a good-looking girl called Rose Leech on his knee. Lennon grabbed Rose's tits. Rose gave him a backhander and Lennon punched her. She went on the floor and Lennon was going to kick her, and all these gobshites were standing round doing nothing. I leapt over this table, and there is a technique where you can get your hand down somebody's collar if they are wearing a tie, fingers down, and you twist, and it is like a tourniquet and they can't breathe, and I had him like that. I had my fist drawn back and I was going to plant him one. He was being a right bastard and he deserved a smacking, but someone shouted, 'Billy, if you hit him, the Fourmost are finished.' He was right, we hadn't even made a record then, and it would have been Bass Player In No Mark Group Beats Up John Lennon."

Dave Lovelady, drummer with the Fourmost: "What Billy did was great and maybe he should have continued. We were the fourth or fifth act in the NEMS stable and the publicity would have done us a lot of good."

Billy Hatton: "He didn't hang around for too long after that. Next time we met, I don't think he even remembered what had happened. He remembered beating up Bob but I don't think he knew the rest of it. Knowing John, he went looking for trouble that night and if it wasn't Bob, it would have been somebody else who couldn't fight back."

Whilst this was going on, Billy J. Kramer had been shouting, "Lay off, John" and pulling Rose away from him. Lennon snarled, "You're nothing, Kramer, we're the top.'"

Brian Epstein took Bob Wooler to hospital and then to Beryl's flat: "I wasn't at the party, but I saw him afterwards. He had marks on his face, his head and his hands. He had a black eye too, but it did look worse than it was."

Allan Williams went round the next morning: "I was aghast when I saw him. He looked as though he had been kicked in the head and he was badly shaken up. I phoned the journalist, Bill Marshall, who had had a row with his wife and was staying at the Caribbean Centre. Bob didn't object because he knew Bill as well. Bill wrote a piece for the *Daily Mirror* and it was the first Beatles story that appeared as a news item in a daily paper."

Bob Wooler: "The story became a national issue because my friend, I repeat, 'my friend', Allan Williams thought fit to contact the *Daily Mirror*." Brian Epstein cannot have been pleased with the national publicity but the feature does have an element of spin-doctoring about it, as though Brian Epstein has told John Lennon to be contrite.

"Guitarist John Lennon, 22 year old leader of the Beatles pop group, said last night, 'Why did I have to go and punch my best friend?' I was so high I didn't realise what I was doing.' Then he sent off a telegram apologising to 29 year old Liverpool rock show compère and disc jockey Bob Wooler. Wooler said, 'I don't know why he did it. I have been a friend of the Beatles for a long time. I have often compèred shows where they

have appeared. I am terribly upset about this, physically as well as mentally.' John Lennon says, 'Bob is the last person in the world I would want to have a fight with. I can only hope he realises that I was too far gone to know what I was doing.'"
(Don Short, *Daily Mirror*, June 1963 - and Bob, of course, hadn't been 29 since 1955.)

The telegram did exist. Bob sold it at a Beatles auction in London some years ago. It read, "Really sorry Bob. Terribly worried to realise what I had done. What more can I say?" Does that sound like John Lennon to you? Exactly. Epstein also apologised for John to Billy J. Kramer but Kramer said, "I refuse to accept a second-hand apology." A few days later, Lennon did apologise to him.

The Beatles left Liverpool straight after the party for appearances in London and Guildford. Two days later Bob received his telegram. On that same day Bob took the stage at the Cavern. Billy Kinsley of the Merseybeats: "We were topping the bill that night and Bob was wearing dark glasses. He took them off to reveal his black eye and he said to the audience, 'I got this at Lennon's Supermarket.'" (Lennon's Supermarkets were prevalent in Liverpool at the time, the Morrison's of their day.)

One reason for John's apology could be that Brian Epstein feared a lawsuit, which Lennon would be bound to lose. Brian Epstein asked the Liverpool solicitor Rex Makin to act for Lennon and as fate would have it, Bob Wooler had the same idea. Bob told me, "I went to see Rex Makin with Ray McFall,and Ray was told to wait in the adjoining room." Both parties, through Makin's negotiations, agreed on an out of court settlement of £200. Beryl says, "He could have got more but he didn't want any fuss made of it." This is probably true, but it is difficult to judge these events in today's climate where Bob could have obtained a huge payment for his silence.

Rex Makin admitted to me that he was acting for both sides, but says that both parties were happy about this. I asked him if he knew what was said in that infamous exchange between John and Bob. "Oh, I can tell you about that," he said, "There was a story circulating that John Lennon was anybody's for £5. Wooler thought it would be money well spent and made a pass at him. Lennon hit him and that punch cost him £200." That sounds out of character for Bob, but, as suggested earlier, it may have been a joke that went wrong.

Bob Wooler did not see the Beatles again until 3 August on what was to be their last appearance at the Cavern: "I had been wondering what was going to happen when we met again. No more spadework, I hoped - are you listening to me, Albert Goldman? It was an awkward situation and he looked sheepishly at me. He didn't put his arms around me and say sorry. I knew then that the telegram had been sent by Brian Epstein."

During the 1970s, John Lennon was sometimes asked about the fight, and his answers make me think that he had seen a psychiatrist. "The Beatles' first national press coverage was me beating up Bob Wooler at Paul's twenty-first party because he intimated I was homosexual. I must have had a fear that maybe I was homosexual to attack him like that and it's very complicated reasoning. I was very drunk and I hit him and I could have really killed somebody then. And that scared me."

Perhaps the fight did some good, because according to a 1972 quote, John became committed to peace after the fight. "That really is nonsense," says Bob Wooler, "Didn't he go berserk with Nilsson in the 70s and there were fisticuffs then? I would hate to think that I was the catalyst for 'Imagine' because I detest the song."

Actually, there are examples of violence after the fight, and indeed some after 1972. John had picked on someone who couldn't fight back, but he was a bully. Did he ever fight with someone who could knock him to smithereens? I doubt it. If Johnny Hutch was in the room, he behaved himself. Maybe that's why he didn't sack Pete Best himself - he thought Best would better him (or batter him) in a fight.

What provoked the attack, how savage it was it and the nature of the aftermath are not fully known. Bob wasn't talking. One minute he would be telling me that the story was unimportant, and the next that it would be worth thousands if sold to the tabloids. It should go without saying that subjects should take their ghost writers or biographers into their confidence, and I'm sorry that Bob was so furtive. Beryl Adams: "Bob played on the fact that everybody wanted to know what had happened. Right up to the end, Bob played along with it. He loved the fact that you wanted to know what it was all about and kept asking him about it."

When I look over this book, I have most of what I need except the story of the fight, which is winning the war but losing an important battle. This is one fight that Bob won. As he said, "I'm not discussing the KO, OK?"

19 THE BEST OF CELLARS

Cavern Stomp - Live recordings at the Cavern - Combo - This Is Mersey
Beat - Sunday Night At The Cavern - Rex Harrison

"It was during the sixties that Liverpool became the city of
pop music. Working people appeared to be coming into
their own at last."
(Eric Heffer, *'Never A Yes Man'*, 1991)

The Beatles' final appearance at the Cavern was on 3 August 1963. Bob Wooler: "It only came about because Brian Epstein couldn't pull them out of an appearance at the Grafton the night before. Les Ackerley said 'I've got them under contract', and Epstein was furious because, by then, he had other things in mind for them. He was calling Ackerley all sorts of names, but he didn't use four-letter words as he never did that. Ackerley had a barring clause preventing the Beatles appearing in Liverpool before but not after that appearance, so Brian asked us to take the Beatles for the Cavern on the following night, which was a Saturday.

"I resented this as he was only doing it to get at Ackerley, to steal his thunder as it were, and anyway, I had booked all the groups for Saturday 3 August. If I'd said no, he would have gone to Ray McFall, who would have said, 'Of course we'll take them.' The Beatles were paid £300, which was quite a bit of money then, and Brian restricted the audience to 500. I can't blame Brian as he had seen how crowded the Cavern got when we had 800 in and he had to think of the Beatles' safety at that stage. The admission price was 10/- (50p) and so that only meant we collected £250 on the door. All the staff had to be paid, and the other groups on the bill too, so we made no profit that night.

"It was more Mercenary Beat than Mersey Beat that night. The Escorts and the Merseybeats still wanted paying for the night: the kudos of being on with the Beatles wasn't enough for them. When I told them that we would be starting the evening an hour earlier, the first thing they said was, 'We're still getting paid, aren't we, Bob?'

"Tony Crane has criticised me on *Radio Merseyside* for suggesting that the Merseybeats performed 'P.S.I Love You' that night. He thought it was a terrible idea. I reckoned that the Beatles wouldn't be doing that B-side in their 45-minute spot and the Merseybeats could have performed it as a tribute to them.

"The Beatles were very professional, there was no larking around and they got on with it. We all felt it was their swan song and that we would never have them at the Cavern again. As it happens, Brian Epstein still owes the Cavern six dates for the Beatles as he kept pulling them out of bookings by saying, 'You wouldn't stand in the boys' way, would you, Bob?'

"One of the most famous pictures of screaming fans shows a blonde girl in leather in total ecstasy. It was taken at the Cavern one Saturday afternoon, and it was faked. She and her friends look very convincing, but you can say the same about *The Jerry Springer Show*. It's a terrific shot though - they put the girls in a certain section of the Cavern and said, 'Scream'. They did a few rehearsals until they got what they wanted.

"Someone from Fleet Street came to the Cavern many years ago and asked me how many times the Beatles had played there. Ray McFall and I put our heads together and came up with 292, but that included some guesswork. That became the accepted figure until Mark Lewisohn's book in 1986, *The Beatles Live!* He had analysed everything very carefully and concluded that the figure should be 274. I accept that figure as more accurate than ours. If you ask me how many times I introduced the Beatles in the Cavern and elsewhere, I would say around 400.

"Ray McFall was treated very offhandedly in the *Anthology* documentaries. He looked after the Beatles a lot by giving them bookings when they wanted £15, which Brian Kelly and Co thought was ridiculous. They played the Cavern more times than all their other bookings on Merseyside put together. I appreciate that the Cavern is famous because of the Beatles and not the other way round, but nonetheless, there should have been some generosity shown towards Ray and he is not even mentioned in the Anthology series.

"Brian Epstein was putting on a promotion at the Tower Ballroom, New Brighton called *Southern Sounds '63* with the Rolling Stones and Jet Harris and Tony Meehan. The Beatles had taken off to such an extent that he no longer had the time to do it. He was farming out the acts to appear elsewhere and he asked me if I would be interested in taking the Rolling Stones at the Cavern and I said, 'Yes, of course.' The contract was for £60 and so I took them. They were overawed to play there as it was the place where the Beatles had started.

"The Rolling Stones came to the Tower Ballroom in New Brighton for the Rael-Brook Contest in August 1964. The company was launching a new shirt with a nationwide beat contest - and the winners would be called the Toplins after the shirt! I told them that I could get the Rolling Stones but their fee had risen in the meantime to £800. It meant nothing to Rael-Brook and they paid up. They wanted a big name to ensure a full house and you could get 5,000 at the Tower.

"The Rolling Stones were the bad boys of rock'n'roll by then, rather like Oasis now, and it was difficult for Dick Rowe from Decca, who was with them, to cope with their peculiarities. In his autobiography, A Stone Alone, Bill Wyman says that there was a fight between the mods and the rockers that lasted for 45 minutes, but that is untrue. We had enlisted some bouncers we didn't know, and there was some trouble with the bouncers fighting amongst themselves, but that's it. The Rolling Stones gave us our money's worth, their £800 worth, but I had to prevail upon them for an encore.

"The Stones' were becoming the Beatles' biggest rivals and I could have destroyed them! Their management wanted to ensure that they could get into the Tower safely and I suggested, not jokingly, the chair lift up to the flat roof. Their management was appalled - 'What if Mick comes tumbling out? You'd better get them in through the back door.'" When I mentioned the Tower Ballroom to Bill Wyman in 2001, he immediately said, "Is that the place with a chair lift?"

Bob Wooler: "The Beatles' four-song appearance on the *Royal Variety Performance* was a landmark. It took place on 4 November 1963 at the Prince Of Wales Theatre before the Queen and the Queen Mother. John Lennon's remark, 'Would those of you in the cheap seats, clap your hands. The rest of you can rattle your jewellery', was fantastic. Like most of the best quips, it was well-rehearsed, although he passed it off as spontaneous."

"Hysteria was made that night with riotous scenes of screaming fans surrounding the theatre. When the *Daily Mirror* reviewed the show, they used the word, 'Beatlemania', which was the first use of the word that neatly encompasses all things Beatle. It was such an apt word for the occasion, which was then televised to the nation." When transmitted, Allan Williams in digust threw a cushion at the TV screen.

"However, according to the Liverpool solicitor, Rex Makin, who had a close relationship with both Brian Epstein and the Beatles, this was not the origin of the word. In the *Liverpool Echo* (22 November 1995), he wrote about defending a Teddy Boy during the early 1960s. He said, 'I was representing a Teddy Boy at Dale Street Magistrates Court and he said that he had been a victim of Beatlemania and very quickly the word became part of the English language.' So this unnamed Teddy Boy is responsible for the word. Perhaps his name was Raymond Jones.

"The Beatles were not put out by not making it in America in 1963 as very few British acts had any luck there, but Brian wanted it to happen. On New Year's Day, 1964, he told me in the White Star that the Beatles were going to America, and I said naively, 'Yes, but what sort of act have they got?' The American acts were always very slick and

I thought the Beatles needed more polish. They couldn't even bow properly and the way they messed around used to irritate me. Brian went very quiet and I thought I had hurt his feelings by saying that they had no act. It was only later that I realised that it was the very informality and throwaway style that endeared them to the Americans. One reporter asked, 'How did you find America?' and George replied, 'We turned left at Greenland.' It's a classic remark and the Americans had never heard anything like that.

"Brian had moved from Whitechapel into new premises in Moorfields but he said that he wouldn't be there very long as NEMS Enterprises was moving to Sutherland House in London and why didn't I join him? He thought that I was wasted at the Cavern, which is true. It was small beer and he was offering me champagne. Why didn't I go? I don't know really. There was security of employment with NEMS, but I am convinced that I would not have fitted in. He couldn't understand why I turned him down. I was a big fish in a small pond, and he wanted me to be a small fish in a big pond. He said, 'You could be a big fish in a big pond', but not *the* big fish of course.

"I had also been present when Brian had blown his top and I knew that he could be very biting and very vicious. I don't like arguments and I wouldn't have liked to have been on the receiving end. Say he had put me on the road with Billy J. Kramer. I would have to send good reports to him - 'It's fantastic, Brian' - and I'm not good at doing that. I once told him about a good performance by Gerry and the Pacemakers, and he sent me a letter thanking me. He only wanted praise, he only wanted to know that the crowd was in raptures.

"It was hectic in '63 and '64. I said to Ray McFall in '64, 'I can't possibly do these lunchtime sessions and book the groups and do the ads all by myself. I need an assistant.' Two people applied for the job, Billy Butler and Mike Ahern. I chose Billy because he worked on the docks as a clerk and could manage some lunchtime sessions. He had been on *Thank Your Lucky Stars* and he was singing at the time with the Tuxedos and occasionally, the Merseybeats."

Billy Butler: "The only time the Tuxedos got top billing at the Cavern was when the Beatles came to Liverpool for the première of A Hard Day's Night. The whole of Liverpool was lining the streets but none of them came to the Cavern. We got about 80 people and I wouldn't be surprised if that booking wasn't one of Bob's jokes."

Bob Wooler: "Tourists didn't start coming to see the Cavern until 1963 when it became an attraction in its own right. Coachloads of young people would come from youth clubs. Then, when the Beatles happened in America in 1964, the Americans took an interest - and have done so ever since. When the Beatles released 'Penny Lane' and 'Strawberry Fields Forever', that clinched it. These were two definite Liverpool landmarks apart from the Cavern that would interest tourists. I did my best to keep up with the mail, but I have some guilt about it. We got letters all the time. A letter might only be addressed 'The Cavern, Liverpool' and it would still arrive."

Pete Frame, the instigator of *Rock Family Trees,* visited the Cavern: "I went to the Majestic in Luton, the Grosvenor in Aylesbury and the California Ballroom in Dunstable but it was different in the Cavern. I got the impression that everyone at the Cavern was mates and this was something they did all the time, whereas it was a big deal in Luton. We only had a dance once a week and the group would be someone totally useless like the Federals."

Bob Wooler: "The Cavern has become the most famous beat club in the world but relatively few recordings were made there. It is not like the Marquee with one album after another, but maybe it was easier to record there as it was located close to the big companies in London. In this chapter, I will mention the Cavern on record and elsewhere, and also other recordings made in Liverpool. So far as I know, none of John, Paul or George's songs ever mentioned the Cavern, even in passing, although it's bound to be one of the places John Lennon remembers during 'In My Life'.

"In 1963 Brian Epstein invited Ray McFall and myself to his office to hear the Big Three's new single, 'Cavern Stomp', as he knew we would be fascinated by a song which mentioned the Cavern. I'm not very good at PR, I suffer from foot in mouth disease, and I said, 'Brian, it doesn't tell you how to do the dance. All the American dance records like 'The Locomotion' and 'The Twist' tell you what to do.' He changed the subject completely because I had dared to criticise something he was involved with, and he didn't play it to us again. To be honest, I didn't care for 'Cavern Stomp' very much: it hadn't got much of a tune.

"The Cavern Stomp, if there really was such a thing, was a cramped version of jive dancing. To do the Cavern Stomp properly, you need a lot of space to swing your arms, and you wouldn't get that at the Cavern. I did have a boy and a girl do it for a photographer one Saturday morning when the club was empty. I had visions of releasing the shots to a magazine with dance step diagrams, rather like the Madison. However, nothing came of it.

"In 1963, after a lunchtime session, we only had the cleaners and the Beatles in the place. George Martin was there with his assistant and also Lionel Bart. At the time, Brian Epstein was keen to have Cilla Black playing the title role in Lionel Bart's next musical, *Maggie May*, but I don't know what went wrong. George Martin was walking round the empty Cavern, clapping his hands and testing the echo. An album of the Beatles live at the Cavern would have been marvellous, but he didn't like its echo and decided against it. It never happened but a few months later, Noel Walker, who came from Liverpool, recorded the Big Three at the Cavern and showed that it could be done.

"The Big Three's recording was on a Thursday. The Cavern wasn't normally open on a Thursday and the whole evening was devoted to the recording session for Decca. There were 600 people in, not quite capacity, although that was still a hell of a lot, and the place was steaming. I knew my introduction would be an ordeal and I am not satisfied with what you hear on the EP. I say, 'Welcome to the best of cellars' and 'the' is prolonged when it shouldn't have been. I was searching for words and I did it better on some other takes.

"The Big Three were taking 'bennies' that day and Hutch said to me, 'Come on, Bob, have a benny'. Johnny Gus would say, 'Go on, man, have one.' He was always saying 'man'. I was drinking like mad when they made that EP but I didn't have any bennies. That's why I announced them as 'The Boys with the Benzedrine Beat' and I'm amazed that Decca kept it on the record. I cringe at my sleeve notes - they are so OTT and so American - 'I was there, were you?' You lose some and you wince some. They offered me a percentage of that EP but I took £25 cash instead. Clearly a mistake on my part.

"*The Big Three At The Cavern* was good musically and very raw. It was much better than what George Martin could have envisaged, but the drums are not properly assembled for the cover photograph. Hutch had already dismantled his drums when the photographer from Decca said, 'Hang on, we haven't taken our pictures yet.' Hutch said, 'Do we have to do this after all we've been through?' You can see that he hasn't bothered to reassemble them, he is just propping them up.

"The Big Three were also on a Decca album, *Live At The Cavern,* with Beryl Marsden, the Dennisons, and Lee Curtis and the All Stars. That wasn't a bad album but they included outside acts like Heinz who had nothing to do with the Cavern. It was simply exploitation for Decca recording artists. Noel Walker put echo on my voice and I recorded the introductions the following day. He came down with a tape recorder and I had worked on my intros like 'It's Dennison time' and 'Here's the bouncy bubbling Beryl Marsden'. They thought that a tinge of echo would add brightness to my voice and I think that it did.

"Although he came from Liverpool, Lee Curtis was also out of place doing 'Jezebel' on that album. Neither Lee nor his brother and manager, Joe Flannery could see that what he was doing was totally wrong for 1963, but he never changed. I remember seeing Lee at a Beatles Convention in the Adelphi Hotel where he was singing 'Jezebel' full-voiced like Frankie Laine and kneeling on the floor with emotion. What he was doing had no connection with the Beatles, so he was making absolutely no impression with his efforts. The fans were leaving the hall and, if he'd thought about it, he'd never have chosen that song. But that's the way he was. I remember him doing 'Let's Stomp' on the Merseybeat edition of *Thank Your Lucky Stars* with all the stops out and he was completely different from everyone else on the show.

"Bill Harry arranged the sessions for *This Is Mersey Beat* with John Schroeder at Oriole Records. The sessions were at the Rialto Ballroom on the junction of Upper Parliament Street and Catherine Street and it was torched during the riots in 1981. It was so sad to see it go up in flames. They had columns outside and there was originally a beautiful ballroom, a big cinema and a restaurant. It was solely a cinema when Bill Harry arranged those sessions in 1963 and Oriole set up the equipment in the disused restaurant. It's a bit like teacher's pets as Bill contacted his favourite groups and he had Faron's Flamingos, Rory Storm and the Hurricanes, Sonny Webb and the Cascades, Earl Preston and the TT's, Ian and the Zodiacs, and the Merseybeats. Nothing wrong with that as Oriole couldn't possibly have recorded all the bands that were around, and they would hardly be one-take wonders as none of them were used to recording.

"The *This Is Mersey Beat* albums worked out very well and they give a good picture of what you would have heard in the clubs. It would have been nice if they had spent some more time on it though as, for example, Derry Wilkie sings nonsense during 'Hallelujah I Love Her So'. He sings, 'And in the evening when the sun comes up.'

"ITV recorded a special all-Liverpool edition of *Thank Your Lucky Stars* with the Beatles and the Searchers. They always had a guest DJ spot in their Spin A Disc section and the producer thought, 'I'll get Bob Wooler. He's the DJ at the Cavern.' It was shot in the Blue Angel and Allan Williams would have been much better than me because he would have been more relaxed. Billy Butler has a copy of the show and he wants to show it to me, but I say, 'Don't even talk about it.' It wasn't my scene to be a DJ."

The complete edition has been preserved and Bob's contribution is fine, although marred by an over-enthusiastic Billy Butler. "No, I don't agree with you," says Billy, "It works fine. I have watched it back on a few occasions. Bob is as smooth as ever and he could have made it as a TV personality, but he wouldn't even try it. He didn't like appearing on television and I spent the day ensuring he'd be okay for the final recording. He did lack confidence and he felt at home in the Cavern because he would be speaking from the band-room where nobody would see him."

Bob Wooler: "I have an audition record which Jack Baverstock did for me, but I did not sound like one of those whizz-kids that you would hear on Radio Luxembourg or later, Radio Caroline. My forte was not in introducing records on radio and the type of programme I would have liked to make would not have been wanted. A programme like Benny Green's on Radio 2 would have suited me fine as he discussed the great songwriters. One minute I would be listening to Frank Sinatra and Ella Fitzgerald and then I would go off to a jive dance and do an Alan Freed - 'And now! - Karl Terry and his Rockin' Cruisers!' It was Jekyll and Hyde stuff.

"In 1964 Geoff Baker from Kennedy Street Enterprises - this is not the Geoff Baker who is Paul McCartney's PR officer today - came over from Manchester and said he could arrange a series at an excellent time on Radio Luxembourg, 10.30 on Sunday evenings. It would be called *Sunday Night At The Cavern* and there would be a group and I would play a few records. More importantly, the programme would be interspersed with plugs for Curry's, the sponsors.

"*Sunday Night At The Cavern* was made by a production company, Ross Radio, and their owner, Monty Bailey-Watson, would drive up the new motorway to the Cavern in a superduper E-type Jag. Despite that, perhaps because of it, Ross Radio made the series on the cheap by recording four 30-minute programmes in a day because they didn't want the expense of staying in Liverpool overnight. It was two at lunchtime and two in the evening, and when they switched to one at lunchtime and three at night, it was no better. They hated retakes and they would say, 'Try not to make any mistakes.' It was in front of a paying audience, so there could be no delays as we would lose the audience. I was quaking and doing them that fast was ridiculous. The programme was being broadcast across Europe on 208 and I was only being paid £10 a show. I had to get Ray McFall on to them when they hadn't paid me for a while.

Ray McFall: "Bob worked hard on that programme. He would select the groups, write the script and present the programme. It worked out very well but Bob suffered from last minuteitis. He would be writing his links for one show while he was recording another."

Pete Frame recalls, "I was working for the Prudential as a surveyor and I came to Liverpool one week in four. I only went to the Cavern once and they were recording the first *Sunday Night At The Cavern*. They were having difficulties with placing the microphones correctly and the Remo Four did 'Sugar Shack' six times. I remember the darkness and the ambience and I felt very lost, a little boy lost from the south, but a local lad asked to me go on the dance floor with him and split up a couple of local lasses. I must have been intimidated as I retreated as soon as the song was over."

Bob Wooler: "Part of the film, *Ferry Cross The Mersey*, was shot at the Cavern and I helped with the continuity. They were filming from 7.30 in the morning and they wanted some Cavernites occupying the front rows, and the same people occupying the same seats at night. The Cavernites asked me if they were getting paid as they could have been in bed. They lined up in Mathew Street and refused to go into the Cavern until the readies were agreed.

"The Cavern was very cold first thing in the morning and I said to the director, 'You want these scenes to match with the ones at 9 o'clock tonight when Gerry is on stage. It'll be an oven tonight and there's no indication that anyone is sweating now.' They brought a bucket of cold water and threw it over Gerry and the Pacemakers to make it look as though they were sweating. This could then be matched with the real sweating scenes later on. Gerry and the Pacemakers can't have thanked me for that.

"The Beatles' press officer, Tony Barrow, researched an illustrated souvenir book about the Cavern by long range from London. He did call into the Cavern when he was here to see his folks in Liverpool, but it was only an afternoon's research. The book, written under the pseudonym of Alistair Griffin, was very pro the Cavern and didn't point out any negative aspects. If you only read the book and had never been there, the Cavern seemed fantastic. It was brilliant spin-doctoring.

"On the other hand, Rex Harrison, who was born in Liverpool, came to the Cavern with his wife Rachel Roberts and someone else from the Royal Court, and it was a very fraught meeting. In retrospect, it is a classic example of 'What shall we do now? I know, let's go slumming it in Mathew Street.' They were ushered in and given the red carpet treatment. They went into the bandroom to see whoever was playing and I went with them as they left. Ray McFall went behind the snack bar and gave them Tony Barrow's publication about the Cavern with our compliments. Rex Harrison was polite, but Rachel Roberts took the book up and threw it on the floor. Ray went white with anger and after the session, he said, 'Can we go to the Press Club?' This was over an hour after the incident but he was still worked up over it. He was hoping some members of the press would be there so he could tell them how she behaved, but even though it was called the Press Club, there were no reporters there.

"The MP Bessie Braddock brought Marlene Dietrich down to the Cavern. She was intrigued by the place so she prevailed upon Bessie to take her. Bessie said it was open at lunchtimes but they didn't arrive until 3.30 and no-one was there. Why didn't they let us know? I would have loved to have met Marlene Dietrich.

"Donald Zec, the showbiz writer for the *Daily Mirror*, decided to cover the Beatles in Liverpool, and he arrived when Ray and I were in London. Ann Hoare was the secretary of the Cavern by then and Ann took him down and switched on the lights and he saw the concrete floor and the bare walls. Reverentially, she touched the stage where the Beatles played. Exit Zec. A devastating piece appeared in the Daily Mirror and Ray said, 'This is terrible. Never let that fellow into the club again.' It was a biting piece but it was accurate with some very clever remarks."

A HARD NIGHT'S DAZE

Bob Wooler wrote this piece for Disc in July 1964. "Ray Coleman was the editor at the time. He accepted it but it is OTT and not very well written. Those papers were terrible papers really, they didn't want any bite."

Oh, how I wish you all could have been in Liverpool last Friday. To see for yourselves just how incredibly fantastic the Welcome Home was. All day long the excitement had been building up. You could sense it everywhere. This was the great day we'd all been looking forward to, when our world-famous prodigal popsters returned home for the Northern première of their film *A Hard Day's Night*.

From the moment their plane touched down at Speke Airport at 5pm to the time they flew out at midnight it was screams, screams, screams all the way. At the airport Press Reception they were caught up in a dizzy whirl of reporters, TV interviewers, cameras and microphones.

I waved a 'Hi' to them and they insisted I join them at their table. It was just like old times. They looked remarkably well considering how hectic life is for them. Paul asked how things were at the Cavern. John enquired how Ray's children were (Ray McFall is the owner of the Cavern and he was with me at the reception). Ringo wished to be remembered to the Cavernites. George said he'd heard my *Radio Luxembourg* programme the previous Sunday night. It was great to have a chat with them again - the same four friendly fellas I had the honour of presenting 292 times at the good old Cavern. How I wish we could have them back again.

More screams, more handshakes, more 'Hellos', more autographs, more questions, more answers, more cameras. And then they were whisked away. A mighty 6,000 strong scream signalled the start of the eight mile Beatle drive to the Town Hall.

Thronging both sides of the Beatle route, like an endless bus queue, were hundreds of thousands of screaming, cheering flag-wavers. People were everywhere, crowding bedroom windows, on rooftops, up lampposts. People with Beatle rosettes, confetti, streamers, balloons. Caps plastered with Beatle pics and 'Welcome home' slogans. Banners hanging from buses - 'We love you Beatles', 'The Beatles forever', 'Long live the Beatles'. Eight miles of this. A sort of ticker tape hit parade. Fantastic, unbelievable. Hail the conquering heroes indeed.

But this was nothing compared to the welcome at the Town Hall. Ten thousand hysterical fans besieged the building. 400 people fainted, 47 went to hospital. The entire city police force was on duty. Bastille day had nothing on this.

Inside the Town Hall the civic reception was in full swing. When the Lord Mayor introduced the Beatles, the 500 guests present cheered and applauded Liverpool's globetrotting ambassadors of song.

More eye and ear boggling followed their departure from the Town Hall to the Odeon Theatre. Here again the streets were jammed with clamouring screaming fans. On stage in the theatre the Liverpool City Police Band played a medley of Beatle tunes to a capacity audience. The house lights went down, the curtain went up and David Jacobs introduced John, Paul, George and Ringo. To accompanying squeals of delight from the audience, they each said 'Hello' and how great it was to be back home. They larked around with David Jacobs, did a little dance routine. The audience was in raptures.

They exited and took their seats in the circle with the Earl of Derby.

Then came the film - a fabsolutely wonderful movie - with the audience applauding each song. Just before the end of the show, the Beatles slipped quietly out of the theatre through a side door. Despite the rain, crowds were still around, especially at the airport. Thus they left as they came: on a wave of screams. History - and hysteria - was indeed made last Friday night. They departed exhausted, I'm sure, but also very, very happy. No other welcome had been quite like this one. After those five fantastic hours in their home town, they must surely have been in a hard night's daze!

Visiting card designed by Bill Tidy.

Keith Richards (The Rolling Stones)
and Ralph Ellis (Swinging Blue
Jeans)

199

20   MAL DE MERSEY
American performers at Cavern - Happenings - Financial problems at
Cavern - End of Mersey Beat - Sgt Pepper - Death of Brian Epstein

"In a rat race, there's no room for the mice."
(Bob Wooler to Karl Terry, 1964)

Unlike the other beat clubs, the Cavern brought several noted American performers to the area. Bob Wooler: "It was a bonus for me to have American acts performing at the Cavern. I was very impressed by the blues musician, John Lee Hooker, who played one Friday night. The audience wanted him to stay on the stage but there was a Merseyside group ready to go on. I should have said, 'Sorry, fellas, you'll get paid but there's no time for you tonight.' I should have kept him on because the audience didn't want to let him go. As soon as he came off, nearly everyone went and the group played to an empty house.

"Sonny Boy Williamson was backed by the Yardbirds, and Sonny Boy came into the bandroom one lunchtime with Giorgio Gomelsky, who was handling them. I said, 'Is that your harmonica case?' He said, 'Yes', and he opened it up and there was a bottle of Johnnie Walker inside. He offered me a drink and I asked a lad for some paper cups and we drank some. He said, 'Let's finish it off', and I said, 'I've got an evening session.' They were staying at the Lord Nelson Hotel, so I joined them there. Another bottle came out and I had to show restraint or I would have been legless. It didn't affect him at all - in fact, it exhilarated him."

Kenny Johnson: "When Sonny Boy Williamson was on, somebody got him a hot dog and a coffee from the snack bar at the back of the Cavern. When he got it, he said, 'Man, is this a hot dog? Back in the States, we got hot dogs one foot long with chili chili sauce.'"

Bob Wooler: "I remember taking Ben E. King to the Blue Angel after the Cavern session at 11.30pm, and I left him at the bar as I had a Cavern lunchtime the next day. I learnt the next day that Ben had thoroughly enjoyed himself at the Blue Angel and even sung there. I was furious about this - we had paid him £120 to play at the Cavern and there he was playing for Allan Williams for nothing. Allan Williams said, 'Well, I didn't charge him to come in.'

"Chuck Berry appeared at the Cavern in February '67. I don't know whether it was a massive comedown for him or if he was in a state of going up to Cloud Nine, but he cut dead Kingsize Taylor who had known him from playing in Germany. Kingsize was very, very annoyed. The vibrations were extremely bad so I was glad when Chuck Berry left the bandroom. He did his act but he only did what was required of him. He wasn't forthcoming like Sonny Boy Williamson or John Lee Hooker, who communicated with the crowds."

John Seddon, then an advertising executive for Radio Caroline: "When Chuck Berry was at the Cavern, he treated Bob terribly. He made Bob stand in the rain while he was in the car talking to him."

Mike Gregory of the Escorts: "Bob Wooler saw us at the Majestic Ballroom and took a liking to us. He wanted us to replace the German Beatles, the Rattles, who couldn't make it one afternoon. We got on the Cavern, but I got the sack for not going back to work. I was going on holiday at the end of the week and while I was away, they sent me my notice. I was a professional musician then."

And then there was Freddie Starr. Billy Butler: "Ray was very staid and if any of the groups made sexy remarks on stage, he would be on them like a ton of bricks. Freddie Starr did an impression of Jim Reeves once by lying on the ground and Ray didn't find that funny at all."

Bob Wooler: "I was always hoping that Ray wasn't around when Freddie Starr was on stage. He worked in the fruit market and he once put an enormous carrot in his trousers and pulled it out slowly. If Ray had seen that, he would have remonstrated with me - 'How could you have let him on stage?' I remember being with Freddie in the Grapes and he saw an attractive girl go into the Ladies. He produced his willie and flopped it on the table. When she came out, he shouted, 'Try this one for size.' Ray McFall hated him and that's not too strong a word.

"The most unusual nights were the avant-garde ones arranged by the Liverpool poet and artist, Adrian Henri. He hired the Cavern one Monday night and mounted Bomb, which was about CND, with the Clayton Squares. Some of the audience were bandaged for that performance, and *The Guardian* quoted me as telling the audience, 'This is not for the feet, it is for the head.' He also did one about anti-apartheid, I'm Dreaming Of A White Smethwick."

Mike Evans, who played with the Clayton Squares, was involved: "We took part in Bomb with Adrian Henri, Brian Patten and Roger McGough. It was a multi-media thing as the band played in the middle where the chairs normally were and all kinds of weird things were happening on the stage - Frankenstein monsters and the like. It was all very pre-psychedelic and it was revolutionary in its own way."

Bob Wooler: "In 1967 Jimmy Duggan, who was connected to the pirate station, *Radio Caroline North*, invited me to a Happening at the Bluecoat. I had read of the Happenings in New York, but the name meant the reverse as nothing really happened, and I was curious about the whole thing. Yoko Ono had a shock of black hair down to her waist and she hardly said a word - her husband, Tony Cox, did the explaining. They had a big sheet of cardboard and they invited the audience to write or pin something on it, as long as it was red, to make a mosaic. Various people did get up, including Adrian Henri, and when you looked at it, it did have something, although I don't know what that something was. I was bewildered by the evening. I spoke with her afterwards and she was told I was connected with the Cavern. I'm sure she'd heard of the Beatles, but she didn't show any interest in seeing the Cavern." I was also there and the highlight to me was when Yoko Ono, covered in bandages and tied to a chair, was heckled by John Gorman, shouting, "You're wanted on the phone." I did some of the bandaging so I am proud to have touched Yoko Ono before John Lennon did.

Bob Wooler: "The most significant groups to emerge from the Hope Hall scene were Adrian Henri's Liverpool Scene and Scaffold with Roger McGough, John Gorman and Mike McCartney, who called himself Mike McGear. Mike coped extremely well with being Paul's brother. He wasn't fantastically talented, but by being in a comedy band, he wasn't trying to challenge the Beatles. The fact that he was Paul's brother must have opened doors for them. Mike was very proud of his brother being acclaimed, and he has a talent himself for taking striking photographs."

Bob did harbour some criticisms of the younger McCartney. Mike appeared on one of my radio programmes in 1998 and when I got home, there was an answerphone message from Bob. I could hear the programme in the background: "Spencer, I am about to turn off this rubbish. I can't stand all this flippancy. It is as though he has something to hide and doesn't want to answer any serious questions. I suspect that he would hate to answer questions about his relationship with his brother truthfully, so he hides behind this ridiculous persona."

Bob regarded the heavy talent in Scaffold as belonging to Roger McGough. "I like Roger McGough's work very much as words come so naturally to him. Like myself, he is a serious-minded person, although much of his poetry is lighthearted and full of quick quips. He wrote accessible rather than obscure poetry, and most of Scaffold's best work is down to McGough. I did have visions of managing another Liverpool poet, Brian

Patten, but it would have meant going round the country and making contacts. He had a vocal impediment, a kind of lisp, that made him sound very attractive.

"I've never fully warmed to Adrian Henri's poetry as his work is too heavily influenced by Allen Ginsberg for me. I like his images but when he dedicated a poem to the Liverpool 8 district, it was ridiculous because most of the things were in Liverpool 1 and Liverpool 7. I first knew Adrian as a painter and his work reminded me of Alfred Hitchcock's as it was full of birds. He even had a dead seagull glued to the middle of a painting.

"Mike McCartney as well as Lewis Collins of the Mojos had been hairdressers and I've never understood why so many rock'n'rollers wanted to open salons. Ringo Starr, Rory Storm and John Kinrade of the Escorts all had that in mind, and Billy Kinsley did leave the Merseybeats for a time to do just that. I did parody *The Waste Land*:

> *"This is the way our world ends,*
> *This is the way our world ends,*
> *This is the way our world ends,*
> *Not with a twang but with a crimper."*

Bob Wooler did have occasional forays into management, notably with the Clayton Squares. "A telegram was delivered to the Cavern offices in 1964, and my face was crushed as it read, 'To Bob Wooler, Congratulations on signing the Clayton Squares. Now take the knife out of my back. Allan Williams.' Ironically, the message came on a Greetings Telegram, which cost him more than the standard version. The Clayton Squares wanted to sign with me rather than Allan because the Cavern had more clout at the time, but they only made two singles, 'Come And Get It'and 'There She Is'. You see, it was reaching the stage where no-one wanted to know Liverpool. It was a case of mal de Mersey with those people down south. By 1965, forget it, chum. It was as though they had drained the Klondike seam and there was nothing worth signing. Of course there was, but they thought differently."

Mike Evans, who played sax with the Clayton Squares, recalls: "Being managed by Bob Wooler meant that we were on every big event that went on at the Cavern. We were on a French television show with Gene Vincent, Manfred Mann and Gerry and the Pacemakers and the whole thing was hosted by Petula Clark. The London manager, Don Arden, was there and when he saw the following, he asked Bob for a 50% share in the band and he would see to it that we recorded the following week with Andrew Loog Oldham. We recorded an amazing version of 'I've Been Lovin' You Too Long' which, with double and triple tracking sounded like a huge soul orchestra. However, Oldham fell out with Arden and it never got released. We made another record and Don Arden said he wouldn't promote it unless we signed over the other 50% of our management commitment to him. We voted by four votes to two to oust Wooler, which was very much against our better instincts and I feel guilty even talking about it today. It did us no good at all as Arden didn't promote the record and moved on to something else."

Doug Evans: "I was managing the Clayton Squares and the Hideaways with Bob. Most people thought I was wasting my time and this made me impatient. People thought that the hit groups from the Cavern had happened and everybody couldn't have that success. We called ourselves Bob Wooler Enterprises and we should have been profitable, but in the end I put more into it than I ever got out of it."

Frankie Connor of the Hideaways: "We played the Cavern nine times in the same week when we went full-time in 1965. We came on the second wave, we were 16 and 17, and we found Bob very trustworthy, and he was putting an agency together with Dougie Evans, the keyboard player from the Blue Angel. They had ourselves, the Clayton Squares, Michael Allen and the Masterminds and they were building a stable like Epstein. They got us work in Carlisle, we were going there once a month three or four days at a time, and we did well on the east coast of Scotland. We were very visual and we were playing R&B, and we weren't a Beatle group. Bob had stopped his 'hi-fi high' stuff by then and simply introduced us by saying, 'R&B as you like it with the Hideaways'. Paddy Delaney had a wonderful voice too and they used to fight in a mock way about introducing us. Bob gave us some advice: he said, 'I don't think you should learn too many difficult chords because the girls don't come to watch you play diminished chords and augmented chords. They are interested in what you are wearing and how your hair is cut. The image is important and should come first.'"

Bob Wooler: "The butterflies of rock come and go. They are colourful but fleeting. They effect a certain wayoutness of garb, of footwear, of make-up, of attitude and of music-making that can be breathtaking and bizarre. They hope that their hairlines will lead to headlines and make them famous. They are left only with the memory of what might have been. Still, as Tennyson said, 'Better to have loved and lost, Than never to have loved at all.' Or, to put it another way, better to be a has-been than a never-was."

And Bob was particularly sorry to see some of them give up: "Chick Graham was a good singer but he quit because he wasn't prepared to put up with the jibes and snide remarks. He was small and people kept calling him a dwarf, which he wasn't. Jimmy Campbell of the Panthers was an inventive songwriter, who could write sophisticated songs as well as rock'n'roll. The group hailed from Kirkby and I suggested that they became the Kirkbys, which would attract publicity for the town and also for them because the second 'k' was silent. The residents would be glad to have a group of our own, and Beryl managed them for a while. They became the 23rd Turnoff because the 23rd turnoff was on the East Lancs Road, but it didn't happen for them."

Some good work came along. Mike Byrne: "When I was with the Roadrunners Mark II, Bob sent us to Switzerland and we got a six week gig in a top ski resort. The Beatles had just done America and Bob had received a call from Nick Lilley of Lilley and Skinner. It was his twenty first birthday and they wanted a Liverpool band. It was £10 a week each with all our transport and accomodation taken care of, and we had a great time. We played for millionaires for six weeks. We met Prince Rainier, Princess Grace and Doris Day and they loved us as we were a novelty"

Billy Butler: "In 1964 I was playing in a football game for the Merseybeat XI and I came off at half-time to give somebody else a game. Bob had been commentating on the first half and he was struggling. He said to me, 'I know nothing about football, do me a favour and do the second half for me.' At the end, he said to me, 'If you're that good on a mike here, what are you like playing records?' I had never tried it, but he asked me to do a night at the Cavern and he said, 'If it works out, you can become a DJ here.' He was under a lot of pressure with his agency and with booking groups and the Cavern. I did a session and Bob was perfectly happy. Ray McFall said that was okay, and Bob christened me Mr. Platter Patter."

Bob Wooler: "The locals stayed away from the Cavern as they felt that it was no longer their club. When the coaches arrived in 1963, I would say on the mike, 'Welcome to so-and-so and we hope you enjoy yourselves tonight.' The Cavernites would say, 'What's the idea?', and I thought at times that they might hammer them. They didn't, but they resented outsiders coming in. That was it really. Some of the regulars stayed but not enough to sustain the club. People were coming because the Cavern was a curiosity. One solution would have been to market souvenirs and to turn it into a Memphis on the Mersey.

"I soon realised the benefits of tourism and I told Ray McFall in 1965 that we should have a Beatles museum in Liverpool, but I didn't appreciate that things were already on the downslide. Dougie Evans, who was the office manager of the Cavern, invited me for a quiet drink one lunchtime and he told me that the Cavern was in the red. I found it incredible, I couldn't believe it. Ray had over-reached himself by getting stars in his eyes over a recording studio. He had rented additional tunnels for that and he had started an agency at the Cavern. Both were to fizzle out."

Beryl Adams: "Although Ray had worked in accountancy, he wasn't well organised and he didn't have any office staff until I came along. I left Brian Epstein when they were moving to London and I became Ray's secretary at the Cavern. He had a back morning room in his house and the whole floor was covered in money from the various Cavern sessions. The notes had been ironed and the coins were bagged with a note of the details of each session. My first job was to get it banked and pay the bills. There was easily a year's takings there."

Doug Evans tells a similar story: "When I got to the Cavern, they hadn't paid any tax. There was a lunchtime session, teatime session and a night-time session Monday to Friday. It was open through the night on Saturday and for every session, there was the door money, the cloakroom money and the refreshment money, all in a room in Ray's house. The accountant told me that I had to count it up and take it to the bank."

Bob Wooler: "The Cavern needed a lot of money to correct its drains and ventilation. The whole place was like a Turkish bath as we believed in BO, and that's Box Office and Body Odour. It was the sweat smell of success. The ventilation was State of the Ark and had packed in long ago and this is why I thought I was going to get TB because we were breathing each other's breath and everybody smoked. It was primitive and really terrible. I'll never forget Ted Knibbs saying to me when the Cavern was failing in 1965, 'You know the trouble with the Cavern, it's suffering from fallen arches.' I wish I'd said that." When I repeated this line to Ray McFall, he said, "Bob might have improved upon it and said, 'McFallen arches'."

"The conduit at the Cavern contained electric wiring and the Cavernites would stand on chairs and hold onto this conduit, and I would say, 'For Christ's sake, get down.' I would say on stage, 'Will you stop doing that? Those wires could be live and God knows what will happen.'

"Ray was very lucky and escaped criticism until a disaster happened at some club in Blackburn. The civic authorities thought they'd better take a look at the Liverpool clubs and unfortunately for Ray, the Cavern was the club in the news. They said, 'You've got no back exit, so you'll have to do something about it. Where's your ventilation, and where's all the waste from your toilets going?' These, as it happens, were very good questions. We learnt that the sewage was just going into the ground and I thought, 'My god, not only am I going to get TB, I'm going to get the plague as well.' You can't blame me for popping a few pills now and then to help me make it through the night.

"I was watching one group at about four o'clock in the morning and the crowd was very desultory; the excitement had happened and they were waiting for dawn to break at six.

Suddenly, there was a scream and ironically the group thought the girls were screaming at them. They were screaming at a rat which had jumped from under the seats and on to the stage."

Billy Butler: "We had been told that the Cavern was going to close in 1965. We had been given a week's notice, and within that week, me, Bob McGrae and Bob Wooler paid off the debtor who was foreclosing. It was only £30 and we had to give it to Ray McFall as a gift for it to work legally, to get the injunction lifted. We asked a London agent Roy Tempest to help us out with an all-night session and he gave us Rufus Thomas, Solomon Burke and the Drifters for free, and so all the money went to the Cavern to keep it open for longer."

But the troubles continued. Bob Wooler: "I used to say to Ray, 'Don't let the phones go off because the outside world might get wind of it and ask, 'Haven't you paid the bill?'' The phones did go off and we had go to the White Star to use their public phone. We drew up a list of people who might help us and we even phoned Murray The K in New York. We needed £8,000 and we didn't get it."

The Beatles played the Liverpool Empire on 5 December 1965 on what was to be their last Liverpool appearance. Bob Wooler: "The Beatles were accosted by the press when they were playing the Liverpool Empire. They had just done *Help!*, but they weren't giving any. The press were asking punchy questions such as 'The Cavern is on the ropes, so what are you going to do about it?' They said they couldn't help out but they could have done, they were rolling in cash. The key is in something Ringo said. He said, 'We owe nothing to the Cavern. We've done them a favour and made them famous.' You can't argue with that, but where was their generosity? It would only have been £2,000 a Beatle.

"Ray McFall had been expecting the bailiffs and it happened on Monday morning, 28 February 1966. He had been told that this time it was for keeps, and the groups played there from three o'clock on Sunday afternoon to eight o'clock on Monday morning. They played the whole night through for free, but to no avail. The Cavernites barricaded the stairs with chairs but they were soon cleared away and if you see photographs, they are either bewildered or laughing, they are not crying."

Billy Butler: "We were told on the Sunday night by Ray McFall that this was going to be the club's last session. My first thought was that we can't shut without a fanfare and Chris Wharton, who was a partner of mine at the time, and myself went round the Liverpool clubs and said that the Cavern was shutting, 'If you want to come down and play, this could be your last chance.' The momentum built up and about half-past eleven, I said, 'Let's block the stairway with chairs and stay here as long as we can, and anyone who wants to leave can go down the side alley. The bailiffs came at nine in the morning and couldn't get in. I went down the alley and went to work at one o'clock because I was working during the day, and, as far as my boss knew, I was at Gladstone Dock doing customs work. I phoned up a few mates, did a little bit to show I'd been there, and then went back to the Cavern, but by then the bailiffs were in."

Bob Wooler: "Bessie Braddock MP was jumping on the bandwagon by saying she would get the Prime Minister, Harold Wilson, to reopen the club if the necessary work could be done. She was true to her word, but she was annoyed that we now had a liquor licence. She saw the Cavern as a youth club, which in a way it was. Like Albert Goldman, she may have thought of me as the scoutmaster. We were selling bits of board from the original Cavern stage and I had an expression culled from the Milk Marketing Board's 'Drinka pinta milka day'. I said, 'Buy a bit of Beatle board'.

"Ray McFall made his exit and the Cavern acquired new owners. Joe Davey of Joe's Restaurant in Duke Street acquired the club and did a deal with *Radio Caroline* to promote it. The Cavern was reopened five months later by Harold Wilson with a lot of ballyhoo and hype, but it was a different scene. It became just another club and I hated the way they served the drinks. It wasn't fashionable in those days to drink out of the bottle. The bottle was poured into a plastic container, which can easily give way. You need both hands on them and I thought how crude it was. It was done because it was safer that way: it stopped people being 'glassed', as they call it."

Frankie Connor: "Ray McFall and Bob Wooler were a very unlikely couple to be running a beat club but Alf Geoghegan and Joe Davey were even odder. Alf was a butcher who liked to be around people in show business while Joe's Café was a landmark in Dale Street. You could get a meal there at half part four in the morning." Alf also spent some time on the boards as Alf the Lightning Cartoonist.

Bob Wooler: "When the Cavern reopened, I spent most of my time working in the office. The window outside the Cavern had been boarded up and we would paste posters on it. One poster from a London agency advertised a group called the Golliwogs, and no-one thought anything unusual about it. Suddenly there was a commotion and someone had thrown a brick down the hallway. There were three lads in the street and they said, 'Get that poster down. It's offensive.' So we covered it up.

"A little later, Billy Butler and Chris Wharton hired the Mardi Gras and they had a lot of coloured people in, which was causing the white clientèle to stay away. They wanted to bring them back and so they closed the club for a couple of weeks. *The Liverpool Weekly News* announced, 'The Mardi's gone white' as they had painted everything in the place white. The implication was obvious and there were ructions in Upper Parliament Street. 'Oh no,' said Billy, 'This has nothing to do with race. The place needed repainting, and white is bright.'

"In the mid-60s, I also did some promotions with Les Lydiate, who wanted to have a big concert at the Empire - '*A Groovy Kind of Show* with the Mindbenders'. Les didn't have an office but I got him to sign a letter that he would be responsible for the payment of all ads as well as the fees for all the groups. Neil Brooks, the manager of the Empire, phoned me and said he had never known anything like this. Kenny from the Dark Ages had been in to pay the deposit and he had used savings stamps and coins of the realm. I nearly started laughing over the phone but he was very suspicious of the whole venture. I told him everything was all right but I was saying that with crossed fingers. The evening was a bit of a disaster because Les wanted two houses and the first house was pathetic. The Mindbenders and Ben E. King got paid but the local groups got nothing.

"I was one of the first on the boy band scene. I had three lads called the Signs, who didn't play instruments and were backed by a local group called the Times. They did a demo of 'There's A Kind Of Hush' but the demo was given to Herman's Hermits, so there's no justice. They did make a record, 'Ain't You Got A Heart' but nothing happened to it. They performed on that Mindbenders show but I didn't choreograph them as they do today: I was never into synchronised swimming.

"Ironically, I view the end of Mersey Beat with a record called 'Please Stay'. 'Please Stay' was a Burt Bacharach and Bob Hilliard song that had originally been recorded by the Drifters. Zoot Money covered it but his version didn't take off. The record producer, Joe Meek, excelled himself by copying Zoot's arrangement and making an excellent record with the Cryin' Shames. Zoot wasn't happy about it when I spoke to him. The Cryin' Shames released 'Please Stay' in 1966 and so I take the span of Merseybeat as being the decade from 1957 to 1966. The Cryin' Shames were the last of the squeal and scream groups. Paul Crane of the Cryin' Shames had a very winning 'little boy lost' personality, ideal to be mothered by the girls. The lead singer of Boyzone has the same quality, and it was a cryin' shame that the Cryin' Shames came apart at the seams.

"Mersey Beat had run out of steam by 1967, but that has nothing to do with the release of *Sgt. Pepper's Lonely Hearts Club Band,* which was pure coincidence. Indeed, there was still a liking for easy-going pop songs as the Monkees were having hits and, just to show you how the pendulum swings, they got their songs from Brill Building writers.

"*Sgt. Pepper's Lonely Hearts Club Band* is the *Citizen Kane* of rock albums. Like *Citizen Kane*, it had all been done before in one way or another, but a concept had never been packaged as completely as this before. The Beach Boys had got halfway to a concept album with *Pet Sounds*, but the Beatles put it all together and created a remarkable album in every respect. It still wins polls as the best album of all-time, although in a recent *Melody Maker* poll with today's musicians, it was voted the worst album of all time. No doubt the stars who nominated the album thought it would be good publicity for themselves: they couldn't possibly believe that it was the worst album of all-time.

"More interestingly, Paul Gambaccini has said that *Sgt. Pepper's Lonely Hearts Club Band* was not the first concept album and has put in a claim for Frank Sinatra's *Songs For Swingin' Lovers* from 1956. It's an intriguing thought, but you might as well put in a claim for *Elvis' Christmas Album* or the Beach Boys' surfing albums. I am sure *Sgt. Pepper* was in a class of its own and certainly no LP had ever been packaged like that with its gatefold sleeve, cardboard pullouts and full lyrics. It was Paul McCartney's album, he had the dominant role, but in a sense, it was George Harrison who had control of the group then. He was the one who had refused to tour and it was because of him they were seeing the Maharishi."

Although the events are not connected, Brian Epstein died shortly after the release of *Sgt. Pepper*. He was found dead in his London home on 27 August 1967. Bob Wooler: "Brian wrote to me when he was in London and I know that he was at his wits' end. The Beatles' management contract was expiring and he was losing them, and even Gerry was contemplating going elsewhere. He should have spent more time with his other artists, but he didn't. The Fourmost asked me to speak to him shortly before he died because they were disgruntled that he was no longer taking any interest in them. I rang him up and he was exuding his charm as usual, even on the phone.

"Brian did have theatrical interests and I went to the world premiere of *On The Level*, a musical he produced, at the Royal Court Theatre in Liverpool in February 1966. It starred Leslie Phillips and was written by Ronald Millar and Ron Grainer. It was a good show and although it transferred to Brian's Saville Theatre in London, it was not a West End hit. Brian had many irons in the fire besides the Beatles, but I can't say how disillusioned he became or whether he committed suicide. So many people connected to the Beatles lived un-Apple-ly ever after."

Beryl Adams: "Bob and I were at my mother's house and we saw Brian Epstein's death on television. If it was suicide, it was totally out of character. It was such a short time since his father had died and Brian would have considered his mother. He would never have killed himself intentionally."

Bob Wooler: "When BE died, I would like to have been a fly on the wall to hear what Lennon said about it. Paul would say, 'Brian has gone, we have got to have a stopgap manager' and Lennon would say, 'Hang on, Paul, it's not your group.'. I'm sure that Peter Brown fancied himself as their manager, but they wouldn't have that. He affected a lot of the style and elegance of BE, but he was no BE. They asked Dr. Beeching because Apple was in such a mess and he had sorted out British Railways. He must have found that rather amusing."

Rhythm and Blues Inc.

Roy Orbison with the Swinging Blue Jeans

BIG! BIG! SESSIONS

FOR YOU AND YOUR FRIENDS AT

THE CAVERN

PRESENTING TOP RECORDING STARS plus FABULOUS SUPPORTING GROUPS

1 SUNDAY, 2nd FEBRUARY, 1964
THE CHANTS (Pye)

2 MONDAY LUNCHTIME, 3rd FEBRUARY, 1964
THE BIG 3 (Decca) plus
DAVE BERRY & THE CRUISERS (Decca)

3 MONDAY EVENING, 3rd FEBRUARY, 1964
THE DENNISONS (Decca) ★ THE FORTUNES (Decca)
LEE CURTIS & THE ALL STARS (Decca)

4 TUESDAY EVENING, 4th FEBRUARY, 1964
THE CRESTERS (HMV)

5 WEDNESDAY LUNCHTIME, 5th FEBRUARY, 1964
THE ESCORTS (HMV)
COLOUR FILMING SESSION FOR "LOOK AT LIFE"

6 WEDNESDAY EVENING, 5th FEBRUARY, 1964
THE UNDERTAKERS (Pye) ★ THE ROAD RUNNERS (Oriole)

7 THURSDAY LUNCHTIME, 6th FEBRUARY, 1964
THE MARAUDERS (Decca) ★ BERYL MARSDEN (Decca)

8 THURSDAY EVENING, 6th FEBRUARY, 1964
HEINZ (Decca) ★ **VIC & THE TTS** (Fontana)
BERN ELLIOTT & THE FENMEN (Decca)

9 FRIDAY LUNCHTIME, 7th FEBRUARY, 1964
THE MERSEYBEATS (Fontana)

10 FRIDAY EVENING, 7th FEBRUARY, 1964
THE REMO 4 (Pye)

11 SATURDAY AFTERNOON, 8th FEBRUARY, 1964
JUNIOR CAVERN CLUB SESSION - 1 p.m. to 4 p.m. for 13 to 16 year olds - VISITORS WELCOME
THE ESCORTS (HMV)

12 SATURDAY EVENING, 8th FEBRUARY, 1964
THE ESCORTS (HMV)

12 EXCITING SESSIONS · 17 TOP RECORDING ACTS
In One MAMMOTH STAR-STUDDED Week at the WORLD-FAMOUS

CAVERN CLUB 10 MATHEW STREET (Off NORTH JOHN STREET)
LIVERPOOL 2.
TELEPHONE · CENtral 1591   DEE-JAY COMPERE : BOB WOOLER

NEW MEMBERS & VISITORS WELCOME . . . . TELL YOUR FRIENDS !!!

The Big Three

SUTHERLAND HOUSE, 5/6 ARGYLL STREET, LONDON, W.1
TELEPHONE REGENT 3261

This Agency is not responsible for any non-fulfilment of Contract by Proprietors, Managers or Artistes, but every reasonable safeguard is assured.

An **Agreement** made the ....20th.... day of ....September.... 1965

BETWEEN .....BOB WOOLER PRODUCTIONS LIMITED..... hereinafter called the

Management of the one part, and ....NEMS ENTERPRISES LIMITED.......

hereinafter called the Artiste of the other part.

Witnesseth that the Management hereby engages the Artiste and the Artiste

accepts an engagement to present
CLIFF BENNETT & THE REBEL ROUSERS

(or in his usual entertainment) at the Dance Hall/Theatre and from the dates for

the periods and at the salaries stated in the schedule hereto.

SCHEDULE

The Artiste agrees to appear for .....One..... evening performance(s) at

£70 (Seventy pounds)
XXXX(Seventy Five pounds): Nett

a salary of { ....------% of the gross **Advance** and Door takings.

The Management guarantees a minimum of £.....------

VENUE	DATE
The Cavern Club, Liverpool	12.0 midnight - 9th October, 1965.

ADDITIONAL CLAUSES

1. The Artistes agree to arrive at the venue by 7.00 p.m. and to perform.....1 x 45 min. spot.
   12.0 midnight

2. The management agree to provide suitable and adequate amplification including at least 2 microphones.

3. The management agree to provide suitable and adequate dressing room facilities.

4. Payment is to be made to Nems Enterprises Limited by cheque, within 3 days of the completion of the engagement.

Signature.......................

NEMS ENTERPRISES LTD

Address.......Sutherland House.......

Cliff Bennett

THE ESCORTS
Representation: Jim Godbolt Agency
Warbour Street, London, W.1   Management: Jim Ireland
Mardi-Gras, Mount Pleasant, Liverpool

The Escorts

Chick Graham & The Coasters

FROM
THE CAVERN - LIVERPOOL
"The Birthplace of THE BEATLES"
COMES THIS GENUINE PIECE OF THE
CAVERN CLUB STAGE ON WHICH
THE BEATLES
PERFORMED 292 TIMES DURING THE PERIOD
1961 TO 1963

212

21   I BLAME THE BEATLES!
Rock n roll songwriting - The Beatles songwriting - Duplicating titles - Bob
Wooler s songs - Today s songwriters

"What are you trying to do, Spencer? Get me lynched
by the Lennonites?"
(Bob Wooler looking over a draft chapter, 1999)

The chapter that held the most interest for Bob Wooler was the one about the quality of the Beatles' songwriting. He said that readers would expect him to be 100% in favour of their work, whereas he had some grave doubts about much of its quality. Time and again, he would compare their work to the masters of the 1930s like Irving Berlin, George Gershwin and Rodgers and Hart and find them lacking. Another time he looked through the lyric of 'Imagine' and said, "This lyric is shoddy, Spencer. Do you think Sammy Cahn would have let this lyric go? Of course not. He would have worked on it." To a certain extent, I would play devil's advocate, defending the songs against Bob's onslaughts.

According to Bob, the fall in standards came with rock'n'roll in the mid-1950s. "I love rock'n'roll but the songs dumbed down during that era. Brian Matthew played 'That'll Be The Day' on *Sounds Of The Sixties* the other day, and I could see how that song influenced both John Lennon and Paul McCartney. Both of them liked its structure. The original rock'n'rollers like Buddy Holly and Bobby Darin were influenced by the people who preceded them and although their songs were regarded as radical, they still retained a Tin Pan Alley feel. Look at that surprising twist at the end of Bobby Darin's 'Eighteen Yellow Roses' when it transpires that the other man who is giving the girl the roses is her father.

"I like 'Twenty Flight Rock' very much which is a good song and very humorous. His girl lives on the twentieth floor and the lift doesn't work. Rock'n'roll is not often cleverly humorous, but they could have improved the song with a little thought. 'All this climbin' is gettin' me down' could have been changed to 'All this climbin' is makin' me frail', which would have given them an internal rhyme. They should have thought of that.

"The niceties and the preciseness of the Brill Building writers with songs like 'Take Good Care Of My Baby' was pure Tin Pan Alley, and all the better for it. They were well-crafted with a beginning, a middle and an end and had good rhymes. The Drifters and then Craig Douglas sang 'When My Little Girl Is Smiling', which is a marvellous song by Gerry Goffin and Carole King. The girl in the song has the winning hand - he gets annoyed with her and then she smiles and 'I just can't win'. The girl also knows that she has the upper hand and I thought that was very touching. He points out negative things about her and resolves it by saying, 'I am so smitten that I have no choice in the matter.' That, to me, is a very well-written song.

"Jerry Leiber and Mike Stoller wrote 'Is That All There Is?' for Peggy Lee, which is so full of feeling and such a quality song that I wonder how they could have written 'Hound Dog' as well. 'Is That All There Is?' has a blasé lyric, the feeling that fame adds up to nothing and the singer is completely drained. It reminds me of a British song from the 30s, 'You're Blasé'. The girl in the song can't inspire her boyfriend at all.

"When I think of the 1960s musically, I think of four people or two songwriting teams - inevitably Lennon and McCartney, and Burt Bacharach and Hal David, who came from the Brill Building. I don't think of the Motown team of Holland - Dozier - Holland or Chuck Berry. I respected Burt Bacharach's quirky melodies and I admired Hal David's ability to write lyrics for them - 'Anyone Who Had A Heart', 'Do You Know The Way To San José', 'Walk On By' - there are so many of them. They lost it when they wrote for the film, *Lost Horizon*: they were terrible songs and that must have contributed to their break-up. I don't know why the songs were so bad, but everybody has their failures.

"I liked the way Lennon and McCartney used an everyday, conversational vocabulary. Paul McCartney's 'Yesterday' was not a rock'n'roll song, and that is why Matt Monro could sing it so effortlessly. I once told Paul that Noël Coward wrote some extraordinary songs. He didn't agree, but I like to feel that all this went into his head, if only subconsciously, and he did record a Noël Coward song, 'A Room With A View' on a tribute album in the 90s. At the Cavern, I used to slip in one or two records of my own choice and I once played 'I Only Have Eyes For You' by Cleo Laine. John Lennon said, 'I'd like to do that song,' and I said, 'Fine, marvellous', but nothing ever happened. He wanted to do it because it was one of Aunt Mimi's favourite songs. I suggested to Ringo that he should do 'Let's Get Away From It All'. It would suit him perfectly and I still hope he will get round to it someday.

"The division between two songwriters was more precise before rock'n'roll. One would do the lyrics and the other the music. It is not the same with Lennon and McCartney. Indeed, it must gall McCartney who is very possessive and self-sufficient that he had to give 50% of 'Yesterday' first to Lennon and then to Yoko Ono. And what's more, John Lennon gets top billing. They agreed that fifty-fifty division in 1962 and they would have never have agreed to it a couple of years later. Paul McCartney's songs are played and performed more than Lennon's so undoubtedly Lennon got the better of the deal.

"If you look at the first single, 'Love Me Do', you will find that it was originally 'McCartney - Lennon' so I wonder who switched it round. It does sound better as 'Lennon - McCartney', but I'm sure to Paul McCartney, it doesn't. Paul would have wanted top billing and I presume it was Epstein's charm that made him accept 'Lennon - McCartney'. The fifty-fifty split did make sense at the time as they were writing a lot of songs together and they weren't thinking two or three years ahead.

"The question of adopting the same name or title as one already in existence can give cause to a great deal of complaint and criticism. Normally a title, unless it is a registered trademark, is not subject to copyright. This has given rise to umpteen books, films, songs, plays and shows with the same title and this is particularly true of song titles. Sammy Cahn didn't approve of songwriters duplicating titles such as when Cyndi Lauper used his title, 'Time After Time' for a new song. Why do people reuse a song title, especially if the definitive song has been written?

"I thought instantly of Jerome Kern's 'Yesterdays' when Paul unscrambled his egg and came up with 'Yesterday'. I wondered what George Martin thought of it as he must have known 'Yesterdays'. And what about the B-side of their first single, 'P.S.I Love You' as Johnny Mercer had previously written a song called 'P.S.I Love You'? George Martin must have had some misgivings about it. As soon as I heard them do 'P.S.I Love You', I mentioned the other song right away. Paul said he didn't know of it and I believe him as I don't think he would have related to it at the time.

"Incidentally, and I'm sure this has to be coincidence, in 1955 when I was a railway clerk, I went to a musical at the Crane Theatre called *Apple Charley*. It was a good show performed by some actors from Chester. The opening song was called 'Free As A Bird' and John Lennon later wrote a song with the same title.

"You can imagine a songwriter duplicating a title like 'Day By Day' by chance because it is so ordinary: it's not like 'Help Me Make It Through The Night' which is so distinctive. When I saw that Dory Previn had recorded a song called 'Mary C. Brown and The Hollywood Sign', I couldn't wait to hear it. 'Don't Let The Sun Catch You Cryin'' is a great title, but it's not minted by Marsden. Ray Charles recorded that song and a few years later Gerry Marsden wrote and recorded a song with the same title. I can't prove it but I don't believe that was anything but a rip-off and that he was hoping it wouldn't be discovered. I sometimes wonder about Gerry - his autobiography didn't contain any home truths as though he was very conscious of his image and how he wanted to appear. I was impressed with 'Ferry Cross The Mersey' as it is a nicely developed song. It is very evocative and well written, and I've always thought it odd that he's never penned anything else as substantial as that.

"Far worse than borrowing a title is stealing a tune, but when I first heard 'My Sweet Lord', I didn't think of 'He's So Fine'. They are in different tempos and the themes of the songs don't in any way connect. One is eulogising a person and the other is eulogising a God. I'm sure that George Harrison made an unconscious mistake. However, I'm not sure that George was a dedicated songwriter - he wrote songs because he was rebelling against the Lennon - McCartney monopoly and because he knew it could make him money. In the old days he struck me as being the most money-conscious of the Beatles and it is significant that he wrote 'Taxman'. One lunchtime session at the Cavern, I asked George to lend me some money, a couple of quid, not much, and the next day I repaid him. Nevertheless, he admonished me by saying, 'You should be more careful with your money.' Funny, but I would never have asked Paul or John to help me out - I wonder why?

"Most people think that George Harrison's 'Something' is a wonderful song, but 'Something in the way she moves, Something in the way she woos me' is hardly commendable rhyming. Okay, Frank Sinatra recorded the song, so what do I know, but he was jumping on the bandwagon. I adore Sinatra but he was totally wrong to record that and also 'Downtown' and 'Winchester Cathedral'. It was not his scene and it would be like the Beatles' recording 'I Left My Heart In San Francisco'. When singers bandwagon, they are out of their depth - they are not liked by the people who revere them and they are disliked even more by the people who don't revere them. Everyone thinks, 'What are they doing that for?' To be fair to Sinatra, maybe the quality songwriters had dried up and were no longer producing the type of songs he preferred to record.

"Like all worthwhile songwriters, Paul McCartney was always conscious of how easy it was to plagiarise. Before he recorded 'Yesterday', he asked a number of people if they'd heard the tune before. He thought he may have unconsciously borrowed someone else's tune. When they assured him that it sounded original, he thought, 'It must be new.' It is nothing like Jerome Kern's 'Yesterdays', a standard from 1933, with Otto Harbach's unusual but perfect rhyme of 'sequesterdays' and 'yesterdays'. It could have come from a rhyming dictionary, and I feel that all songwriters, especially from the rock era, would be well advised to have one. Songwriters who don't use one are usually pathetic rhymers.

"Even John Lennon's songs have their faults. He had the talent to write them properly but he wasn't prepared to spend enough time on them. He wasn't a dedicated songwriter - I use 'dedicated' for want of a better word. A more dedicated songwriter would not have allowed 'Working Class Hero' out as it was. It's not the 'fucking' in the song that I object to - in fact, that makes his point rather well - it's the poor rhyming. John Lennon, along with lots and lots of other songwriters, was not prepared to find a better way of saying what he wanted to say. 'Working Class Hero' should have been expressed much more skilfully - as it stands, it is long-suffering and phony. I don't want to say any more as I don't want to be lynched by the Lennonites.

"The songwriting on John's solo albums is slacker than on his work with the Beatles and maybe Paul acted as an editor and said, 'Hey, John, you can tighten this up' or done it for him. A good example of how they worked is 'I Saw Her Standing There'. Paul had written 'She was just seventeen, Never been a beauty queen' and John changed it to 'She was just seventeen, you know what I mean'. That was an invaluable change as it is full of innuendo and it's like Eric Idle going 'Nudge, nudge, know what I mean?' Yes, of course we do.

"I wrote a lyric like that, 'Etcet'ra, Etcet'ra, Etcet'ra', three syllables, three notes, which was the phrase that Yul Brynner used in The King And I, and one verse went:

> *You worm your arms around me like an octopus*
> *Then I know I've got a gal with everything plus*
> *And all I wanna do is to start lovin' you*
> *Etcet'ra, Etcet'ra, Etcet'ra.*

"You hear the first 'Etcet'ra' and you think, 'I know what's going on', and then there's another one, and another one. It is double entendre taken to extremes.

"If you write songs for musicials you can be more adventurous in your references and rhyming. Stephen Sondheim has rhymes that you couldn't put in pop songs, the witty 'Gee Officer Krupke!' from *West Side Story* being a case in point. One of my own songs was 'Too Good To Be True' about a girl who was out of this world, 'You're what one can see, On a bright Christmas tree', but there's a twist at the end,

> *But as I have thought all along,*
> *You're just like a popular song,*
> *Your love is synthetic,*
> *I need an emetic,*
> *Too bad you're too good to be true.*

"You could get away with 'emetic' in a musical or revue number but not in a Tin Pan Alley song.

"I like 'When I'm 64' very much as there is such an absence of humour in rock'n'roll songs, and I don't know why that is. 'When I'm 64' is both satirical and ironic. I've read that Paul wrote it during the time I knew him, but he never showed it to me. If he had, I would have asked why he had chosen '64'. 65 was the retirement age for males, and he was using poetic licence because there are more rhymes for 'four' than 'five'. There are only a handful of genuine rhymes for '65', but why didn't he pick '63'?

"I sometimes wonder if people think, 'This must be a fantastic song because it's written by Paul McCartney' or some such celebrity. If it was written by an unknown writer, would they think it was so fantastic? I doubt it very much. To me, it's a clear example of how people think today and have done throughout the rock years. The credo which they follow is the singer, not the song.

"John and Paul never wrote for Eurovision and was that because the songs had to be submitted blind and it wouldn't do for a Lennon and McCartney song to be turned down. Many of the Lennon - McCartney songs are mundane and ordinary but some are superb. My favourite Beatles track is 'Here, There And Everywhere'. It is so well-written that I can't credit that a Beatle wrote it. Sammy Cahn singled it out as being extraordinary, and I don't think Paul McCartney will write a song as good as that again. He is normally much stronger with melodies than lyrics but here both are perfect. That marks his zenith and ironically, the song was written for Jane Asher rather than Linda, although she is not named in it. I would put that song alongside Hoagy Carmichael's 'Stardust' and Horatio Nicholls' 'Among My Souvenirs', and I can't praise it any higher than that. That song is wonderful so how can you explain 'Dance The Do', a pathetic song that Mike and Paul McCartney wrote together for the McGear album? The Goodies' 'Funky Gibbon' was bad enough but this is a parody of a parody.

"The Beatles were writing and recording quite simple songs and then they got more complicated. Either the Beach Boys were an influence or they wanted to be a step ahead of them. They produced songs that were not really capable of being performed live at that time, although almost any Beatle tribute band can perform them now.

"'Penny Lane' is a mass of contradictions, not that I object to that because I go in for contradictions. It is not meant to be realistic - the girl is selling poppies in the pouring rain and yet there are blue suburban skies. When I took people on Beatle tours, they were always surprised to find that the fire station was not in Penny Lane. One boy thought that the roundabout would be a merry-go-round, a carousel, so you never know how people hear and interpret songs.

"What are 'The Fool On The Hill' and 'The Long And Winding Road' about? You would be hard-pushed to explain them. Why has Paul McCartney 'been there before' in 'The Long And Winding Road'? The song doesn't tell you. Why did 'Yesterday' come suddenly? I don't know, the song doesn't tell you. I think he threw it in because it seemed to rhyme. Both 'Yesterday' and 'The Long And Winding Road' are full of pining for lost love and I wonder if it is because he lost his mother when he was young. Perhaps he doesn't know himself.

"'Strawberry Fields Forever' is so oblique, so obscure that I would bracket it with Procul Harum's 'A Whiter Shade Of Pale'. I think they were all as high as kites when those songs were written. I hear 'A Whiter Shade Of Pale' and I realise I am being conned as it makes no sense at all. No-one has ever explained 'Strawberry Fields Forever' to my satisfaction. I do like the line, 'Nothing is real', and I wonder if John intended that it should be a pun with 'reel' as though he was watching a film unwind.

"Talking of conmen, what about Bob Dylan? I can think of no better example of the Emperor's new clothes, but there are many people whose opinion I respect who think he is tremendous. Spencer, are you taking this down? I feel that Bob Dylan's songs are like those Magic Eye pictures which contain another picture but I can never see them. I did like some of the protest records, but I thought Barry McGuire's 'Eve Of Destruction' was better than any of his. P.F. Sloan who wrote 'Eve Of Destruction' also wrote 'Take Me For What I'm Worth' for the Searchers, and it was their drummer Chris Curtis who was having such a profound influence on their repertoire and chose that excellent song for them.

"Ray Davies of the Kinks put some wry humour in his songs, and I like that very much. I also like the music-hall influence. I have reservations about 'Waterloo Sunset', which many would say was his greatest song. He should have been more specific about the importance of London to him in that song. He could have captured his feelings about London when he was looking over that bridge. I don't expect him to be John Milton but look at the books of Ernest Raymond, who was very observant on the 1930s and 40s in London. In the same way, Ewan MacColl's 'Dirty Old Town' didn't tell you that much about Salford. It does mention the gasworks, but it could have had a real *'love on the dole'* feeling about it. Lorenz Hart's wonderful 'Manhattan' is far more specific about its subject.

"I felt that Cilla Black's boyfriend Bobby Willis had potential. He wrote B-sides for Cilla and his talent should have been nutured and encouraged. He wrote both words and music and all credit to him. All his songs are intricately and properly rhymed. I used to discuss songwriting with him in the Blue Angel and we liked the same sort of songs.

I am surprised that Cilla didn't do more of his stuff. After all, she had the authority and the clout to record what she liked. I do think that she should have recorded more Burt Bacharach and Hal David's songs after her success with 'Anyone Who Had A Heart' and 'Alfie'. 'A House Is Not A Home' is a remarkable song and no one has ever had a hit with it in the UK.

"Another songwriter with potential was Lally Scott, who was with the Phantoms and then Denny Seyton and the Sabres. He came from Prescot and was married in Rome and had a hit in Italy with his own version of 'Chirpy Chirpy Cheep Cheep'. That was a No. 1 for Middle of the Road so he must have done well out of that. He also recorded a single called 'Jakaranda', note the 'k', and I wish I had talked to him more about songwriting. He was killed in a motorcycle accident on the day the Queen was celebrating her Silver Jubilee.

"I did write a few rock'n'roll songs, but even they may have been too sophisticated. The groups were polite if I mentioned them, but I drew a blank because of CV, and that's not Curriculum Vitae but Cover Versions. That's all the groups would do, cover versions. The Big Three were playing the Iron Door and doing R&B songs like Ray Charles' 'Lonely Avenue'. I told Johnny Hutch, their drummer, that I had written some songs and one was a waltz, 'At Least You Might Have Told Me', which he said he would set to music.

> *At least you might have told me*
> *That you could no longer care,*
> *But instead you let me think that*
> *We had a future to share.*

"There's a twist at the end:

> *But I still think there's a chance, dear,*
> *For us to live happily,*
> *So the least you can do is tell him*
> *That you're coming back to me.*

"I couldn't imagine a rock'n'roller doing a waltz, but I wish I'd let him do it really.

"I owe my songwriting debut to Brian Epstein, which was 'I Know' for Billy J.Kramer with the Dakotas. The credit on the record - I never succeeded in getting the sheet music published - was shown as 'Martin - Wooler' - my name is often misspelt. I was dreaming that George Martin and I were going to have a partnership like Lerner and

Loewe or Kander and Ebb, but that was the only song we wrote together. Maybe he didn't think much of my lyric, but he was involved in so many other things. The title came from a film with Alan Ladd, *The McConnell Story*. He is testing a plane and when ground control asks him how he is, he says, 'Now I know how the angels feel.' The song was originally called 'Now I Know', but the music publisher, Dick James, altered it to 'I Know'. It caused me some anguish, but I thought, 'You're in there, you're in there, don't complain.' I get royalties from Polygram who acquired the Jaep catalogue - James/Epstein - and there's somone on the radio in Spain who keeps playing that record, which was the B-side to 'I'll Keep You Satisfied'. My last royalty cheque was for £25, and I'm hoping that its inclusion on the CD, *Billy J.Kramer With The Dakotas At Abbey Road,* will bring me a little more." As the illustrations show, the sheet music of 'I Know' was published, but sadly, Bob never knew it.

Bob Wooler:"I saw a rodeo movie called *The Lusty Men* where Susan Hayward asks Robert Mitchum something and he says, 'I guess I got sidetracked on the way'. I expanded that into a country and western lyric called 'Sidetracked' and that was recorded by Phil Brady and the Ranchers. The lyric is the story of my life - I've been meaning to write the story of the Cavern for years, but I guess I got sidetracked on the way. I am still writing songs, by the way, which is ridiculous. At my age, what am I writing them for? It's something that's in my system and I can't get it out.

"If I had had a collaborator who was on the ball and geeing me up, I surely would have written better lyrics. I couldn't find anyone to write the kind of music I wanted and I'm sorry that I didn't know Willy Russell then. He is a words and music man but he has so many talents that he has never concentrated on writing songs. I went to see *Blood Brothers* at the Empire and it received so many ovations. I wasn't used to seeing actors applauding the audience, but I was told that they were applauding them for their applause and encouragement. I would have preferred more songs, because the songs, as they stood, weren't the centre of the show. The essence of the show was the interplay between the two boys and their circumstances and the people surrounding them. It is a fantastic musical and I am very impressed that Mrs. Johnstone has been played by Barbara Dickson, Carole King, Helen Reddy, Kiki Dee, Petula Clark, Lyn Paul and Stephanie Lawrence. There is no-one else really doing musical plays on Merseyside, or at least there is a huge gap between Willy and the others.

"A talented songwriter from the Wirral, Colin McCourt, wrote a musical based on *The Devil Rides Out* but why on earth did he choose that? It is such a terrible book and such a terrible film. The highspot is when the horse arrives with the Devil on his back. Christopher Lee is telling them not to move out of the circle while he recites some mumbo-jumbo and the horse flees. Why didn't he come out with this mumbo-jumbo right at the beginning? It was the natural thing to do, but we wouldn't have had the film then. It's like the way people in films go into apartments at night without the lights on. It's such nonsense: the first thing you do when you go into an apartment is to switch the light on.

"My biggest disappointment, and I used to nag Paul about this, is that Lennon and McCartney didn't write a proper musical. I was telling them to write one in 1962. When the Lifelines feature appeared in the *New Musical Express* the following year, John Lennon said his ambition was 'To write a musical', which he might have said to appease me. It never happened and the nearest they got to it was *Sgt Pepper's Lonely Hearts Club Band* which had a reprise as well as a beginning, a middle and an end. I would still like Paul to write a musical and he is very ambitious. However, he took a bad tumble when he became a filmmaker with *Give My Regards To Broad Street*, and he is bound to be cautious. He will have seen the disaster surrounding Paul Simon's Broadway musical, *The Capeman*, and he wouldn't want his ego to take another pounding.

"I call this chapter, *I Blame The Beatles!*, partly to be provocative and partly because I do. The Beatles have a lot to answer for because they sparked off this dreadful tendency to write your own songs. The Beatles emerged as songwriters of note, but nearly everyone else was so ordinary. I blame the Beatles because, unwittingly, they have made songwriting seem so easy - so many untalented musicians write their own stuff and it is diabolical. In my book, OM stands for Own Material which has to be OMinous. Unlike the Tin Pan Alley and the Brill Building writers, today's songwriters have no grounding in music and know nothing about the correctness of crafting a song. To my mind, the Beatles opened a Pandora's box and we have had to suffer the consequences for over 30 years.

"A true songwriter concerns himself with the songs of any era: it doesn't mean that he has to like the songs but he should be intrigued by the way they're written. That is how you learn. They take no notice now - and implicit in that is that they know it all. When I was young, I knew I didn't.

"I find the repetition in today's rock music so irritating. When someone has nothing to say, why don't they let it go? They repeat titles endlessly, and the records are just chewing gum for the ears. The public don't mind as some university in California confirmed that the majority of people do not listen to the words. I personally go numb with the repetitions, although I accept that they may be okay for a singalong and that many jazz singers like Bessie Smith and Joe Williams have repeated lines over the years.

"Good songs are so scarce today. Young people show little awareness of the lyrics of songs: it's as though they don't matter. I remember playing 'Ruby, Don't Take Your Love To Town' to a Beatles' fan. He had heard it many times before, but he didn't know what it was about. What was he listening to? That is a very good short story. Ruby, an attractive girl, is married to a paraplegic who has been in the war. He's at home and he's begging her not to go to town and hence, to another man. I love the image of the shadows on the wall, and the drumbeat and the slamming of the door is so effective. The song reminds me of Lady Chatterley, who was frustrated by her husband and found solace in the arms of the woodman.

"Most of the time today, the songs hardly have lyrics, they are just something to enable the front man to sing and, in many cases, the records are effectively instrumentals. It's the beat that's reet for the feet that interests them, and that's what I have against the majority of rock songs. I also don't like the repetition: so many songwriters run out of ideas and repeat themselves. The skill is not so much in how to start a song, but in how to end it, how to build up to a climax.

"Frankie Connor and Alan Crowley come from the Mersey Beat generation, but I enjoyed the album they wrote, Many Happy Returns, as much as anything I have heard recently. Artists like Billy J. Kramer, Billy Kinsley, Albie Wycherley and Faron sing the songs, and I was particularly impressed by 'Call Me Tonight', which is performed by Mike Byrne. The theme is the same as 'We Can Work It Out' but it is much better. In 'We Can Work It Out', Paul McCartney sneaks in that he is more in the right than the girl - 'Try to see it my way'. I resent that: he is saying he is superior to her.

"People may read my observations and say, 'Who the hell does he think he is coming out with things like this?', but all too often people measure the quality of a product by the quantity it sells. That is putting hype above excellence. That's what rock'n'roll has taught us - LCD rules and the HCD is for unfashionable fools. I don't want to come over as a clever clogs, but that never happens in my book. 'My Ding-A-Ling' was a No. 1 for Chuck Berry, but that doesn't make it a worthwhile rock'n'roll song."

Paul Murphy and Allan Williams, during proceedings regarding the release of 'The Beatles Live At The Star Club Hamburg 1962'

OUTSIDE PICCADILLY'S Caprice Club after a reception to announce the German release of The Beatles Live! At The Star Club in Hamburg Germany 1962 are Lingasong record company boss, Paul Murphy, and former manager Allan Williams, the self-styled "man who gave the Beatles away", holding self-awarded platinum discs bearing the legend: "The world's most important platinum oldie."

Paul McCartney 2001

John Lennon 1969

22 A BURNT-OUT CASE

Marriage and Divorce - Ice Rink - Bingo

"Strictly entre nous,
Darling, how are you
And how are all those little dreams
That never did come true?"
(From 'Thanks For The Memory' by Leo Robin and Ralph Rainger)

"Call it my guilt-edged insecurity, if you like, but I don't wish to discuss these matters," said Bob Wooler. Nearly always dodging the question, Bob Wooler had been very reluctant to talk about his sexuality with me or, indeed, it would seem, with anyone else. Beryl Adams: "Bob told me in 1963 that he was gay. I'm not aware that he did anything outrageous and he didn't want to draw attention to himself in this respect. He hated being gay, it was the bane of his life. I knew he was gay but I also knew that I loved him and that I wanted to look after him. In spite of all his friends, Bob was very much a loner, the biggest loner I have known and yet he could get on with everybody. My family liked him a lot, they thought he was very amusing."

Doug Evans: "Bob was pedantic to a fault and so, in almost any conversation, he would end up having a row with somebody. He was hard work and not the easiest person to spend a couple of hours with. He had to be in control and yet he was so impatient. When we had the agency together, he would say from time to time, 'There's a nice young feller in such and such a group', but it was never anything more than that. There was no man talk with him. He wouldn't comment on the girls he saw."

I suspect that Bob Wooler was envious of the way that Yankel Feather certainly and Joe Flannery and Brian Epstein to some extent flaunted their sexuality. Homosexuality was illegal and Bob, a very law-abiding man, would have been horrified to have been arrested. The *Liverpool Echo* often reported the shame of homosexuals who had been caught. A professional man was arrested on Otterspool Prom but strangely, he got off while his partner was found guilty. I asked Bob how this could be and he said, quick as a flash, "Maybe he swallowed the evidence."

Yankel Feather, who owned the Basement club in Mount Pleasant, recalls, "At the time there were no places for homosexuals to go for entertainment and so they would hang around pubs and clubs and it was inevitable that they might meet people who would cause trouble. Brian Epstein was beaten up by somebody with a milk bottle in a park.

225

One day I went into NEMS and I said, 'Brian, I wish you would look at me and not over my shoulder.' He said, 'I am looking at that young man on the corner. He has just come out of prison and he is the young man who attacked me. I said, 'You'd better ring the police then.' He said, 'Oh no, I am taking him out to lunch.'"

Because of both the legal position and the social stigmas, Brian Epstein could not tell the truth about his relationships in his autobiography, *A Cellarful Of Noise*, in 1964. Yankel Feather, however, was quite open about his sexuality. "Being gay has never been a problem to me. Indeed, it has been a blessing in many ways. I wouldn't have chosen to be gay, but one does not have a choice in these matters. I liked making love and I still do and I can find no fault with it at all."

Yankel, who is now 81 and recently had an art exhibition in Liverpool, told me that he had once gone to bed with Bob: "I expected roast beef and I got jelly." Beryl Adams: "Maybe I am looking at life through rose-coloured glasses but I don't think that Bob was like that. He was very, very ashamed of being gay. If he did anything out of character, it will be because other people led him on. He might have been curious, I don't know."

Also, Bob Wooler didn't like talking about the later years, in his case, the years after 1966. He felt that it was full of missed opportunities, and that he wasn't able to control it. "I was a drained person by 1967, a spent force, as the novelist Graham Greene would say, 'a burnt-out case', although that refers to leprosy. I was at the end of my tether, nothing interested me and I was blasé and looking for some new excitement or enchantment. It was not forthcoming at the Cavern because it had all happened there. I used to say to Beryl, 'The rock'n'roll years have finished as far as I'm concerned.' I had pushed Billy Butler forward and Brian Kelly used to say to me, 'Why are you pushing Billy Butler? You should be doing this yourself.'"

On 19 August 1967, at the height of the Summer of Love, Bob Wooler and Beryl Adams were married. Doug Evans: "It was a marriage of convenience and he didn't seem the marrying type to me. I knew Beryl from the Cavern. She was a very nice girl but highly strung, which meant that they argued endlessly, a bit like himself and Allan Williams."

Frankie Connor: "I didn't go to the wedding and I don't know anyone who did, apart from his bride. We were in town that night and he and Beryl were in the Blue Angel. We didn't drink, and Bob partook of the grape and was certainly the worse for wear. The fact that he got married was a big surprise like hearing Epstein was getting married. Really? We knew Bob's persuasion but we had no proof of it. We loved girls, that was what the Hideaways was all about, but I never saw Bob with a lady at all. We knew Beryl, but I can't even recall him dating Beryl."

Beryl had lived with Bob for six years on and off before they were married, so she knew what she was taking on: "He was out nearly every night, but I was out too, doing bar work at the Embassy Club in Prescot Road. He would go to the venues on the bus unless he got a lift from one of the groups because he was never interested in driving. He liked to drink and he couldn't drink if he was driving. There were lots of ups and downs before we were married. There was one New Year's Eve where Bob had promised to take me for a meal. Instead, he had been drinking in the White Star and he said to the writer, Stanley Reynolds, 'Stan, will you take Beryl for a meal?' I was annoyed but we went for the meal and we came back to the Cavern. Bob was drinking Dubonnet and whiskey. I had a bottle of Dubonnet for him and I flung it down the bandroom steps. Ray McFall went bananas as I might have injured his DJ, but I didn't mark him. However, the accounts of his drinking are exaggerated and generally speaking, he was not obnoxious when he was drunk. He was just more theatrical. He had insomnia in that he would work late and then be up and out in the morning."

Bob Wooler: "I had met Henry Henroid at the Cavern when he was the road manager for Gene Vincent in 1962. He was a very impressive person and part of the Don Arden organisation. We kept in touch and he sent me a telegram suggesting I should do an audition for BBC Radio 1. Again, there is a legend that I showed up drunk for an audition at Radio 1 and didn't get a job that was mine for the asking. It never happened. I never pursued it because I didn't see myself as a Radio 1 DJ. I have never regarded myself as a DJ. I was simply a DJ because there was no one else to introduce the groups."

Billy Hatton: "Nobody had taught Bob his style. He had developed it all for himself and he had been ahead of his time. He could have become a big-time DJ and presenter, but he didn't want to leave Liverpool. He felt he would be a minnow in the ocean rather than a big fish in a little pond."

Bill Harry says that Henry arranged that Radio 1 audition for Bob and that the job was his for the asking. He knows that Bob had come to London the night before and worked himself into a nervous state in Piccadilly. Beryl Adams: "I'm not sure whether Bob did an audition for Radio 1, but I don't think that he was interested. He didn't like the limelight. He was okay when he had had a few drinks, but when he was sober, he shied away from it. He also wouldn't have been happy in London. Liverpool gave him that bit of security and he did love the place and didn't want to leave it. After the Cavern, he had a job in the Clic-Clic in Southport, which was a teenage club with live music. He did want to live in Southport at one stage but that was as far as it got. He reckoned that if we had moved to Southport, we would never have split up, but I'm not sure about that."

Bob Wooler: "We were married for only three years as our love tale didn't dovetail. If you think that this is a flippant dismissal, remember that I was born on the flipside of life. I was in such an unsettled state, and Beryl used to go on and on about my drinking. I did drink but not as ridiculously as some people have made out. I would never have lasted seven years at the Cavern if I had. In that respect, I'm like Dean Martin - he was able to drink and yet still maintain a professional attitude.

"Then the Iceman cometh. I was given a job by Derek Jeffrey as the DJ at the Ice Rink in November 1967. It was work, but I was so jaded. I get so hopelessly in ruts. I have said to Beryl, 'Why weren't you firm with me? Why didn't you say, "You've had your time, you've come to the end of the line, you must do something else."' She agrees now, so why didn't she do it at the time?

"The Ice Rink was all right on the serious skaters' nights as I was able to play Billy Eckstine, Ella Fitzgerald and all sorts of nice tunes at a reasonable volume. However, pop skating sessions were needed for the Ice Rink to survive, and they were terrible. All they wanted was what was in the charts. The skaters would go round hugging the barrier and shout, 'Hey, mate, put on the Monkees', and they would come back fifteen minutes later and shout, 'You haven't put on the Monkees.'

"I presented Bill Haley and his Comets at the Ice Rink and I said, 'What we have on stage are the very beginnings of rock'n'roll. Forget about Elvis Presley, forget about Carl Perkins, forget about Gene Vincent, these fellows started it off.' Bill Haley was received well but the punters were bewildered by them really. They were doubling that night at a club in Leigh. We went to the bar and the drummer was so pleased that he bought me a drink. He said, 'We've never been introduced like that before', and started talking to me about Louis Jordan."

I asked Beryl if one specific incident had brought about the end of their marriage. "Yes, one evening he got carted off to the police station from the corner of the road where we lived. The police came and told me, and this was totally new to me. I had never experienced anything like that and I didn't know what to do. I didn't think that I should go and get him and I left it until the next morning. When Bob came back, he was most upset that I hadn't got him out. He never forgave me for that and I never found out why he was arrested. He said that he was just looking in a window. Things started to get awkward for us after that.

"We broke up at the beginning of 1970, and I didn't have anybody else then. I was taking driving lessons and the instructor, Peter Mullins, dropped me off at a flat I wanted to see. He found out my situation, as driving instructors do, and we became friendly. Bob and I got divorced in 1971 and I married Peter right away, with our son Simon being born on our first wedding anniversary. That too ended in divorce, but again we remained friendly. I call myself Beryl Adams now as I didn't like the name Mullins."

Beryl had tried to expand Bob's wardrobe. "He was very reluctant to spend money on clothes. When we were married, I bought him some shirts and a few things. He got a new suit for the ceremony, but once we split up, he only bought the clothes he needed."

Frankie Connor: "He grew a beard and he looked like Captain Bird's Eye on a bad day. He was well but there was a forlorn look about him. He was still hanging around Canning Street. The Hideaways had broken up, I had a real job and was paying tax like everybody else. Then I lost track of him for several years."

Billy Butler: "I didn't bump into him that much as I was here, there and everywhere, trying to get work for myself once the Cavern shut. I was doing things in Warrington and Wigan. He was working at the Ice Rink and he was very unhappy. When he got a job as a bingo-caller, I thought, 'What a waste'."

Bob Wooler: "The Ice Rink folded in 1970 and by then, Beryl had gone and I was in trouble with the Revenue over tax. Like a lot of musicians, I didn't declare all I should, but I haven't told anyone about it until now. I can't understand these people who go on TV talk shows and let it all hang out. Yesterday I saw some beggars saying that they collected around £100 a day. That's a lot of money - it's £35,000 a year! - and surely someone from the Inland Revenue will have seen this show and be contacting them. Mecca, and not Macca, offered me a job as a bingo-caller. Bingo was not my calling but I did that for three years purely to clear my back taxes. I'm totally in the clear now.

"I was a curiosity as it got round that the caller was the Beatles' DJ. I soon realised that a bingo-caller is subjected to dreadful insults. If the punter wins, the caller is fantastic. If the punter doesn't win, and the vast majority don't win, they say in a loud voice as they are leaving, 'The sooner they get rid of that caller the better.' It's as though the next one in line would make them a winner.

"If you didn't hear them call 'House' or 'Here you are' and moved onto the next number, it invalidated their claim and there were ructions. It was a very tense situation and I would say before the session started, 'You don't often win, so make sure you let everyone know, especially me, if you have a winning card.' The assistant would put the card on the camera and it would show up on the screen so that the numbers could be checked. Sometimes they hadn't got the right numbers, and the audience would shout, 'Get on with it', as some of them would be sweating on one number.

"I was at the Granada in Dovecot which was an old cinema and it meant I could go to the projection room and peer through the ports and see how wide the screen was. Then I got a move to the Olympia in West Derby Road alongside the Grafton Rooms and I went all around that building too. On one occasion, I finished the bingo at 3.30pm and went into the Grafton Rooms where Joe Loss was rehearsing his orchestra, and the manager introduced me to him. I was interested in Chick Henderson who used to sing with him and was killed during the war. He sang 'Begin The Beguine' and Joe Loss simply said, 'A nice man'. I felt he could have been more forthcoming.

"Even when *BBC Radio Merseyside* started in 1967, I wasn't interested in seeking programmes on local radio. In the late 1970s, I did submit an idea to Roy Corlett at *BBC Radio Merseyside* called *Chartbeat*, and I concluded by saying, 'Don't spike it, like it.' I had suggested Billy Butler as a presenter and I only wanted a credit at the end, rather like Roy Plomley and *Desert Island Discs*. Roy Corlett wanted me to do it myself and it was effectively Juke Box Jury with a panel of three."

Billy Butler: "Bob was totally at ease and knowledgeable in *Chartbeat* and he also knew how to put his guests at ease, which was important. I did try and get him a series with Allan Williams, just talking about things that had happened or what was in the charts. You only had to put them together and something happened and I felt that if I produced them, we could have had a very funny weekly radio series. I never saw him lose his temper with anyone except Allan Williams. It never lasted long but it happened all the time."

I couldn't agree more, but they would have argued over their billing - whose name should appear first? I was once in Keith's Wine Bar when Allan Williams said he had been thrown out of a sauna. Oh, said Bob, you are now persauna non grata. Frankie Connor: "Wooler and Williams were a wonderful double act. They were like characters in a play. They were always larger than life, always extremely entertaining and always grouchy. They did Beatles conventions together but they could have been radio stars."

Bob Wooler
bending the ear of
Billy J. Kramer

Tony Barrow. 1999

Bob Wooler,
1998

Beryl Marsden with Brian
Farrell of Colonel
Bagshot

231

23 BEATLEMOANIA
Beatles Conventions - WW Associates - Tribute bands

"My hor-moans."
(Bob Wooler, 1998)

Bob Wooler: "Beatles Conventions are now an industry, and a highly profitable one. Cavern City Tours present their convention with immaculate planning in Liverpool every August Bank Holiday, and regular conventions are also held in London, Derby and even Manchester. The American conventions are, like most things American, on a grander and vaster scale than anything in the UK and one convention can attract 20,000 Beatle fans. So far as I know, no A-team Beatle has ever appeared at a Convention because that would look like an official endorsement. Pete Best has no such qualms, however, and regularly plays at Conventions.

"One of the first Beatles Conventions took place in Norwich in 1976, simply because it was the organiser's home town. It was in a church hall and it did pretty well, perhaps because of its novelty and small scale. However, this caused the organiser, Dave Chisnell, to become ambitious and, with Allan Williams, he promoted a two-day event at Alexandra Palace in London in December 1976 which was billed as Europe's First Christmas Beatles Convention. It was forlorn, dreadful and a total disaster. One reporter said that I was walking round in an alcoholic haze, and who could blame me? I did get my money, £35, but I had to wait several months.

"The Convention did so badly that the doors were opened for free on the Sunday. The image that sums up the Convention has to be of the four inflatable Beatles, each about 30 feet high, which started leaking and beginning to droop. One photographer caught the Beatles hanging their heads in shame as so few people were attending the Convention in their name."

Despite the setback, Allan Williams felt that there was mileage in Beatles conventions and he teamed up with Bob to create them. "The Liverpool Beatles Conventions started in a very modest way in the late 70s with Allan Williams and myself. Allan wanted to call us Williams - Wooler Worldwide Promotions, but I wanted something more sedate. We settled on WW Associates, and you can decide for yourself whose 'W' comes first.

We called ourselves 'entertainment entrepreneurs' but we didn't have a phone in our office at first. We would take our papers to the main post office in Victoria Street and use their call-boxes. We would load in the coins to prevent people from knowing it was a call-box and we would say, 'I'm making this call very quickly as I'm due to meet somebody.' Call-boxes were marvellous then as you got limitless time for your money, but when the new-styled, STD ones were introduced, the pips would be heard as you were about to run out and that would give the game away.

"This first Liverpool Beatles Festival was held at Mr. Pickwick's Club in Liverpool in 1977 and inside the programme, we included the English Tourist Board's guide to Liverpool. It looks like a satire to include it in the programme, although it hadn't been intended that way. The Spinners are in the official guide but the Beatles are only given a passing reference alongside The Liver Birds comedy programme. The powers that be had no interest in the Beatles and weren't even aware of the commercial possibilities.

"I didn't enjoy the Conventions because of the amount of stress and worry and the 101 things you had to attend to: Allan could cope with all that but I couldn't. I wasn't going to do the second one, also at Pickwick's, and his initial publicity only shows his name, but then I agreed to come in. Frank Sharrock, the manager of Pickwick's, said, 'These Beatle things are no good for my bar takings', and I said, 'Come off it, Frank, Allan and I do our best for you.' I remember Allan leading a conga up Fraser Street into Islington, down Islington, into Camden Street and then into London Road. They were all singing 'Give Peace A Chance', and we had to hasten to the bar after that. Allan is very good at these events as he can be the life and soul of the party, whereas I appear too long-suffering. The fault is not in the stars, dear Brutus, it is in myself and I shouldn't blame outsiders.

"The press hung around the VIP bar in Pickwick's, waiting for the Beatles to arrive, but nothing happened. When we moved to Zhivago's, Allan got on the mike and said, 'And guess what, folks? We have a real live Beatle here for you today.' Everybody was agog, and Allan said, 'And here he is - Tommy Moore.' I remember you mocking us in *Lancashire Life* for implying this casual drummer was a key member of the group. I thought it was a funny piece but Allan took a different view.

"We held five Beatles Conventions, four in Liverpool and one in Sheffield. Sheffield was the last one in May 1980. We weren't getting good attendances and the interest in the Beatles was largely negative, especially from the Merseyside area. Most people who came to the Conventions were from outside Liverpool."

Allan Williams: "We did two Beatles Conventions that went well at Mr. Pickwick's but they didn't want the third one there. The bar takings were down so much that they didn't want another day of Beatle fans. We then went to the Top Rank in Lime Street, but there was a change in management who gave us a hard time. We were going to have an all-night film show at the Forum, but Harry Livermore who headed the Watch Committee refused us permission. The Chinese and the Indians had had all-nighters but it was a no-no when it came to the Beatles."

That might have been the end of conventions but for one thing. Bob Wooler: "Consider this. He was a well known musical figure and he died when he was 40 and he wore glasses and he died in unusual circumstances in December. Any reader will instantly think of John Lennon but it is also Glenn Miller, who died in December 1944. You don't think of John Lennon of being 40, at least I don't, but Glenn Miller seemed rather older than 40. A lot of major figures died young - Fats Waller was 39, George Gershwin 38 and Buddy Holly only 22.

"The death of John Lennon at the end of 1980 transformed everything with regards to the Beatles. Everyone became Beatleised. I don't have much to say about the day of Lennon's death itself except that I had a fearful cold. I wasn't on the 'phone and didn't hear of his assassination until I caught the midday news on the radio. I went down to the Grapes in Mathew Street and Bob Cook, the manager, said, 'Thank God you're here. Everyone's looking for you.' Allan had been at *Radio Merseyside* since dawn and done one interview after another. I then did all sorts of programmes and interviews for the newspapers, radio and TV. The Liverpool playwright Alan Bleasdale was in a pub that night and some old-timer said, 'They're making all this fuss over John Lennon. Just think what'll happen when Ken Dodd dies.' I take back what I said - not everyone was Beatleised.

"Sam Leach organised a very big candlelight vigil on St.George's Plateau in Lime Street. I was there helping out and so was Allan Williams. It was Sam's do and I didn't want AW to take over, and I didn't go on the mike at all. We stood on the steps leading up to St George's Hall and there were candles galore. David Shepherd, the Bishop of Liverpool, was there with other luminaries. There was a two minute silence, although the traffic didn't stop. The weather was kind to us, it was free, it was extremely well attended and it was very touching. I felt then that there was a rebirth, a renaissance of the Beatles. It got dark very early and then there was a parade of groups throughout the evening."

"It's extraordinary really but from the moment that John Lennon was shot by a crackpot, the whole attitude towards the Beatles changed. Beatles Conventions have done very well since that date. Allan and I have not organised any since 1980 but we have appeared at several, often as a double-act. In moments of absolute truth, I say to Allan

Williams, 'We strike people as has-beens and curiosities. They look at me and they can't believe I was a DJ all those years ago.' I have an expression, which I put on my wall at home, 'Put it this way - At least the has-been has been but the never-was never was.' Billy Butler called us Tweedledee and Tweedledum, and I said, 'Who's Tweedledee, Bill? I want top billing.' Really, Allan and I are chalk and cheese, but don't ask who is the cheese. Cheese is supposed to be better than chalk, and yet you can write with chalk and not with cheese. Allan and I have a love-hate relationship but at times it is more like a loathe-hate relationship."

Allan Williams: "When we did the Conventions, people used to think our arguing was for real, but after the appearances we would be getting drunk together. We would be still arguing though, this time about whose round it was." Much of the time though, their drinks would be bought by the fans. I've bought them drinks myself and it comes into the category, "Buy me a drink and I'll tell you a story about the Beatles."

Bob Wooler: "People laughed at us because we drank so much. The next stop with Allan and I was always the nearest pub. Allan and I were invited to Paris by a French television station. Allan invited everyone in the restaurant to have free drinks and said, 'They're paying for all this.' Our bill showed all the things we had eaten or drunk, and the manager said, 'We had President Nixon here a while ago and his bill didn't come anywhere near yours.' Our fee was used to pay the bill and we had nothing left. When we got outside, I nearly strangled Allan Williams, I said, 'I don't like flying and I have come all this way for nothing.' He said, quite philosophically, 'But you'll never forget your time in Paris.'

"I have needed AW because his enthusiasm is constant, he is seldom on a downer. The bottle is half full with him and half empty with me. I need a person like him to keep things going for me. Without him, I know I would think, 'Oh, is it worth it?'

"We certainly differ over one thing. I am a one-off person. If something is successful, I don't want to follow it with something similar. Alan Jay Lerner wrote in one of his songs from *My Fair Lady*, 'The sequel is never equal': I wouldn't go as far as that but I would say, 'The sequel is seldom equal.' Allan has had bonanza nights with the Glenn Miller Orchestra and Mersey Beat reunions, but he has followed them with floperoos. I didn't want to follow up an all-night beat boat in 1966 but he persuaded me and it wasn't a success. I came across a picture of the Titanic sinking and wrote across it, 'Another AW promotion'.

"There are so many tribute bands now, and they play at the Conventions. Some people devoted their lives to impersonating Al Jolson, so I suppose it's nothing new, but no other group had evoked this kind of adulation and interest. A lot of the tribute bands come from this area such as the Premiers, who were named after their drumkit. I also liked the Moondogs who were an Eric's group who modelled themselves on the Beatles, but eventually dropped the Beatle tag. I am fond of the way that groups derive their names from the Beatles - in the 60s, you had the Byrds and the Animals, although to be fair, the Beatles had based their name on the Crickets. Now you have bands like Rubber Soul, Revolver and Paperback Beatles. Oasis probably derived their name from the Oasis Club in Manchester and I have one of their newsletters from 1962 with the Beatles on the cover.

"I was instrumental in bringing Gary Gibson's group, Cavern, from Preston or thereabouts into Liverpool for a performance at a Yates's Wine Lodge near the State Ballroom. They were very keen to play Liverpool. Gary Gibson looked like Lennon, much more than the rest of the group looked like the others, and he went solo. Whenever I see Gary Gibson, I wonder what is going on in his mind. His whole life is spent trying to be someone else, namely John Lennon.

"The Bootleg Beatles emerged from the Beatlemania! stage show. They are very impressive and have gone out of their way to sound as close as possible to the Beatles, and look at the duration and prestigious venues for the Bootleg Beatles' current tour. They even play with Philharmonic Orchestras. Paul Cooper, who is Paul McCartney, lives in Liverpool and I asked him, 'How's your mother? Have you bought her a new house yet?' He said, 'It's on the way', and I said, 'Good for you. You looked after your parents in the 60s and that was what the Beatles did.'" Paul Cooper has since left the Bootleg Beatles.

Bob Wooler: "I don't think that there will ever be anything as big as the Beatles again. Every time there is a new musical phenomenon, the media calls them 'the new Beatles' whether it be Oasis or the Spice Girls, but they never last. Oasis are often compared to the Beatles but I hope they develop into some other guise. Oasis took a year off in 1998, and I couldn't imagine Brian Epstein allowing the Beatles or Gerry to have a year off in 1965, although the Beatles started the trend for not playing live when they became a studio band in 1967. You see, everything can be directed back to the Beatles.

"The media loves all this. Journalists knock the Beatles from time to time, but that is only to get two bites of the cherry, to get as much mileage as you can out of them and to attract attention for yourself. I contrast John Lennon's death with all the grief surrounding the death of Princess Diana in equally tragic circumstances. The press and the public went mad, but I am convinced that the tributes to Diana are going to fade - I can sense that even now. On the other hand, the Beatles' legacy will go on forever and I can't praise them any higher than that."

CARRY THAT WEIGHT

Tribute bands can be big business, especially if you are the Bootleg Beatles. If you look at your local theatre listings, you will see around 25% of the acts are ersatz - there are tribute bands to the Beatles, Elvis Presley, Abba and Queen, to name just the favourites. They often have amusing names (Elvis Mcpresley, Bjorn Again) and here are some of the Beatle tribute bands. Most of them have appeared at the Beatles Convention in Liverpool and I thank Ray Johnson of Cavern City Tours for his assistance.

The Blue Meanies appeared at the George Harrison tribute concert at the Liverpool Empire in 2002. They were photographed with Paul McCartney, the first time that any tribute band had been pictured with a Beatle.

Abbey Road (Spain)
Aleph (Mexico)
American English (USA)
Apple (UK)
The Apple Band (Brazil)
Apple Scruffs (Italy)
Australian Beatals (Australia)
The Backbeat Beatles (UK)
Banned on the Run (UK)
The Beat Boys (Slovakia)
The Beatcombers (UK)
Beatlemania (UK)
Beatles For Sale (UK)
The Beatless (UK)
The Beatolds (Italy)
The Beats (Argentina)
The Bells (Slovak Republic)
Berliner Beatles (Germany)
Black Maria (UK)
The Blitz Beatles (Georgia)
The Blue Meanies (UK)
The Bootleg Beatles (UK)
The Bootleg Rutles (UK)
Andrew Bowers (UK)
British Import (USA)
Cavern (UK)
The Cavern Beatles (UK)
Chattanooga (Italy)

Clube Big Beatles (Brazil)
Damstadt Beatles (German)
Dark Horses (UK)
Det Beatales (Norway)
The Fab Faux (USA)
The Fab Four (UK, three different groups from Liverpool, Nottingham and Oxford)
The Fabz (UK)
The Flying Postmen (Moldova)
The Fools On The Hill (Finland)
Friends (Brazil)
Rolando Giambelli (Italy)
A Hard Day's Night (two US bands, one New York, one Ohio)
A Hard Night's Day (USA)
Hare Georgeson (UK)
Harrisongs (UK)
Hitcher (UK)
Hocus Pocus (Brazil)
Get Back (UK)
Gary Gibson (UK)
Lawrence Gilmour (UK)
The Imagine Band (UK)
Instant Karma (UK)
Itchycoo (UK)
Johnny and the Silver Beatles (Germany)
Liverpool (Spain)
Liverpool (Sweden)

Liverpool (UK)
The Machine Guns (Brazil)
Billy May (UK)
Freddie May (Germany)
The Merseybeat Band (USA)
The Mersey Beatles (UK)
The Meatles (Japan)
Mojo Filter (UK)
The Moondogs (UK)
The Moptops (Canada)
Museum (Kazakhstan)
1964 (USA)
No Reply (UK)
The Norwegian Bootleg 'Bootleg Beatles' (Norway)
Norwegian Wood (Norway)
The Overtures (UK)
Lenny Pane (Sweden)
The Paperback Beatles (UK)
The Parlophones (Italy)
The Parrots (Japan)
Los Pasontes (Spain)
Patchwork (France)
The Patriots (UK)
The Pinkies (Germany)
The Premiers (UK)
Profumo Affair (UK)

The Quarrymen (Ireland)
The Quarry Men (UK)
Ready Steady Go (UK)
Redhouse (UK)
Refer to Drawer (UK)
The Remnants (USA)
Reunion (Italy)
Revolver (UK)
Ringer (UK)
Dr Robert (Italy)
Roots (Japan)
Rubber Soul (UK)
The Rutles (UK)
Los Saltamontes (Spain)
Billy Shears (UK)
The Silver Beatles (UK)
Sgt. Pepper (Brazil)
Strawberry Jam (UK)
Swings (Norway)
Chris Tassone (USA - looks like Ringo, sings like John!)
Tunel do Tempo (Brazil)
Walrus (UK)
Scott Wheeler Band (USA)
Wishing (Japan)
Marco Zappa (Switzerland)
Zeatles (New Zealand)
Zeebra (UK)

Cavern Walks,
Mathew Street
Liverpool

Bob Wooler
15 Grove Park
Liverpool
L8 0TL

Mr Ron Ellis   Monday 13 August 1984
116 Churchgate
Southport
Merseyside

Dear Ron:

Thank you very much for phoning me this morning. I think I explained to you on the
phone just how I feel about this business of 'telling it all' about the Mersey Beatle
scene. As far as I am concerned, Ron, and please don't get me wrong on this point,
these various writers are doing it in the main for money. Ego comes into it, but they
are primarily doing it for the money. This can amount to a great deal - I know of one
person who is virtually a millionaire as a result of writing a Beatle book at the
right time. A lot of effort goes into writing an 'in depth' book about such as The
Beatles. Of this I have no doubt and I don't diminish the fact. But the rewards can
be very, very considerable. I could ask for a piece of the 'action', a percentage,
and why not? On the other hand, I could ask for a fee for my contribution. It does
get me, Ron, and I believe I am perfectly entitled to think this way, that none of
these writers is willing to mention a fee to me. It could be as low as a fiver, for
all they know. But the fact that it seems they want something for nothing - the money
grabbers that they are - my fee is now in the region of £50,000.

See what you can extract from Albert Goldman on the lines suggested by yourself.
But no pawnbroker syndrome, please. He must come up with a price, in black and white,
and in turn I hope you will let me see his letter, as you have promised. I must
emphasise, Ron, that whilst I must ask what's in it for me, I am really quite indifferent
to the fact. I am now rather insulated against being ripped-off, as I have been in
the past. This inevitably makes it rather difficult to get through to me, I freely
admit. I even may be contrary about the matter, and this must make it extremely
difficult. The truth is I've really got nothing to lose, have I? Always beware of the
person who has little to lose; he can be very obstinate, so much so that he may even
be unforthcoming completely.

Enough at this stage, otherwise I will be writing as copiously as Albert, and that is
not my object. Do try and see it my way, after all I have been putting up with various
'invasions' for twenty years now. It does begin to pall and make one prickly, you know.

Stay in touch.

Best wishes!

Sincerely,

Bob

Bob Wooler

GREETINGS FROM
BOB WOOLER
"THE BEATLES' DJ"
CAVERN CLUB 1961-1967
COMPERE OF OVER 400
BEATLES' SHOWS

Enclosure

Billy J. Kramer single

OFFICIAL SOUVENIR PROGRAMME
FOR THE FIRST - EVER
LIVERPOOL
BEATLES
CONVENTION

Presented by Allan Williams & Bob Wooler at
MR. PICKWICK'S CLUB,
FRASER STREET, LIVERPOOL L3
Saturday & Sunday 8th & 9th OCTOBER 1977

From "Love Me Do" to "Let It Be"

Acknowledgements

The promoters of the Liverpool Beatles Convention gratefully acknowledge
(alphabetically) the generous advice, assistance, co-operation, efforts and
ideas of the following people:

Billy Butler, of BBC Radio Merseyside, Liverpool.
Dave Chisnell, of Britains Beatles Appreciation Society, Norwich.
Bob Crook of The Grapes (Higson's), Mathew Street, Liverpool
Brian Holland, of Mr. Pickwick's Club, Liverpool
Ron Jones, of the Public Relations Office, Merseyside County Council, Liverpool.
Freda Kelly, former secretary of The Beatles Official Fan Club, Liverpool
David Matlow, City Public Relations Officer, Liverpool.
John O'Mara, of the North West Tourist Board, Bolton.
Richard Quick, of the English Tourist Board, London.
Cyril Richardson, of CBM Advertising, Liverpool
Ken Shipton, of The Corkscrew, Liverpool

The promoters are also indebted to The Lord Mayor of Liverpool,
Councillor Paul Orr,
for very kindly agreeing to open the first ever Liverpool Beatles Convention
at 1 p.m. on Saturday the 8th October 1977

Paddy Delany
and Ted Knibbs

Arthur Dooley's
sculpture in
Mathew Street

24 THE ALLAN AND BOB SHOW
Allan Williams and Bob Wooler at a Beatles Convention

This is the transcript of Allan Williams and Bob Wooler on stage with Spencer Leigh at the Merseybeatle Convention arranged by Cavern City Tours on 31 August 1998. It is typical of their appearances together.

ALLAN: We've only got half an hour and we're the godfathers. You don't get grey hair for nothing.

SPEN: We're going to start the afternoon with The Man Who Gave The Beatles Away, Allan Williams, and Bob Wooler, the DJ at the Cavern for so many years. (Applause)

ALLAN: I wonder if they'll be clapping at the end of our talk as you'll get the truth and nothing but the truth here.

SPEN: From Bob.

ALLAN: You're getting sacked before we start.

SPEN: Let's start with your first impressions of the Beatles.

ALLAN: I regarded them as coffee-bar layabouts. I had a coffee-bar downtown in Liverpool called the Jacaranda. By the way, I wouldn't advise going there today. It's not a very nice place and I hate the owner. He has put a painting of me upside down over the ladies' toilet. He's even crossed the word 'Ladies' out and put my name there.

BOB: Hang on, Allan, you promised not to say things that would be out of line. Someone may sue us and I'm not capable of it at my age.

ALLAN: Okay, so what do you want to know, Spen?

SPEN: First impressions of the Beatles.

ALLAN: John Lennon and Stuart Sutcliffe were at the Art School, and the Jacaranda was about four minutes away from the art school. They used to miss lectures and come down to the Jac because a lot of groups used to rehearse in the Jac. John was always cadging free coffees and cigarettes, and I was having problems with the ladies' toilet that I had to share with the sweet shop next door. All the girls were writing obscene graffiti on the walls. Knowing these lads were from the art school, the first job I gave them was to decorate the ladies' toilets.

SPEN: First impressions of the Beatles, Bob.

BOB: Right. We're in 1960. It's December. The Beatles had come back from Hamburg. Allan Williams had sent them over there. He had established a Hamburg / Liverpool connection for rock'n'roll groups. The Beatles came back in disgrace because they had been hounded out of the country, but you will know the accounts of that. Allan had finished with them as he wanted to concentrate on the opening of his Blue Angel club, which was not a rock'n'roll club. He knew a north of Liverpool promoter called Brian Kelly, who had a string of halls, and he told me to get them bookings. I got them that rather memorable booking, if I may so, with Brian Kelly at Litherland Town Hall on Tuesday 27 December 1960. Paul McCartney has recorded in *Who's Who*, no less, that it was a turning-point in their career. Brian Kelly thought, 'My god, what have I found with this group?', and signed them up for a long series of dates.

SPEN: But what about your impressions of them?

BOB: When I put them on stage, I didn't know what they were going to be like, but the crowd went crazy over them. It was like a big fight had broken out in the hall. I'm still trying to fathom out what they did to people that night - and every night after that. They had such a magical influence on people. That's why you're here today and that is why, in 1998, we're still holding Beatles conventions, not us although we started them off in 1977, but the Cavern City Tours people are. It's your turn when I've finished, Allan, and let's find what is so special about the Beatles.

SPEN: Had you any idea before they performed how good they were going to be?

BOB: No idea at all. I was relying on what Allan Williams had told me about the group: he had sent them over to Hamburg and said they were marvellous, and I believed him.

ALLAN: (To audience) Has anybody got the record, *The Beatles - Live! At The Star-Club in Hamburg, Germany; 1962*? (Many say Yes) Right, well, can you honestly say that that group would be the phenomenon of the century? We knew that were great, they had great personalities, but nobody could have predicted that.

SPEN: Do you think George Harrison was right in wanting to stop that recording being released on CD?

ALLAN: Yes and no. When it was first released, it was on vinyl and I was involved with it, and the judge said that he was giving permission for this to be sold as a piece of history and not as a quality recording. Now, 20 years later, someone wants to do it on CD as a quality record. I agree with George Harrison who said the Beatles never put out rubbish, and this was rubbish. By the way, I never got paid a penny for this. I got ripped off by X (name given) and he's a con-man. (Sings) "I'll be suing you in all the old, familiar places."

SPEN: And would you call yourself a con man, Allan?

ALLAN: No, I am a honest man and that's why I'm on stage here. (Audience laughter)

BOB: Listen to me, the horse's mouth speaks. Here comes a vital question which many people have asked me over the years about Allan Williams. I'm going to ask him in front of you all, and I want you to answer this truthfully, Allan.

ALLAN: If I feel like it.

BOB: I'm not getting at you.

ALLAN: You'd better not. You're walking with a stick now.

BOB: The question is this: if you thought the Beatles were so extraordinary, why did you let them go?

ALLAN: The second time I sent them over to Hamburg, Stuart Sutcliffe wrote to me and said John Lennon wasn't going to pay my commission. They said that they had got the job themselves the second time, and my point was that they wouldn't have even got to Hamburg if I hadn't sent them the first time. He had no right to get the booking: it was in the contract.

SPEN: Does that mean that John Lennon was the leader of the group at the time?

ALLAN: Oh, definitely. Paul was jockeying for the position, but it was John's group. It was John who had the Quarry Men. Paul joined them.

BOB: I'm visualising the Beatles at the Cavern. If you were looking at the stage, it would be George on the left, Paul in the middle and John on the right, so I got the feeling that Paul was the radiant person in that group and John couldn't give a damn about it.

ALLAN: If Paul hadn't been successful as a Beatle, he would have been a good public relations man. He could smooth the troubled waters.

BOB: I am going to make a statement about the Beatles. If Lennon and McCartney had not been a great songwriting duo, the Beatles would have been another come-and-go group. The songs that they wrote were the vital thing about the Beatles.

ALLAN: How about some of the myths about the Beatles?

BOB: Well, you're the one who started them off!

SPEN: Let's take one from a couple of weeks ago, the story of Lord Woodbine and his place in the early Beatles' history, which seems to be kicking you out of the story, Allan.

ALLAN: Yes, I was hurt over that, but Woody was led by the nose. He didn't say all those things. Lord Woodbine and I were partners on various things including the famous strip club in Upper Parliament Street. When one girl wanted to strip to live music, the Beatles - I think it was just three of them then - backed her. The strip club wasn't our scene and I said, 'Let's sell it' and with the money we made, we went to Hamburg. Woody knew the Beatles through his association with me and the story has got out of hand. I am not going to fall out with Woody because of a stupid newspaper report.

BOB: But you are not using the language you used to me when his article appeared in *The Observer* and *Daily Mail* and you were annoyed because you hate taking a back seat, Allan.

ALLAN: Calm down, Bob, calm down.

BOB: And he's got the best mike, I've got the lousy one. You are letting Woody off so easily, Allan, and he was calling you all sorts of names.

ALLAN: "Sticks and stones may break my bones, but words will never hurt me."

BOB: Is that original?

SPEN: Bob, when Allan had given up on the Beatles, didn't you think of signing them?

BOB: The Beatles were a very difficult group to handle…

ALLAN: Hear, hear.

BOB: McCartney, Lennon and Harrison could close ranks against you - Pete Best was much milder in the background, but he did chip in. But it was impossible for me, an ex-railway clerk with no finances and no car…

ALLAN: I was only an ex-plumber, I wasn't Brian Epstein with a silver spoon in my mouth.

BOB: Exactly. Brian Epstein had a car and he had money and he had clout, and so they gravitated towards him. Other people were toying with the idea of managing the Beatles: there was Ray McFall, who owned the Cavern, Sam Leach quite seriously, your friend Bill Harry…

ALLAN: (Blows raspberry) As George Harrison said, he knew nothing about the Beatles.

SPEN: Hang on, George said that about Kingsize Taylor, not Bill Harry.

ALLAN: Bill Harry is a plastic Scouser who lives in London like so many of them . (Laughter) He's a fart. So sue me, Bill Harry. (More laughter)

BOB: Is that it?

ALLAN: You don't want any more - you're frightened of being sued.

SPEN: So the difference between Brian Epstein and you two is that he had a cheque book.

ALLAN: Oh, no, no, to me he was like a fifth Beatle. He did it for the love of the Beatles and he wasn't just being "a professional manager". He made mistakes over the merchandising.

BOB: I can't believe what I'm hearing from you.

ALLAN: I've never knocked Brian Epstein!

BOB: You said to me when you eventually got the Blue Angel going, "Look, Bob, the Blue Angel is a cabaret club and I don't want you bringing in any of your fucking rock'n'rollers." (Laughter)

ALLAN: You didn't hear that, folks. Go and wash your mouth out with alcohol.

BOB: And guess what, folks, within two years you were signing groups up, and I got a bad name from the resident band who were playing the likes of George Shearing. Allan said to them, "Wooler did it. He brought the groups in here." Anyway, we're digressing. The point is, you didn't talk about Epstein like that in the Blue Angel.

ALLAN: Well, Brian told me that he was thinking of managing the Beatles and I said, "Don't touch them with a f'ing bargepole." That's better than what you said.

SPEN: And he took no notice of you.

ALLAN: Well, you could say that, yes. (Laughter) Everybody makes mistakes. It's just that my mistake was the biggest mistake in show business. (Laughter)

SPEN: How do you think Brian managed them, vis-à-vis the way you would have done it?

ALLAN: I think they killed Brian in the end.

BOB: Come off it, Allan!

ALLAN: I didn't say they assassinated him. (Laughter)

BOB: Philip Norman in his book *Shout!* suggests that the Mafia killed Brian. Do you think that's right?

ALLAN: Oh, that was to sell the book, wasn't it?

SPEN: (Trying to get control) Let's take the Beatles one by one and have a favourite reminscence about them. Allan, Paul McCartney.

ALLAN: Oh, yes, this went on for ten years. I acquired Paul McCartney's leather trousers and first of all, Paul said they were stolen. We proved that they weren't. Then he decided that they weren't his bloody trousers - he said, "Look at the size of them, I haven't grown six inches." The truth is that Faron, who is my height, five foot nothing, had the trousers after Paul and he cut the trousers down to fit him. That's why the legs were different. I wasn't going to give in as I knew that they were Paul's trousers. By the smell. (Laughter) I suggested a DNA test and he backed off. He refused to go into court and so I got the trousers back, which I have still got if anybody wants to make a bid for them. (Laughter) I'm charging a pound a sniff. (More laughter) Anyway, after ten years it was thrown out of court. My bill was £8,000, so you can imagine what his bill was like. Those trousers must have cost £25,000.

SPEN: And you do hope to sell them at a high price?

ALLAN: Oh yes, well, I have got to pay for things like my big Frank Sinatra night next week - it's on 6 September at Maxine's Club in Wigan. Tickets are still available.

BOB: Of course they are. This is one of your Titanic promotions. (Laughter)

SPEN: And your story about Paul.

BOB: Right, we are in '61, the pubs weren't open all day as they are now so at three o'clock, Lennon, McCartney and I decided to go to the Mandolin Club for a drink. This was an old cinema near the Cathedral. I was amazed by the person who ran the club as he had a bowl of purple hearts and pills, which they popped in those days. I know you have never popped and you have never smoked, and you don't believe in that, Spen, but we did. John was on a sofa with a girl and Paul went over to the upright piano on the stage and he played a tune. I asked him what it was called and he said, "'Suicide'". I learnt from Spencer that years later, 'Suicide' emerged on a tape he sent to Frank Sinatra for him to record. Sinatra thought a song called 'Suicide' was a pisstake and turned it down.

ALLAN: Bob was talking about Sinatra. Does anybody know the size of the wood that they used for Frank Sinatra's coffin?

SPEN: Go on.

ALLAN: (Sings) "Two by two by two." (Allan cackles, much laughter)

SPEN: Let's move onto George Harrison.

ALLAN: Oh yes, it's rather sad. George told me in the Blue Angel that he was extremely upset that he wasn't included in the songwriting team. He said, "You know that we all wrote songs in Hamburg." He was very upset that Brian had chosen Lennon and McCartney as a team.

BOB: Hang on, you're going a bit berserk here.

ALLAN: No, I've got a witness, his girlfriend, Bernadette.

BOB: But they didn't write songs together.

ALLAN: Yes, they did, in the Hamburg days.

SPEN: And a George Harrison story from you, Bob.

BOB: Well, I could tell you about one in Brian Epstein's home, but I won't do that now, I am saving it for the book.

ALLAN: Oh yes, folks, finally Bob is writing a book and I am between the two of them. Spen is writing it and Bob is doing the talking. A few years ago Bob was saying that he had written a book and that it wasn't going to be published until his death, but that was just to get people off his back. Now he has the tenacity of this young man who's pushing Bob, and at last we're going to have the book to end all books. I want a galley proof by the way.

BOB: I hope you've got a smart lawyer! (Laughter)

ALLAN: I sure have - Rex Makin - and you can't get any smarter than that.

SPEN: Let's have the George Harrison story that you are going to tell us.

BOB: Okay, 'cause you are watching the clock of course. George came to me one Saturday night at the Cavern when he was late. He was just in time for the middle spot, which was the best spot to have. I said, "Are you all right, George? Where the hell have you been?" He said, "Don't tell Eppy, but I've been having sex with a girl." I'm afraid it's a very short story.

SPEN: Well, it brings us back to time. A drummer's story now - Pete or Ringo.

ALLAN: I was around when Pete got the sack and like most of us in Liverpool, we were very upset. He had been with the Beatles all through the hard times, in the Hamburg days, in the Cavern days. Now they'd got their feet on the bottom of the ladder and they sacked him. That comes under the Dirty Tricks Act. Why did it take two years to discover he was no good on the drums?

BOB: Why do you think they really got rid of them?

ALLAN: The most popular story is that he was too good-looking and that Paul McCartney was jealous and he was the instigator of the sacking.

BOB: But do you believe that?

ALLAN: No, I don't really. I don't think Pete was a Beatle socially.

BOB: Spen has written a book about it, *Drummed Out!*. It has just come out, he has talked to a lot of people and there's a hell of a lot in there that neither of us know, Allan.

SPEN: There's a stall selling it in the other room.

ALLAN: This is the commercial break, folks. (Laughter)

SPEN: And who was plugging his Sinatra night five minutes ago? (Laughter) Let's get back to the stories. Allan, John Lennon.

ALLAN: They're too dirty.

SPEN: Do we mind them being dirty?

AUDIENCE: No!

ALLAN: No, no, there are some children here, I can't tell these.

BOB: Okay. John did cherish Aunt Mimi and he was under her umbrella, her protection, as it were. She decided to come to the Cavern with a friend one lunchtime. John told us that she was coming and he said, "No swearing, behave yourselves." I thought that was rich coming from John who was the most outrageous person around. I'm not saying that John wasn't a nice person but he was very wayward, very rebellious, very assertive and this is what Paul McCartney didn't like about him.

ALLAN: This week in the paper there is a German lady, woman, member of the opposite sex, I don't know how to describe this dreadful person who is claiming that she is John Lennon's illegitimate son…

SPEN: Daughter. (Laughter)

BOB: She's a transvestite. (More laughter)

ALLAN: Uncle Charlie said on radio that he had seen the birth certificate and he has accepted her. But this birth certificate is completely phony! This is from Hamburg and where it says 'Father' on the original, there is a blank, and she has added 'John Winston Lennon, Occupation - Musician, Address - Weybridge, England.' She is a phony and she has been barred from The Beatles Shop and from the Jacaranda.

SPEN: So she has that in common with you.

ALLAN: I am surprised that the press fell for this one.

SPEN: But, Allan, considering the way the Beatles behaved, aren't you surprised that there aren't illegitimate children around?

ALLAN: Yes, they did sow their wild oats when Bob and I knew them.

SPEN: It's gone half-past one and we will have to move onto the next guest, so can we thank Allan Williams and Bob Wooler. (Much applause)

ALLAN: There's a collection box on the way out.

SPEN: Allan has got a stall.

ALLAN: Yes, we hope to see you there and by the way, the Stuart Sutcliffe painting never sold yesterday at the Auction. It didn't fetch its reserve, so if you want to have a look at one of the best paintings Stuart Sutcliffe ever did, it's there and I want offers over £2,500. (Laughter)

BOB: There's no stopping you, Allan.
(More applause)

Allan Williams and Beryl Wooler, 2002

Bob Wooler with old friends Ray McFall, Joe Flannery,
Bill Harry and Paddy Delaney,

The Grapes, Mathew Street, 1999

25 MYTHEW STREET
Films and books about the Beatles - Loves and hates

"I was just someone who liked hearing his own voice, but unlike
most people, I got the chance to do so. I wasn't all that impressed
with what I heard."
(Bob Wooler, 1999)

From time to time, films about the Beatles are shot in Liverpool. Bob Wooler: "There have been so many films made about the Beatles. One of the first, *Birth of the Beatles*, should have been okay. It was made by Dick Clark, the presenter of *American Bandstand*, and had Pete Best as an advisor, but they took so many liberties. They used a place in Penny Lane for the Blue Angel and it was nothing like it physically. Pete may have said, 'It wasn't like this', and they would have replied, 'Don't worry, we're looking after you.'

"I didn't see *Backbeat*. I received an invitation for the Liverpool première, but I didn't go, and when it was on TV, I went to sleep. That was nothing to do with the film, it was broadcast too late for me and I don't have a video. Ian Hart who plays John Lennon keeps saying, 'It's all dick', but that's a fabrication. It wasn't something he said.

"When the American network NBC came to talk with me about the Beatles, I said, 'Is there any money in this?' They said that they never paid anybody, and that is often the way. Instead, they invited me to dinner at the restaurant at the top of the Beacon in Liverpool. It was an extravagant affair but I'd have liked some cash. Andrew Solt who produced the *Imagine* film sent one of his underlings to the Albert pub to see Allan Williams and myself as we had both been helpful. We were each given a cheque for $500. That was nice: it was thank you very much. It was not the £10 touch, but $500.

"I enjoyed Willy Russell's play about the Beatles, *John Paul George Ringo...And Bert*. He invented some very sharp dialogue for them and that play was a turning point, not for the Beatles but for all the rock'n'roll musicals, which started in Liverpool. Not to be outdone, Alan Bleasdale wrote *Are You Lonesome Tonight?* about Elvis, and there has been *Cavern Of Dreams* about the Cavern and musicals about Billy Fury, Roy Orbison, Eddie Cochran and Gene Vincent. We've even had the rock'n'roll TV producer, Jack Good telling his life story in *Good Rockin' Tonite!*

"Mark Lewisohn's book, *The Beatles Live!*, is a very impressive work and he is praised for his factual accuracy. However, he includes early bookings that are unverifiable and repeats Allan Williams' fabrications about the Beatles at the Jacaranda. He includes all this and yet he is quick to nail me on my 292 appearances for the Beatles at the Cavern. When the Beatles appeared with the Pacemakers, he says that 'someone' suggested the name, the Beatmakers. Someone! It was me! I have got to take offence at that as I was helping Mark as much as I could. He calls the Royal Iris 'infamous' without saying why and he praises Sam Leach for his 'true innovation'. I gave the book a very good review in *Merseymart* when it came out - maybe I should revise what I wrote.

"Albert Goldman wanted me to talk to his researcher, Ron Ellis, for *The Lives Of John Lennon*. He wanted me to 'come clean' but why should I? I wasn't being offered any money. I am not obsessed with money but if money is being passed around, then I feel I should have some. Goldman is doing it for money - otherwise, why the hell is he doing it?

"After the shooting of Lee Marvin in *The Man Who Shot Liberty Valance*, James Stewart and John Wayne are left standing. We know that John Wayne shot Liberty Valance but it was rather confusing, and the apprentice reporter says to his editor, 'Who shot Liberty Valance?', he replies, 'When the legend becomes bigger than the truth, print the legend.' Brilliant, that puts it in a nutshell. People go for the legend, they want the legends about the Beatles and there's disbelief in their eyes if I say, 'That isn't true. It wasn't as exciting as that. It was rather mundane.'

"There's a great temptation for an author to put in ridiculous speculations in order that he can sell lots of copies of his book. Philip Norman's book, *Shout! - The True Story Of The Beatles* is very skilfully worded, but the inference is that the Mob killed Brian Epstein because he refused to cooperate with their merchandising plans. Why did he come out with such guff? Isn't it sufficient that he should write accurately and exhaustively about the whole Beatles' phenomenon?

"You can say what you like about someone once they've died without fear of reproach. People are intrigued as to whether there was a sexual relationship between John Lennon and Brian Epstein. I have to say, 'Hang on now. Were you there?' Of course they weren't, so how can anyone talk about it authoritatively? I can say nothing about it either. *The Hours And Times*, that two-hander film about Brian and John, was well done, but although Brian may have looked at John with longing, who knows whether anything happened?

"I must make one major criticism of John Lennon that, as far as I know, is not in any of the books about him. John was constantly saying how great Stuart Sutcliffe was as a

253

painter. With his vast wealth, he could have mounted a Stu Sutcliffe exhibition that could have gone around the world and perhaps too, there could have been a permanent exhibition in Liverpool. Several people worked for him so John wouldn't have had to do the organising. John Lennon could have put Stu Sutcliffe on the international map, but he didn't. It's typical of his behaviour, and I hold it against him. In 1969 JL decided to fly the flag for James Hanratty, the alleged A6 murderer, but that too petered out because he had moved on to something else.

"The first person to do something about a permanent Beatles memorial in Liverpool was the *Radio City* DJ, Pete Price. He arranged the finance for Arthur Dooley's sculpture, *Four Lads Who Shook The World*, which is opposite the Cavern in Mathew Street. Arthur Dooley was a devout Catholic and a Commie too, and, like Graham Greene, there's a religious angle in all he did. He put the four Beatle dolls in Mother Liverpool's arms and one day I noticed McCartney was missing. I said, 'He must have taken Wings' and that one-liner ended up in the *Daily Post*.

"The first people to want a full-sized Beatles statue in Liverpool were three lads - John Chambers, Gene Grimes and Leslie Priestley. Allan Williams and I supported them, although Allan was probably thinking, 'Why didn't I think of that?' I have my reservations. I am not fully in favour of statues of personalities - the trouble with putting people on statues is that you can see that they have feet of clay.

"In the end, a statue by John Doubleday was funded by Royal Insurance and opened in the new Mathew Street shopping centre called Cavern Walks. It costs tens of thousands of pounds and it is a monstrosity. As Mike McCartney succinctly said when he unveiled it, 'I wouldn't have recognised our kid if he wasn't playing the guitar left-handed.' Perhaps I will meet someone who will put me wise as to why it is excellent and entirely befitting of the global phenomenon it is supposed to depict, but until that happens, I will continue to think of it as pathetic. They don't look like the Beatles and why do they have their backs to each other?" As all four Beatles look alike, I suspect that an Everyman point is being made, but as the four Beatles all look like the sculptor, John Doubleday, it may be simply wish-fulfilment.

Bob Wooler: "I must put in a good word for Tommy Steele's statue of Eleanor Rigby in nearly Stanley Street which he sold to the Council for half a sixpence. As if it wasn't enough to be an all-round entertainer, he is also a crime novelist, a painter and a sculptor. I remember taking some tourists one Sunday morning to see Eleanor Rigby and I was appalled that the Saturday night revellers had dumped the remainder of their curry and chips on her head. The tourists insisted on taking photographs so heaven knows what sort of impression that created." In later years, the statue was kept in good condition through 'Mad Margie', the owner of the themed café, Lucy In The Sky With Diamonds, who often put flowers in her arms.

Bob Wooler:"Nowadays everybody wants to get in on the tribute act. They have dedicated the Nepture Theatre in Hanover Street to Brian Epstein and I can only ask why. As far as I know, Brian never went there, and he had no connections with it. Indeed, it was called the Crane Theatre in his time and Crane's was NEMS' rival for record sales. The Council chose it simply because it was the only theatre they had available to dedicate to him. If they had to dedicate something to him, they should have picked a place with more class and more relevance.

"I would like to see a plaque at Brian's family home in Queen's Drive or on the site of NEMS in Whitechapel. That is now an Ann Summers shop, which I'm sure would amuse Brian, but the Council should never have allowed it to happen. Thousands of tourists go to Whitechapel each year to see where NEMS was, and they find a sex shop. It would never have been allowed in Memphis, but when Spencer questioned the Lord Mayor on *Radio Merseyside*, she praised Ann Summers for bringing jobs to the area.

"The city has started to appoint cultural ambassadors. These are people of good standing who will promote the city and its benefits. So far there has been Joe Flannery, Sid Bernstein and Julie Goodyear, who played Bet Lynch from *Coronation Street*. Sid Bernstein commutes from New York as though he were coming in from the Wirral on a Merseyrail train, and he is planning an enormous festival in the city to celebrate the Millennium. He is 80 years old and I admire his energy and enthusiasm as I do so little now." All the Council's good intentions fell apart. The Cultural Ambassadorships were withdrawn and then restored, but no more have been created. Sid Bernstein's love affair with the city paled as he met resistance to his plans. Even though Sid had staged the Beatles at Shea Stadium, I thought his new plans were mostly hot air and I couldn't see what he would gain if his plans to have, say, Barbra Streisand at Aintree didn't come off.

Bob Wooler: "People think they are doing me a favour by asking me to go on the mike again. All I can say: 'Thanks, but no thanks.' I did record an introduction at the Albert Dock for the Bootleg Beatles to use on their 1998 tour, but that apart, I've well and truly hung up my Reslos, and I have no intention of taking them down. This is my Reslo resolution, and if anyone really wants to do me a favour, all they have to do is to stop trying to persuade me to do otherwise. Period. End of conversation.

"Being a DJ can be so profitable now. The top DJs in Liverpool are like footballers and can earn several thousand a week. Albert Dunlop, who used to play in goal for Everton, told me that he used to earn £15 a week. He would say, 'Look at what they are getting now', and this was in 1970s which was nothing compared to what footballers are getting now. An 18 year old like Michael Owen can clear £1m a year. Easy.

"Fortunately, I have stopped drinking and smoking. I sent Allan Williams a note when he had angina and was in hospital. I said, 'You can only give up your habits by changing your lifestyle. If you go round with the same cronies as before, it is so hard to give anything up.' People thrust cigarettes and drinks upon you and it is difficult to say no. You may want a tomato juice, but if someone puts a vodka in, you're back where you started.

"I don't think the drinking led to my ill health: that was down to worry and stress. I never had a stable job and when I was writing for the *Maghull Review* and it went to the wall, I thought, 'What am I going to do now?' I had a stroke in 1982 and I have also had a heart attack, plus the complications of diabetes and arthritis. It is not surprising that I have lost my sense of humour." I think this book is proof that he hadn't.

Bob Wooler: "Ironically, Allan Williams now lives with my former wife, Beryl. It was the Town Crier, Eddie Porter of Cavern City Tours, who told me this. I said to Allan, 'Why didn't you tell me?' He said, 'I didn't tell you because you might have exploded.' I said, 'Exploded? Why should I? It is so many years ago and it is over and done with. It's not as though I am Mick Jagger and she wants my £7m house. I've got no money and there's no bricks and mortar.

"In 1998 I was so embarrassed to find my name in a telephone poll in the *Liverpool Echo* for Merseyside's Greatest Entertainers. I thought, 'I hope Allan Williams doesn't see this because he would hate me to be included and not him.' I was certain that DJs like Pete Price would say on air, 'What the hell is Wooler doing on that list?' I couldn't imagine anyone ringing in to give me a vote, but I could imagine a lot of people wondering why I was there.

Bob Wooler was a keen supporter of local charity such as the Roy Castle Foundation and Merseycats: "I applaud Don and Lin Andrew - Don was with the Remo Four - was setting up the Merseycats charity in the 1980s. Many groups like the Fourmost, the Dennisons and Earl Preston and the TT's have reformed for Merseycats events. So many musicians have come out of retirement and when they announced the Big Three at the Philharmonic Hall, nine musicians came out to play! I admire them for the thousands they have raised for charity, but I didn't attend when they made me an honorary member of the Merseycats at a show at the Grafton. They offered me a lift, but I do hate a fuss being made of me.

"I was also very impressed with the Merseybeat edition of *Rock Family Trees* on BBC-2 during 1998. They picked a very positive bunch of people, some of whom were comfortably well off and some of whom like Mike Pender of the Searchers looked extremely good for their age. I did, however, detect a degree of sadness about the whole thing, and I rather liked that undertone. Even Geoff Nugent of the Undertakers who is normally very enthusiastic came out with penetrating observations."

Bob enjoyed programmes where people detailed their likes (*Desert Island Discs*) or hates (*Room 101*). "If I were on *Desert Island Discs*, I wouldn't pick any Beatles or Mersey Beat records. I would pick songs from stage or film musicals like *Seven Brides For Seven Brothers*. I would choose Duke Ellington, who wrote marvellous music, and Frank Sinatra and Ella Fitzgerald. If I was forced to choose Mersey Beat records, I would take the Beatles' 'Here There And Everywhere' and something from the Escorts, who were very raw to begin with but matured very well. I would include Earl Preston and Faron and I like the catch in Tony Crane's voice on the Merseybeats' records of 'It's Love That Really Counts' and 'Don't Turn Around'.

"There are lots of things I could nominate for *Room 101*. For example, what could be worse than being forced to watch film after film with Bud Abbott and Lou Costello? I liked Laurel and Hardy but Abbott and Costello were a torment. I would put Bob Dylan in *Room 101*: he is the musical con-man of the century. However, my pet hate for *Room 101* is closer to home. Nothing could be worse than being closeted in a room for days on end listening to someone endlessly fabricating stories about his days with the Beatles."

One day I found the term, "False Memory Syndrome", in *The Oxford Dictionary Of New Words*. This is where you convince yourself that something happened, although it did no such thing. Bob wondered if the researchers had come to Merseyside, "but," he added, "this is not confined to Liverpool. I've been shown an article from an American newspaper in 1998 in which Brian Hickton, the owner of the Middle River Auto Sales, claims he took over as the lead singer of Rory Storm and the Hurricanes in the early 60s. I can just see Rory agreeing to that! He says he worked under the name of Lee Shane and adds, 'Ringo was always coming up with some pranks. Back then we were just kids having fun.' I have never heard of him and presumably he told this tale because he knew that the journalist would not be able to check it out.

"More than anything, I hate people who do not tell the truth about the past. People take liberties with things, and they think, 'No-one will remember, I can say what the hell I like.' I told Allan Williams, 'You'll be glad when I'm dead. There'll be no-one to correct you when you come out with your ridiculous statements.' He said, 'Well, I won't be the only one.' Of course, Allan is by no means the worst culprit. He may embroider his tales to make them more entertaining, but others do it to make themselves seem more important.

"Well, I have news for them all. This is my o-bitch-uary: I am coming back to haunt them. I am the Ghost of Mersey Beat Past. My demise will end the lies."

Billy Butler: "Bob had this wonderful line that Mathew Street should be renamed Mythew Street and it was only by talking to him that I appreciated the damage that was being done by people not telling the truth. Other people pick up on it and repeat it and something that is untrue becomes the accepted fact." In a similar way, Bob has made me wonder about the history I learnt at school. Who's to say that we are not being given the 15th century equivalent of Beatle myths? History, it is sometimes said, is written by the winners, but much of the Beatle history comes from the losers.

Truth was one of Bob's preoccupations: "I am convinced that we would have no crime if we all told the truth. We would have no need for court scenes as we would know what had happened. There is also nothing more terrible than knowing what the other person is thinking. It would be *Room 101* if we all knew what others thought about us."

Bob retained his interest in Liverpool music: "I was very impressed with Ian McNabb, who played in City Lights and specialised in Beatle numbers at one of our Beatle Conventions. He was on keyboards and the McCartney of the group and he developed into a very good songwriter. I liked the image of the La's, whom I saw in Sefton Park on a glorious summer's day but they soon fell out. Pete Wylie has written some impressive songs, but they are too aggressive for me. He is a marvellous conversationalist and maybe he will become this generation's George Melly. Up And Running have filled the big Liverpool theatres without a hit record and Phil Jones has cultivated a rock star image, all lean and mean, but he has trodden on too many toes to ever make big. I admired Up And Running but I hated their use of backing tapes. Live music should be live."

He could be both funny and bitchy about the 60s acts. "The old bands keep going but the Searchers are like automatons, going through the motions with their hit singles. David Garrick sent me his operatic CD and I admire him for recording that, but I didn't like his unshaven look. Designer stubble is only okay in young people. The Klubs were the first Liverpool group to wear make-up on stage and I see that they have reformed. Why do they bother? It will all end in tears so it could be streaky mascara." Bob wrote the tongue in cheek notes for the first LP by the Class of '64.

Once when I was with Bob in Mathew Street, we looked at Cavern Walks. "What does the top part of the building remind you of?" he said, "It is a tall building in a narrow street and it reminds me of the Dakota. You can see it at the beginning of Rosemary's Baby, although it had no particular significance then. I asked the architect David Backhouse about it and he said that he had modelled it on a Victorian building, but I think that the Dakota, which is of the Victorian age, may have been subconsciously in his mind. I am impressed by the new Cavern and I appreciate that they have had to add all the trappings and trimmings. I am very glad about the air-conditioning, but the absence of the band-room with all its fond memories is too much for me to accept."

Bob Wooler was happy in 34 Pelham Grove in Aigburth, but the landlord wanted the property for other purposes and he was moved to a flat a few hundred yards away at 21 Waverley Road. His friend, John Seddon, conducted the move: "There were mountains and mountains of files and we moved them into this flat. It was a shambles from the start and he had locks everywhere and he would use blocks of wood to shut the doors. I tried to pack the files tidily so that he could find things, but he would have been quite glad to give them away. I did ask Granada TV if they would like them for their archives but they said that there were too many. Bob got paranoid when he was in Waverley Road. He would complain about the neighbour upstairs and he would bang on the ceiling, but when I went to see her on his behalf, she was really nice."

Allan Williams: "He was a hoarder and you couldn't get into his bathroom. The bath contained boxes right up to the ceiling and there were even files in the wash-basin. There was a narrow pathway to the lavatory. Yet he was always clean, he would wash his body over the sink in his kitchen. You could hardly open the door to his bedroom for memorabilia. He had a file for everybody he knew. His telephone book included comments on people and he would write 'RIP' by the ones who had died. He had a sad ending, but in a hundred years, the guides will be saying, 'This is where Bob Wooler lived' and 'This is where he had a fight with John Lennon'."

Doug Evans: "If you don't keep a place tidy, you eventually get past the point of no return, and that happened with Bob. My grandson is a Beatles obsessive and he had been delighted to meet Bob. I asked him to give me something that I could pass on for his birthday. He said, 'I will get down to it, don't push me,' but he never did. He had so much stuff and it annoyed me that he wouldn't part with something."

Although Bob Wooler collapsed at his home in January 2002, it was a day or two before he was discovered. He was taken to the Royal Liverpool Hospital. When I went to see him, he was in a terrible shape physically, but his mind was still alert. "I am tired of people coming round with their cheesecake grins," he said, "I can't read and the radio stations here don't include *Radio 4*. I know I am dying and I want to die. Can you help me out?" "Bob," I said, "I will get you anything you want, but doing time in Walton Prison for you is not on the agenda." Little did he know that I had already killed him off as I had already written his obituary for *The Independent*.

John Seddon: "I was sorry that there were arguments beween Bob and Beryl and Allan in the later years. He was very upset that she was going to Beatle Conventions with Allan Williams and speaking as Beryl Wooler, and there was a time when he didn't speak to Allan for about a year. It was over something trivial - Bob had been to see someone and not told Allan about it." Almost certainly this is when Terry Sylvester from the Escorts and the Hollies was visiting Liverpool. Bob wanted to see him after my live radio programme and he was insistent that I must not tell anyone about it "in case word gets to Allan and he decides to come along". Bob had a marvellous evening - he was so delighted to see Terry again.

Shortly before his death, John had tried to persuade Bob to move into retirement accommodation and both Allan and Beryl wanted him to take a flat in the very pleasant Alfred Stocks Court like themselves. However, if Allan and Beryl thought something was good for Bob, he wouldn't accept it, and I would have felt sorry for any senior citizen wanting a quiet life and finding Bob and Allan arguing in the communal dining room. John Seddon: "Even in the hospital at the end, there were arguments and the Sister told me that Bob wanted me to be the one who would be notified about his health, not Allan and Beryl. By way of contrast, Joe Flannery went to see him and he was really considerate. I remember him rubbing his back. Just before he died, the *Daily Post* published a terrible article about Bob urinating in front of visitors and it was very degrading. It may have been written with the intention of getting him more respect and privacy but it was the wrong way of going about it."

Bob Wooler died from kidney failure on Friday 8 February 2002. The next day I bought an *Echo* in the city centre. I saw the headline, "Princess Margaret Dies", and said in passing, "A sad day." "Not half as sad as yesterday, mate," said the news-vendor, "Bob Wooler died."

A few weeks later Allan Williams stood up in The Grapes and said, "I have the ultimate Beatle possession for sale - Bob Wooler's ashes. What am I bid?" The patrons were shocked - well, not really, this was, after all, Allan Williams - but it was a jibe that had gone wrong. How one person would have loved Allan's behaviour; how Bob Wooler would have laughed.

26 THE JUDI SPIERS SHOW
Another Allan and Bob Show

BBC Radio 2's *'Judi Spiers Show'* came to Liverpool on Saturday afternoon, 15 November 1997 for a two-hour, live programme from the Cavern featuring the Bootleg Beatles. I was a guest and I mentioned in passing that it might be better to interview Allan Williams and Bob Wooler separately. "I'm sure Judi can handle it," said the producer, "After all, what can go wrong in five minutes?"

JUDI: Here at the Cavern Club in Liverpool, we are celebrating the 60s with the Bootleg Beatles. Now a lot of people put up their hands and say, "I was there when the Beatles first started," but the next two guests really were there. They are Bob Wooler, the DJ at the Cavern Club when the Beatles performed their early sets on stage, and Allan Williams, the Beatles' first manager. You two know each other pretty well, don't you?

ALLAN: Yes, very well. We have only got a five minute slot, Judi, and it normally takes Bob Wooler that long to start to insult me.

BOB: This can be arranged very quickly if you want.

JUDI: Allan, how did you get to meet the boys?

ALLAN: I had a coffee-bar downtown called the Jacaranda, there were a lot of coffee-bars then, and the Beatles to me were coffee-bar layabouts. I first met them when I had to have the ladies' toilets decorated because of the obscene graffiti on the walls. Then I put on a big show with Eddie Cochran and Gene Vincent at the boxing stadium. Unfortunately, Eddie Cochran was killed so I put Liverpool groups on for the first half, but I didn't even know that the Beatles were a group. After the show at the Stadium, they approached me and asked me to be their manager.

JUDI: And you took them to Hamburg?

261

ALLAN: Yes, Bob doesn't agree with this, but if it wasn't for Hamburg where they learnt their trade, we wouldn't be here talking on the stage. They were working six to eight hours a night seven nights a week.

JUDI: Why don't you agree with that, Bob?

BOB: It's highly contentious this. If Hamburg made such a transformation on the Beatles, why didn't it transform - hang on, Allan, don't interrupt please! - Gerry and the Pacemakers, the Big Three, Rory Storm and the Hurricanes, Derry and the Seniors, etc etc etc.

JUDI: Oh, good point.

ALLAN: Because they weren't in the same league as the Beatles. Gerry and Rory were the big name groups in Liverpool until the Beatles came back. You, Bob, didn't recognise the potential of the Beatles before they went to Hamburg.

BOB: But when they came back from Hamburg in December 1960, why did you finish with them and hand them over to me?

ALLAN: Because I had a club called the Top Ten and it was going to be the Cavern of Liverpool and you gave up your job to work there as my manager, but unfortunately after five days, the Top Ten burned down which left me up shit creek, yeah.

JUDI: Remember me, hi, this is Judi. Bob, you made a record about the Cavern club, didn't you?

BOB: Say that again please.

JUDI: You made a record about the Cavern club, didn't you?

BOB: Ah...

JUDI: 'Hi there, all you cave-dwellers.'

BOB: Oh, the Big Three were recorded here in 1963. I did the intro to that record.

JUDI: At what spot did you think that the Beatles were geniuses then?

BOB: I thought that they were extraordinary and I couldn't understand why Allan had finished with them. He had nothing to do with them in '61 or '62 or even '63.

ALLAN: Okay, Bob, well, why were you interested in rock'n'roll music? Your music is the Glenn Miller type of music, so why were you interested?

BOB: Because, as I explained to Bob Spitz who is doing this book about the Beatles, my interest was as a songwriter. I thought if Lionel Bart can make it through Tommy Steele, let me try that road.

JUDI: But let me just say, Bob, they were happy days here?

BOB: Ah, this is it.

JUDI: (Despairing) Oh, lord.

BOB: Now the word 'magic' has been applied to the scene in those days, but I don't know the definition of the word 'magic', because there was another side to the whole scene, I call it the Mercenary Beat. It was the promoters, I am not pointing at you, Allan...

ALLAN: You are pointing at me, you fart!

JUDI: Please, please, please, for heaven's sake. Can I just say what a joy and a pleasure it has been to meet you and I'm glad everything has been explained so succinctly and clearly. Allan Williams and Bob Wooler, thank you very much indeed. (Applause)

Half an hour later, it was my turn to be interviewed by Judi Spiers. As I made my way to the stage to talk to Judi with her audience of two million listeners, Bob Wooler handed me a piece of paper to give to the producer. It was for his expenses.

WOOLERTIN

To: For the record

Friday 14 October 1983
11.05 a.m.

Re: **JAMES BOND 007**

Subject: Proposed James Bond Convention

The following is for record and any apprpriate action.

1) Allan Williams was told about BW's idea for a James Bond Convention in
   Liverpool during the summer of 1984 in the Railway Pub at lunchtime on
   Friday 7 October 1983. Philip Key was present. AW thought it was a good
   idea and wanted to know when it was to be done. BW, as the originator
   of the idea, said it would be done properly, in writing, and that this
   would inevitably take time. BW made it clear to AW that he would not in
   anyway be pressurised, and that the promtion must take its natural course.

2) BW spoke at length with Roy Carson at the re-vamped Village Country Club,
   Cantril Farm about the JBC idea. This was at about 12 noon on Saturday
   8 October 1983. RC said he would put up an appropriate sum of money, for
   which he would come in on the idea as a partner and receive a third of
   the profits, if any. BW made it clear that the other partners were
   himself, as the originator of the idea, and AW. There would be no ego
   tripping by any of the partners. The wole idea, said BW, was done to make
   money. If profits looked like they were not forthcoming, then any, if not
   all of the partners, were entitled to pull out. BW said, in due course,
   he would get out a proper profit and loss sheet, which all the partners
   would study and decide upon. BW said there was, in his book, no other way
   to do it. The one-dayer is due to be presented at the most suitable venue
   on Merseyside next summer, say, towards the end of July. This would allow
   the promoters about 9 months in which to tie up properly all the details,
   in writing. The majority of this essential work would be done by BW.

3) At this early stage it is vital that this whole idea is kept
   under wraps. We do not want anybody else to "borrow" the idea,
   do we? I cannot emphasise too strongly the need for absolute
   circumspection - no irresponsible, precipitate action should
   be indulged in, purely to show off and ego trip, or bandyied
   around in pubs, etc. Let's ensure that this completely original
   idea is, as James Bond himself would put it:

FOR YOUR EYES ONLY

4) The cautionary note that prevails in this memo is really for the benefit of
   AW, who is often given to 'blowing the gaff' in pubs, etc. when he's had a
   few drinks. I really must empasise that at this early stage the utmost
   confidentiality be observed by all concerned. It is so very easy to steal
   an original idea and I don't want that to happen here. _BW_

(14 Oct 1983)

POP SECRET

CAVERN CITY TOURS
present
"THIS IS MERSEYBEAT"
Saturday 28th August 1993

ROYAL
COURT
THEATRE
ROE ST.
LIVERPOOL

A Benefit Gig
for Mr Cavern
BOB WOOLER
£8.50

MERSEYBEATS
TONY JACKSON (ex-Searchers)
KARL TERRY & THE CRUISERS
FARON'S FLAMINGOES
MERSEYBEATS ON STAGE 7.30pm PROMPT

DOORS AND
BARS OPEN
7.00pm
CONCERT
BEGINS 7.30pm